July 25, 2011

The laugh makes me comfortable – a hearty burst he lets loose easily. It reminds me of his son's distinct, high pitched chuckle I remember from high school.

Landrin Kelly is 42 years old and not particularly big, considering the size of his son. He's clean shaven with short hair, dressed casually in shorts and a t-shirt. He snorts, coughs, spits, howls, smokes a cigarette, clears his throat or makes some form of aggressive noise at all times. Rough around the edges is an understatement.

Landrin has very little academic background, but is nevertheless savvy. He feels people and situations out through instinct and experience. His voice is distinct – deep, raspy, rough. You can see the pain in his eyes – bottomless wells of emotion.

I've waited seven years for this interview. I'm relieved that our conversation starts lighthearted and smooth. We're in 'TK's room,' a shrine on the second floor of Landrin's modest home dedicated to his son. It's cluttered with posters, trophies, pictures, tributes, accolades and awards.

Landrin begins with the troubles of his late teens and early twenties. His wife Mary brings us food – chicken and shrimp enchiladas. He growls menacingly at one of his grandsons to leave us alone when the tiny child interrupts. My head spins as Landrin rattles off a web of names – the village that raised his son.

1

We walk to a local convenience store to grab beers. It's a chilly, windy night in Suisun City, California, 30 miles northeast of Landrin's hometown of Richmond. He moved here after the tragedy because it was affordable and far away from the memories back in Richmond.

We approach an intersection. I wait for the crosswalk while Landrin walks boldly across the highway. I follow his lead. Headlights appear in the distance. Landrin laughs and breaks into a sprint.

"C'mon, they ain't gonna slow down!"

He is a God-fearing man. I follow his lead.

On the way back, we stop at Landrin's beat up car. Inside, he plays a recording of his younger cousin Malik Carr as he raps in tribute to TK immediately after the funeral. It's called *The Day You Went Away*. Landrin softly whispers the lyrics in rhythm. We listen to it three times.

Back in the garage, we crack open beers as Landrin takes me through more memories and pictures that adorn the walls. He walks me through the period when TK enters high school. Landrin's deep voice occasionally trails off as he recalls this time, as if it were all in a different life. He speaks fast as we approach the tail end of Terrance's senior year of high school. Then his voice loses strength and fades. He abruptly changes the subject.

We open new beers and Landrin lights a cigarette as he relives the night of August 12, 2004. Tears stream down his cheeks and his eyes redden. He's in a different place now, inches away from my face. He appears bigger and more imposing than before. His face contorts wildly and his voice BOOMS. He hasn't gone back here in years. He stares at me wide eyed and his bellows echo off the garage walls. My heart pounds. I'm scared, but I don't move. Then Landrin lets out a long, deep cackle that relieves the tension for a moment.

I laugh, cough and fight to breathe when his voice deepens again – guttural, raw, full stream of consciousness as he delves back into the moment. The story finally ends to Landrin's hoarse, choking coughs. He stares into my soul. I apologize for not keeping it together, my voice weak with emotion.

"It's alright man," he says.

"But it's rough every day.

"I think about 'what if' every day.

"What if he were here?

"What if?"

CHAPTER ONE

Man, Where You At?

AUGUST 12, 2004. An eerie night in Richmond, California's 'Iron Triangle.' Named after three railroad tracks that delineate deadly turf boundaries in the shape of a triangle, the area is four miles west of million dollar hillside homes with views of the Golden Gate Bridge, and 10 miles east of some of the most expensive real estate in the world in Marin County.

The San Francisco Bay Area is renowned for spectacular views. While you can see San Francisco and several different bridges from Richmond's shoreline, the flatland neighborhoods have a different type of skyline – the massive Chevron refineries' tall smokestacks. The refinery casts a shadow over two rival areas of the city with reputations for fierce violence and desperate poverty – Central Richmond and North Richmond.

It was calm and still in Central Richmond that night, like the wilderness when a predator approaches. For an area where violence is endemic, Central was particularly on edge at this moment. In the fall of 2003, a traffic incident between young men had re-ignited longstanding tensions between Central and North and resulted in at least six killings. Various street elements in Central, to this point organized by block or corner, coalesced into a larger entity to protect themselves from their better organized foes to the north. In the spring of 2004, a high profile Central Richmond 'shot caller' was gunned down at a local park. Over the course of the summer, the body count grew as groups of young men rode into opposing territories and opened fire with automatic weapons.

Terrance Kelly was aware of these events as he drove down a lifeless street to pick up his de facto stepbrother Brian James, but the 18-year-old had been insulated from them. His father Landrin and grandmother Bevelyn had worked tirelessly to send him to private schools. After he accepted a full athletic scholarship to the University of Oregon in January, a sea of groupies, male and female, latched onto him. Towards the end of high school he had a social calendar packed with places to go and people to see, whether it was in the majority white suburbs where he attended a private high school, or in the different sections of Richmond. Tonight, his friend Jeremy knew of a party in the safer area of Hilltop Richmond.

But first he had to grab Brian.

TK noticed a pile of candles, flowers and empty bottles on the street as he drove deeper into Central – a makeshift memorial to a young black male slain in the recent feud. The memorial sparked voices in his head. The countless warnings he had heard from family and friends.

"Stay out of Central."

"Call your friends and tell them to come over here, I'll order pizzas if ya'll stay home tonight."

"Granny Bev don't like you being over there in C-side."

"I'm takin' the car away if you keep going down there."

TK knew it wasn't the best idea to drive around in Central at this hour, but Brian needed a ride and no one else could do it.

Brian was Landrin's girlfriend's son. TK and Brian had their issues, but he felt like Brian was a little brother, with all of the pains and annoyances that come with any brotherly relationship.

TK rolled down the passenger side window in his dad's white '72 Oldsmobile Cutlass Supreme to break the silence because there was no radio to play music. As he neared the corner of Seventh Street and Nevin Avenue, his thoughts drifted to the young kid from Central who egged his car and got in his face at a house party. The boy often hung around this corner. He was half TK's size and three years younger, but he dressed in heavy clothes, acted hard and had an attitude.

TK didn't have a problem with Darren Pratcher. He was over any petty beef that may have flared up on the basketball court or at the house party. Besides, he would whup the boy if it came down to it.

But it wasn't the boy's fists TK had to worry about. In this part of Richmond, kids like Darren had to be respected, or at the very least, avoided. It didn't matter how small or how young they were.

*   *   *

Landrin paced around the kitchen table. Where was he? He'd already called twice. How many times did he have to tell TK to get home? Two days before his flight and he's out screwing around at night? In this city?

He sighed and dialed TK's number again.

"Man, where you at?"

"Dad. I'm pickin' up lil' bro."

"Man, get your ass home."

"Why you trippin'?"

"Mama called she want you come home you gotta finish packing your stuff. It's dark. You don't need to be hanging out. Just come home."

"I'm cool dad, I'll be home soon."

A second after Landrin hung up the phone, it rang again – yet another call from his mother. For the past 16 years, Landrin and Bevelyn had worked to give TK the best despite the hardships and circumstances of the immediate area in which he was raised – nicer clothes, a better education and more attention than any kid in the neighborhood. TK was Bevelyn's pride and joy – her first grandchild and first opportunity to devote a majority of her attention to a kid rather than multiple hourly jobs.

"Hey mama."

"Landrin, where your baby at?"

*   *   *

Seventh Street and Nevin Avenue. TK arrived at the corner and dialed Brian's number. He eyed his surroundings carefully.

"I'm outside."

Through the passenger side window to the right, he observed four young black men huddling around a car parked on the driveway. They looked restless. Tense.

"Who that?"

Inside, TK relaxed a bit recognizing two of his old teammates from Central. He called out:

7

"Larry check it out."

Larry Pratcher approached TK's passenger-side window. Behind him, his 15-year-old younger brother Darren disappeared towards a side yard.

There, Darren Pratcher grabbed a .22 Marlin bolt-action rifle and turned back around towards the street.

CHAPTER TWO

This Your Baby

"BRING THAT BABY OVER HERE," Bevelyn Kelly said.

Short and round with a soft voice that never cursed, Bevelyn was also stern and not one to mince words.

The year was 1988. Richmond, California.

Landrin Kelly, nineteen, shifted uncomfortably as his mother scooped up the infant boy. As a junior at John F. Kennedy High School, he had made a name as a no-frills crack dealer in Southside Richmond's burgeoning street economy. But Landrin was also using his product on the side and far from ready to be a father.

Bevelyn held the infant in her arms and inspected his hands and feet.

"Landrin, this your baby."

"Naw mama naw. He ain't mine, that ain't my baby."

Bevelyn placed the infant on the ground, who waddled towards Landrin and hugged him, wanting to play like they had many times before. The baby was the product of a two year relationship between Landrin and a woman who lived around the corner in the local housing projects. Though the relationship had since ended, Landrin hid the boy from his family because he was scared of what his mother would do. As Bevelyn looked into her first grandchild's eyes, she fell in love on the spot.

"Shutup boy, you lyin. This your baby. You gonna have to get what he need, and Imma get him everything he wants."

One week later, a blood test confirmed Bevelyn's hunch. Two-year-old Terrance "TK" Kelly was Landrin's son.

CHAPTER THREE

One Foot In, One Foot Out

AFTER TK **MOVED** into Bevelyn's house in 1988, his life was similar to many other kids in the neighborhood. Bevelyn ran a day care out of her home. Every morning at 6 a.m., the other kids arrived. Soon, they were all playing together. In the afternoons, TK napped in cots with the other toddlers or engaged in Bevelyn's early child care development routine.

Landrin had learned from an early age to change diapers, cook and wash clothes for other kids working in the day care. Now 20, he spent more time at the day care with the other little boys and his own three-year-old son. As the kids developed physically, Landrin taught them the fundamentals of his favorite sports in the back yard – how to throw, swing and catch.

But Landrin was still very much 'out there' in the streets. Nearly all of his friends were involved in the local drug trade. Landrin's best friend and teammate, Paul Webster Sr., had earned a scholarship to play baseball at Pasadena City College in Southern California and pursue his dream of playing professional sports. But then he also had a son, Paul Webster Jr., who was coincidentally the same age as TK. Paul Sr. eventually dropped out of school and returned to the Bay Area to help raise his boy.

Paul Webster Sr.: "For the first couple years, me and Landrin was still messing up. Both of our moms did so much for our kids until we were ready to step up and be men. For a young parent, it doesn't really kick in – the baby isn't really a reflection of yourself – until they start walking and talking. Then, when they start asking questions, you better have some good answers."

Landrin Kelly: "We grew up together, us and our boys. There's no script for raising a child."

After TK moved in with his mom, Landrin took a step in the right direction and enrolled in classes at Contra Costa Community College. He maintained a 3.0 grade point average. Then, he took a giant step backwards after a routine day of selling crack in the housing projects around the corner from his mother's house turned upside down.

TK was born in these projects, which were also known as 'Globetown.' Globetown was typical of government-subsidized housing projects gone wrong in cities across the country: a massive, 199-unit, circular, one-way-in, one-way-out cluster of red and beige apartments surrounded by tall perimeter fences. The projects were designed as cutting edge architecture that would foster low income community development in the post-World War II years. Instead, they became a prison that trapped its inhabitants in a whirlpool of misery. The sounds of cars racing up and down the streets, emergency sirens, gunshots and the smell of burning rubber were routine.

Residents had complained for years about crime, murders and heavy street traffic in Globetown. Lawsuits had been filed against the buildings' owners and against the city. The police had raided the projects before, but Landrin's crew had lookouts planted at every entrance and exit. When the police arrived, they melted into various apartments where family and friends provided safe harbor.

Bevelyn's little sister, Sondra Dempsey, lived in Globetown and recalls how things turned in the mid-1980's.

Sondra Dempsey: "It was like things had just changed overnight. I came home from church one night, and when I pulled into my parking lot there were guys lined up standing on both sides of my car yelling, 'Rocks! Rocks! Rocks!' My apartment building was flooded with drugs. The street traffic – there was no police officers, nothing. It was amazing. They had just sort of taken over. It was scary. We became prey to these people. It changed our lives. Bevelyn and I grew closer. We stood by each other. There was a bond there. We were one. We were very watchful with our children. We didn't want them to be a part of that."

Unfortunately, Sondra's nephew Landrin was very much of a part of the problem. The Richmond Police changed their tactics by sending undercover and surveillance units inside the complex. An informant told one of these undercover units where and when Landrin would be selling crack one day.

Landrin Kelly: "Sometimes, I'd sell it myself so I wouldn't have to pay my workers. Or, the addicts could come directly to me if they didn't have the money at the time – I'd give it to them on credit. But I wouldn't let my guys give any credit out. That's why I was doing the transaction when it happened."

An undercover officer approached Landrin, who sold the officer rocks. As Landrin walked away, he heard the screeching tires of an unmarked patrol car. He ran and undercover officers arrested him. Landrin pleaded that he was just a user, but they found additional crack in his possession.

Landrin watched from the back of the car as he was paraded through rival neighborhoods, then booked and charged with possession for sale of crack cocaine. Officers recorded Landrin's voice to help track his whereabouts before Bevelyn bailed him out of jail.

There is never a good time to get arrested for crack possession, but this was a particularly bad time. In 1986, President Ronald Reagan signed the Anti-Drug Abuse Act, which appropriated $1.7 billion to fight America's War on Drugs and created mandatory minimum penalties for drug offenses. The law resulted in harsher sentences for crack offenders than powder cocaine offenders, and a disproportionate amount of racial minorities earned long prison sentences as a result.

Landrin faced a three-five year sentence in California state prison for possession of cocaine base, the legal term for crack, with intent to distribute. At his preliminary hearing, Landrin requested permission to apply for an alternative work furlough program. The judge ordered three years' probation and that Landrin apply for the work furlough program instead of serving a mandatory 120 days in jail.

The judge had offered him a deal. A wave of relief hit Landrin as he digested this second chance and walked out of the courtroom. Outside, Bevelyn was solemn.

"You gonna have to change," she warned. "And you gonna have to change now."

CHAPTER FOUR

I Was Gonna Do Everything Different

IN 1990, Landrin was out of jail and on track in the court-appointed work furlough program. Through the referral of Bevelyn's little brother Billy Dempsey, Landrin now cleaned dishes at Vale Care Convalescent Hospital in San Pablo – working the 5 a.m.-2 p.m. shift.

Billy Dempsey had always been the man in Landrin's life when his own father, Lanny Sr., wasn't around. Lanny Sr. and Billy Dempsey had known each other since they were eight years old growing up in Berkeley. Both had veered towards the streets as young adults.

Inmates in Landrin's program could leave the Contra Costa County detention facility in Richmond for a maximum of 10 hours, giving him one hour each way to travel to and from work. After his shift, Landrin had to find a ride back to the facility where he shared a room with 10 other inmates providing labor in exchange for jail time. He was also required to pass two drugs tests at the facility and attend two drug classes per week.

Life consisted of trips back and forth to court, the convalescent hospital and the detention facility. After he had shown good behavior and the deputy signed off on his class attendance and drug tests, Landrin got an eight-hour pass to go home where his family tried to facilitate his transition out of the streets. Younger sister Latonya picked out a new wardrobe and made him cut his hair in a more professional style.

Bevelyn and Lanny Sr. stepped in as TK's surrogate parents. As TK aged and his vocabulary increased, he called Bevelyn "mama" and read a children's book to her every night before bed. Lanny Sr. had a second chance to be the full-time father that he had never been with his own kids. He had missed many of the major events and games in their lives, and instead showed up around holidays or birthdays. With TK, he didn't want to miss anything. Whenever his grandson needed a ride, a meal or anything else, Lanny Sr. provided it.

Bevelyn also had a second chance with TK. Her perseverance through extreme hardship led to her day care business. For years, she had worked three jobs to put a roof over her four kids' heads and pay the bills. After hurting her back working at the Berkeley Co-Op supermarket, Bevelyn underwent surgery, took disability and briefly went on welfare. She used this time to earn a degree in Early Childhood Development and eventually opened the child care center out of her garage on Florida Avenue.

With the day care filled to capacity at 20 kids, Bevelyn's house became the neighborhood's unofficial preschool. Lanny Sr. drove half of the kids to school in the morning, while the younger group stayed home with Bevelyn and Paul's mother Janett to work on educational activities such as flash cards, numbers, shapes, colors and Hooked On Phonics. This group would become TK's brothers and best friends, beginning with Paul Webster Jr.

Paul Webster Jr.: "Every day I pass Grandma Bev's house where we grew up and learned our ABCs, 123s and our colors, where we took naps, where we played in the backyard – it takes me back. Our grandmas' focal point was making sure all the kids in the day care were brought up the proper way. Their emphasis was education – knowing how to read, knowing how to write, knowing how to spell."

Jamie Richards Jr. grew up on Ohio Avenue, two blocks from Grandma Bev's house. He started in the day care when he was 1 years old. Josh Dozier attended day care with Richards and TK. Louis Montgomery, Quinton Ganther and Josh Harvey also grew up in the neighborhood.

Richards: "The grannies taught us everything. If you were wrong, they checked you on that. If you did something right, they applauded you and rewarded you. It was a real family-oriented place."

Dozier: "Bevelyn was what I knew. She was the only woman in my life that my mom allowed me to call mom. She was very sweet, but very stern."

Montgomery: "Miss Bev? They don't make 'em like that anymore."

Harvey: "It was love at Bev's house. TK had a whole lot of love. That was TK's mom right there. TK was real spoiled, but it didn't bother me because his grandmother loved him – that was like her son."

Ganther: "Miss Bev was so loving and encouraging. You could go to her for anything. She was a part of raising all the kids who played at Nicholl Park. She was like everyone's grandmother."

TK was Bevelyn's first grandchild, the family's first great-granchild, and Landrin's first child. Bevelyn went overboard to ensure he felt at home. TK loved the Teenage Mutant Ninja Turtles and watched the *Teenage Mutant Ninja Turtles* movie on repeat. Bevelyn had a ninja turtles costume tailored for him and did the same with a batman costume on Halloween. At Christmas, family members such as Bevelyn's nephew

17

Johnny Dempsey flocked to the house to watch the spectacle of TK opening his presents.

Johnny Dempsey: "It was like a scene you see in a movie, with the choo-choo trains going around the track, bikes and stuff. My Aunty Bevelyn lived and breathed Terrance. He was like an only child there for a while. My little brother and I was around 14 years old, and we would go over there just to watch him open his stuff. A lot kids would be selfish with their things. TK would say, 'Here, you can play with this. You can play with that.' "

Paul Webster Jr.: "TK was spoiled to death. Anything he wanted, anything he asked for – he got. He was the first kid to get everything. But he wasn't a spoiled brat. He never threw it in other kids' faces. He was far from selfish. When he got something, we was all happy, because that meant we had a new toy too."

Jamie Richards Jr.: "It depended on what toy you talkin' about. At the day care, it was his stuff that everybody was playing with. He had his special things hid in the back. Certain of us could go back there and play with him."

Louis Montgomery: "It wasn't just Miss Bev and Landrin spoiling him. It was his aunties, uncles and everyone. Everyone spoiled him because he rubbed off on you the right way."

*　　*　　*

Landrin eventually passed through the work furlough program and moved home. After a shift at the convalescent hospital in the morning, he ate lunch at his mother's house and played with the day care boys in the back yard. These sessions got more organized over time. Landrin lined up the little boys in an infield formation and hit whiffle balls at them from a mock home plate.

TK's closest friends in the day care – Jamie, Josh and Paul Jr. – became the core of Landrin's first T-ball team, the Playschool Angels. Bevelyn sponsored the team and paid for their uniforms.

The president of the league, Jarvis Brown, knew Landrin's background and encouraged him to continue coaching. Jarvis was best friends with former Major League Baseball player Willie McGee, who provided funding and support to the youth leagues in Richmond.

The Angels practiced in Bevelyn's backyard and at nearby Nichol Park. With Paul Webster Sr. home after playing college baseball in Southern California, the two old friends now coached their boys alongside Jamie Richards Sr. and Josh's father Donald Dozier.

Josh Dozier: "Our dads were trying to make us better, not only as athletes, but as people. All of our dads made sure they were teaching us more than sports. If somebody dropped a cuss word, we'd get pulled aside and talked to."

Jamie Richards Jr.: "They taught us how to play and the mentality of being an athlete, even though we were young. It was like a real baseball practice. Throwing with form. Catching. Taking infield and outfield. There was no games out there. You had to be on point."

Paul Webster Jr.: "We knew the fundamentals of the game when we were 5. Landrin was a big runner. If you miss a ball he'd say, 'Drop your gloves and take a lap.' We'd play catch for hours. If you made an error, my dad took infield shots at you until you got it right."

For Landrin and Paul Sr., the challenge was personal. Both had the talent to play professionally – Paul's father had played tight end for the Chicago Bears before a car accident ended his athletic career – but both had been swallowed up by the street environment instead.

Paul Webster Sr.: "We wanted our kids to be better than us. We was good to a point but we dropped the ball. We wasn't going to let them drop the ball. Our mindset was, 'Let's take the bullshit out of they lives, and let their talent take them where they need to go.' One of us attacked the physical, the other attacked the mental. We had a script planned and trust me we rehearsed it daily. If nothing else, at the end of the day, we knew our kids weren't gonna be in no streets."

TK played multiple sports as a child, including basketball, gymnastics, ballet and karate. Landrin even took him to Berkeley Iceland to try ice hockey.

Landrin Kelly: "My dad wasn't there for me. He didn't teach me how to be a man. I was gonna do everything different than my dad did. I was gonna be in my son's life. I'd go everywhere he'd go, I'd do everything he'd do, and I'd be there for him. And if I can't be there, I can't be there. I ain't gon' lie to you if I can't make it. That's where I learned how to be a man.

"It was around 1990 when I got my second job. I wasn't gonna have my son standing out on no corner to make money. The first job was for my standard of living, the second job would pay for TK's education and activities. I found a position doing inventory with the night crew at Home Base, which was before Home Depot. We brought all the items down from the shelves, counted them, wrapped them properly and put them back in place."

Home Base had recently hired a good-looking female cashier. Two of Landrin's coworkers – his manager and his cousin Tavio – bet Landrin that he couldn't get her number. And, he had to touch her chest.

Landrin strutted to the checkout line thinking of what to say and told her, "Hey you want me to bag that for you?" Mary smiled and said sure. Landrin had seen her play softball at the park. He asked about her games as he bagged items. Landrin was a talker and a charmer, and it wasn't long before he got her number. Then he asked Mary about the

New Edition Bobby Brown shirt she was wearing, pointing at her chest as he did, "Who's that?" "And what about right there?" "What about this?"

Mary answered, pointing down at her chest, "That's Bobby, that's Ricky, that's Ronny, that's Mike."

From down the aisle, Landrin's friends laughed – he had won the bet.

The bet turned into much more. Landrin and Mary went on a few lunches at work and began dating. Terrance was 4 by now, while Mary had a 2-year-old daughter, Tra'Meka, and was also raising her 8-year-old niece, Lajada. Mary lived on Chanslor Avenue at the time, on the border of South and Central Richmond. The young couple made plans for their kids to meet at Mary's apartment.

*   *   *

"This ain't your son, this your brother," Mary said.

Landrin and TK joked around in Mary's apartment, playing and wrestling like brothers.

"Terrance, tell her I'm your dad," Landrin said.

TK flashed a smile, "Uh huh."

The next day, Landrin invited Mary to Bevelyn's house to meet his parents.

Mary Kelly: "At Bevelyn's house, I really fell in love once I saw how Landrin cared about his mother. He treated her like she was his queen. He worked two jobs when I met him, but any burden he could take off of her, he would do. 'Do you need me to put gas in the car? Take out the trash?' He'd tell me, 'I'm gonna come by and see you but I got to make sure my mom's OK.' That right there stole my heart."

Landrin moved in with Mary and her girls. TK, Lajada and Tra'Meka got along like regular brothers and sisters. Lajada was the oldest, TK the middle child and Tra'Meka the baby. TK and Tra'Meka were too young to remember anything different.

TK would now call two places his home. Bevelyn's house on Florida Avenue was his primary residence, and wherever Landrin lived his second home.

Landrin and Mary, early 1990's

CHAPTER FIVE

One More Time

LANDRIN WAS GOING LEGITIMATE, but the transition was far from complete. In his teenage years he had easy money at his disposal from drug sales and the freedom that came with it. Still in his early 20's, he now earned every cent through a loaded schedule, most of which went to TK's various needs. Landrin wanted the money and flexibility to get TK everything he wanted. After moving in with Mary and the girls, Landrin wanted to provide for them as well.

Bevelyn Kelly watched TK during the week at the day care, but on the weekends, the boy was Landrin's responsibility.

Landrin Kelly: "It was hard. I had to give up the nice things – the clothes, the cars. Sometimes we needed to wait a paycheck or two before I could get him something. I couldn't get everything that I was used to having right then and there. So I'd tell him, 'No. Wait 'till Daddy get paid.' After that, it was about the quality time I could spend with him. There were other things we could do, even if we didn't have no money. I took him to the park and we played baseball. We'd go to the arcade, or we'd rassle [wrestle] because he loved to rassle. He thought he was the Ultimate Warrior. I'd be Andre the Giant or The Claw."

With money and time constraints, Landrin eventually succumbed to temptation.

Landrin Kelly: "Opportunity came. I took it and tried to do it one more time. I was used to that fast money and it wasn't the same."

It wasn't a good time to go back 'out there.'

Richmond's devastating 1991 total of 62 homicides in a city of less than 100,000 people brought increased attention from the Richmond Police Department and a buildup of the police presence in Richmond's housing projects. Globetown's infamous reputation led to intensified police patrols and raids, and once again, Landrin was in the thick of it.

While selling crack in Globetown, he heard one of the lookouts call out, "ROLLERS! ROLLERS!" Police sirens wailed as a task force blew through the front entrance of the projects. Helicopter blades swished overhead and a spotlight illuminated the parking lot behind the apartments where Landrin fled. He scampered towards an emergency escape route in the form of a hole cut in the chain link fence. He squirmed through the hole and could see Bevelyn's house down the street when a separate group of officers approached from behind. After a brief foot pursuit, they caught him, slammed him to the ground and roughed him up a bit.

"You're a known drug dealer now. Do you know what that means?"

This time, Landrin had priors, which enhanced his sentence to a minimum of five years and a maximum of nine years.

In court, the judge offered Landrin a third and final opportunity. He could serve 120 days in jail now, with five years' probation. Another hiccup and he was going to California state prison for nine years.

*   *   *

Landrin called Bevelyn from jail. She knew what he had been up to and prayed that he would change. But no talk from his mother could amount to what happened that Memorial Day weekend at Contra Costa County jail.

Mary waited somberly on the other side of the glass at the visitor's area as Landrin walked in with his head down and grabbed the phone.

"Baby it's gonna be alright," she said.

Landrin didn't know that 6-year-old TK was hiding behind the counter on the other side with Mary. Before Landrin could respond, TK popped up from underneath.

Landrin Kelly: "I couldn't touch him. I couldn't see that. I couldn't let my baby see me behind no bars. I turned my back to them and told the deputy, 'Let me go back to my room.' I knew I had to change. I couldn't be like my daddy.

"It was give it all up, die or go to jail, and I didn't want to spend another day in jail."

TK and Landrin

CHAPTER SIX

Two Steps Forward

"E-L-E-P-H-A-N-T. ELEPHANT," Landrin pronounced into the phone. "H-Y-D-R-O-P-L-A-N-E. HYDROPLANE."

A machine on the other line authorized Landrin's voice.

Landrin came out of jail in 1992 with a new lease on life and a court-ordered monitor around his ankle. He knew he had to be busy all the time. Too busy for any side trips to the projects to make fast money. Too busy to return phone calls from his old crew, who weren't happy with the decision.

Landrin Kelly: "It wasn't like the mob or anything, where you go to jail or you die trying to get out. But they didn't like it. They told me, 'You're out? You got the connects! You got the car!' I was like, 'Ya'll can have it. I'm gone. I gotta think about my son.' I didn't want to get out of jail and realize I've wasted nine years of his life."

Each day of Landrin's new schedule began at 4 a.m. with a shift at Vale Care Convalescent Hospital. After a nap, he coached TK's baseball practice, ate dinner and clocked in for the night shift from 7-11 p.m. at Home Base.

Paul Webster Sr.: "Landrin started working and being better before I did. I didn't believe him because I'd never seen it. That drug stuff was something that everybody got mixed up in down there. Drugs was rampant in Richmond and there was peer pressure. Eighty-five percent of the kids I grew up with went through that phase. A lot of people didn't make it. They either died or went to jail. I have very few friends that made it. When Landrin started being better, that actually helped me. It was peer pressure actually working in a positive form. I never thought he'd be right. If he could be right, I could be right."

Paul Sr. and Landrin both lost an important male role model at the age of twelve after Paul's father James passed away from a stroke. James Webster's goal was to keep his four kids and their friends away from Richmond's street element. As the boys' father figure, James provided whatever they needed, whether it was dining out, trips to the batting cages, home-cooked meals and presents. Actively involved in non-profit and charity work, he also had the boys pack lunches and work as volunteers for the less fortunate.

James Webster was determined to provide the best for the boys despite discrimination and prejudice, of which he experienced plenty. He was a 6-foot-3, 250 pound black man that married a 5-1 white woman, Janett, in the 1940's South. Janett's family disowned her after the marriage, so the couple moved north to Chicago, and later, west to Richmond.

Paul Webster Sr.: "My dad had worked on the railroad out in Chicago. You couldn't own nothing back then if you were black, so he had a good white friend help them get an ownership percentage of the railroad. My father bought three properties when he got to Richmond, but he carried the black struggle with him."

Crosses burned in the front yard after the family arrived, but James was determined to remain in his new California home. He always dressed in suit and tie and showcased a registered .38 on a visible harness across his chest.

James had a degree in psychology and wanted the best education for his children. Instead of attending King Elementary School in South Richmond's flatlands, he had his kids bussed uphill to the predominantly white Kensington Elementary School, which had the highest test scores in the city. Paul Webster Sr. was thus part of the first group of black children to integrate white schools in Richmond.

Paul Webster Sr.: "Being a part of that was life changing. It was always on TV and the newspaper. You could feel the animosity. The TV mini-series *Roots* had just come out and educated a lot of black people on slavery. People were saying stuff. I remember going to school as an athlete, people would ask me, 'What side you gonna be on, the blacks or the whites?' I be making jokes. I'd say, 'Whoever wins.'

"When Landrin and I came up, there were people that was always there and then you had people that would come and go. We knew a strong man and we knew when a man not present. My father made us know what was going on, what men had to do. You had other people into the street stuff who don't stay around. We knew the difference. Of the team we coached, there were about five dads that were there, and the rest was single mothers."

If Landrin and Paul's street friends showed up for the boys' games, it was for a few innings before they went back to hustling. Some were restricted geographically because of turf issues.

Landrin Kelly: "Some of our friends couldn't go everywhere their kids could go. So I told them, 'When your kid with me, he's my kid. Imma dog him out, Imma treat him like my kid.' They knew how I was and what I was about. We were well-connected. We had played in that league and grew up in that neighborhood. I knew all the parents and they knew me. They knew how I coached. If their kids got out of line, they gave me the right to whup their kid's butt."

Landrin made it clear that his son would not receive special treatment.

Landrin Kelly: "I told Terrance, 'On this field, between these lines, I'm not your friend. I'm not your daddy. I'm your coach. Don't call me daddy at practice. Call me Coach Kelly. Or Coach Landrin.' We were harder on our kids. We wanted them to be better so there couldn't be no talk that there was any favoritism."

Tra'Meka Kelly: "My brother was a big crybaby when he was younger. I watched a lot of their practices at Nichol Park and my dad didn't give Terrance no special treatment. He'd tell Terrance, 'You wanna cry? Go run the ramp.' 'You not gonna be soft.' "

The boys were now in the 7-8 age group of the Richmond Pinto Baseball League, where young pitchers are allowed to throw. The team had a new name, the White Sox, with matching uniforms. Practices took on a new intensity.

Landrin is not particularly big, but to this day he has no problem commanding a room or silencing a crowd. When angry, he seems to grow bigger and more menacing because of his booming, raspy voice.

On the team's first day of practice at Nichol Park, Landrin parked himself at home plate with a bat and a bucket full of balls at his side. He addressed the team bluntly, as if they were grown men:

"Everyone earns their position on my team, and the best players play. If you make a bad throw, you run to the fence. If you make an error, you run to the fence. Now get set."

When his players stood in straight-legged positions, Landrin's voice rang out:

"You better get your asses down. **GET DOWN**. Ready. Set."

Josh Harvey: "Landrin, he don't play. He hit those balls *hard* at us man. He was scary. He was a great motivator. You make any type of error, you had to run to the ramp and back 20 times."

Louis Montgomery: "Coach Landrin was aggressive. Fair. You earned your playing time. Him, my dad and Paul's dad, they wanted the best out of us. Landrin was more aggressive than anything. Not in a bad way. In a great way."

Paul Webster Jr.: "Landrin brought a 16-inch tire to home plate. We threw the ball probably 50 times a day to hit the circle. He'd have us stand like a flamingo with one leg up for 10 minutes straight to practice maintaining our balance."

Paul Webster Sr.: "A lot of raw people came out of Richmond playing baseball. There's ghosts and legends out there. When you go to the park growing up in Richmond, you get heckled. You gotta be able to take that. We did that to everybody so the kids learned how to laugh."

Postwar-Richmond had produced black Major Leaguers like Willie McGee, Mike Felder and Marcus Moore, while the nearby cities of Berkeley and Oakland churned out more talent including Curt Flood, Frank Robinson, Joe Morgan and Rickey Henderson.

Then there were the local athletes from Richmond that everyone knew had the talent to make it, but got swallowed up by the environment instead. Both Landrin and Paul Sr. fell into this category.

Paul Webster Jr.: "We heard that a lot. 'Landrin was *this*. Big Paul was *this*. Are you as good as your dad? Or is you not as good as your dad?' Growing up, TK and I were mediocre. We had our moments. But we was the fat boys. We were the biggest, slowest kids on the team. That's part of why we connected, because we got talked about a lot. Other kids told us, 'Ya'll suck. Ya'll sorry. Ya'll fat. Ya'll slow.' "

Paul Webster Sr.: "A lot of pressure is put on these kids. You walk into the park, they know that's my son, that's Landrin's son. They expecting you to hit the ball out of the park. Our kids caught on to that. When they first started, they wasn't that good."

Paul Webster Jr.: "When we went to the batting cages on the weekends, my dad said, let me see your hands. If he saw blisters, he'd say, 'OK, go in there and swing until they pop, and when they pop, we can leave.' We're 7 years old. Ain't no way we should be in the batting cages until our hands bleed. Ain't no way that should be put on kids like that. But, it made us stronger. It made us better."

Paul Webster Sr.: "All the coaching in the world is not going to make a kid good. But when they start telling they self, 'OK we gonna go out ourselves and play,' that's when me and Landrin know we had 'em. Ain't nothin' *you* the dad can actually do. You can show 'em, but whoever goes out there and participates the most in that activity, nine times out of 10, is going to be the best. In baseball, you don't have to be the biggest or strongest, you gotta have the most repetition. Being around us, you gonna get it. If you practice for three hours, you're going to be mentally and physically tired, but there's a sense of accomplishment. The kids kept winning, so we kept doing it."

In a big game against their cross-town rivals from Central Richmond, the 'Bad Boys,' TK hit a few deep shots and drove in some runs early in the game. But in an important late inning at-bat, he struck out on a high pitch, threw his helmet and walked off the field with tears in his eyes.

Josh Dozier: "At that age, I don't remember one time where, after he struck out, he didn't cry. He cried every time."

Landrin's eyes smoldered from the dugout:

"What is your problem? Why are you crying? It's not over, you've got another at-bat. Now you threw yourself out of the game. If you don't wanna be here you can go sit in the stands with your grandma."

"C'mon dad I wanna play."

"NO. You did what you did. You threw the bat, you know we don't throw no bats. Go home. *Bye*. Get out'a here."

Mary Kelly: "I watched plenty of games where that happened. I'd tell Landrin, 'You don't need to be yelling at him like that!' And he'd holler back, 'You can get the hell up out'a here too!' Sometimes I'd leave, and sometimes I wouldn't. I watched that since Terrance was 4 years old. That's what made him the sportsman that he was as he grew older."

Louis Montgomery: "We'd go back to Bevelyn's house after games. People were bragging. TK had hit a few shots and had a few good hits. All his dad could say was, 'What about those errors?' But it had a purpose. They knew what type of environment we were in. They wasn't hard on us for no reason. They kept us out of trouble, I can say that."

Paul Webster Sr.: "When parents coach, we personalize stuff. TK could have two home runs, but strike out a couple times. Landrin mad about the two strikeouts."

Landrin Kelly: "I had to make an example out of Terrance to show those other boys that I ain't even playing with my own son, so why do you think I'm playing with you? And I love this boy."

After being tossed out of the game by his dad, TK sulked off the field towards his grandmother Bevelyn.

33

Mary Kelly: "We get back to the apartment and Terrance tells me how his dad embarrassed him. I reassure him, 'He's only doing it because he loves you.' Then Landrin and I get into it. I say, 'You are harder on him. Harder on him than anyone else on the team. You don't have to make an example out of him.'"

Landrin Kelly: "He's my son, and he's gonna do what I say. If I can't get him to respect what I say, how can I get anyone else to show respect?"

Mary Kelly: "Just don't embarrass him in front of everyone."

Landrin Kelly: "Fuck that! In between those lines, those boys are mine. If you or anyone else wants to say something? They can go home too. You go deal with some girls, I got this here."

When Landrin finished with Mary, he went to TK's room and prodded him to turn his head over from the pillow; that booming, grating, raspy voice softer now:

"Hey man. I wouldn't have to get on you if you was doing what you was supposed to do. I need you out in front."

"I know daddy I was – "

"– I don't care. Man, how can I get these 14 other boys to listen to me and respect me, if you don't respect me and you do what the fuck you want to do? You play hard whistle to whistle. And never let 'em see you cry. You come home and cry on my shoulder, don't ever let 'em see you cry on that field."

"I'm sorry daddy I'll never do it again."

CHAPTER SEVEN

Raising Champions

WHILE BEVELYN ENSURED TK had the best academic instruction in the area, Landrin obsessed over the boy's performance on the field and dedicated limited free time away from work to one-on-one training sessions.

Landrin Kelly: "Any problems I noticed or heard anyone else talking about, we'd go out in the yard and attack them. We worked on his individual weaknesses together 30 minutes before every practice. Over time, the other kids picked up on that and showed up early for individual coaching as well. So I told Terrance, 'Do your homework before, and we'll do our own thing after practice.' I'd take Terrance to 7-11 and get a Slurpee when practice ended. We'd come back and work on his game one-on-one after.

"Terrance was a dead fastball hitter because he had quick hands, but he reached for the curveball. So my older brother and I went out to

Nicholl Park and threw him a hundred curveballs until he learned to sit back and wait for it."

Over time, Landrin's pressure and individual work with TK had the desired effect, as the boy's skill, gamesmanship and mental stamina improved. But other parents were bothered by Landrin's booming, raspy voice and hard-nosed coaching style.

Landrin Kelly: "I told them to they face, 'You don't want your son to play for me? Take him home.' When I coach and compete, it's off. I don't teach that pretend game, I teach the fundamentals. I ain't like these hip hop parents and these PlayStation coaches, how they coachin' today – favoritism – 'I know your daddy so I'll put you at running back.' You got to earn what you gonna do and where you're gonna play for me. I'm gonna put the best nine out there that'll help me win. I don't care if my son's the 10th. I ain't tryin' to satisfy no egos or nothing like that."

Tra'Meka Kelly: "My dad told parents, 'If this not how you want me to coach your kids, then take him off the team.' Obviously his way of coaching worked or my brother wouldn't have gotten as good as he did. My dad wanted all of his players to succeed. He gave the foundation to all the boys, and it was up to each kid to decide how to build on that foundation. Terrance did what he was supposed to do with it."

Mary Kelly: "He didn't want the boys to be soft. In the stands, parents said, 'Who does he think he is talking to my son like this?' I would turn around and matter-of-factly state, 'He thinks he's their coach. If you want him on another team, then put him on another team.' Because these kids came home with us after practice a lot. We fed them, took care of them, took them to the batting cages. If we do all that, then Landrin can have some words with them as well."

Some parents may have had issues with Landrin's aggressive style, but he commanded unconditional respect from the players. He was a rare male role model in Richmond that genuinely cared about the boys. The players improved as athletes and won big games under his lead.

After winning the 7-8 year old Richmond Pinto League Championship with the White Sox, Landrin was selected to coach Richmond's all-star team and pick the best players to represent Richmond in the California Little League World Series tournament. While other coaches couldn't control the more talented kids on these teams, Landrin never had a problem with discipline.

When the coaches left, however, TK and Paul Webster Jr. remained the topic of conversation as the chubby kids.

Paul Webster Jr.: "It was a lot of talk-about sessions. We was known to get on one another. If you had a bad game, it would be like a roasting session afterwards. If you messed up that day, you was the person to talk about. If you had a real good game, can't nobody say nothin' about you. So don't mess up, because if you do, you're dealing with it during the game, after the game and when we get home. It was relentless competition. TK and I were the punching bags for a while because we was the biggest, slowest guys on the team. They called us, 'Fat boy!' "

Josh Harvey: "We all got into it with each other. It was serious, but it wasn't. TK was always laid-back. He was never one to talk shit."

Paul Webster Jr.: "TK was an easy target because he'd take it. He'd let people talk about him. He didn't really come back with jokes, because he wasn't the physical type or the fighter type. He laughed a lot, he smiled a lot. He wasn't a confrontational dude. At a certain point I'd tell them, 'Shut your mouth or I beat you up.' "

Mary Kelly: "Terrance wasn't into conflict. When he was young and playing with toys – he'd just share the toy rather than have a problem. As he got older – he was bigger and taller than most of the other kids, so he could have taken them on. It wasn't because he knew he couldn't win, he was just like that. He'd say, 'Go on man, go on. I'm not trippin.' That was his thing, he wasn't trippin.' ''

TK also heard talk when he showed up at practice in a private school uniform. TK's younger cousin, Lanny Kelly III, attended the same private elementary and middle schools as TK.

Lanny Kelly III: "Kids told us, 'Aw look at the little school bitch.' 'You look cute in your little uniform.' 'You not a real nigga.' 'You too scared to go to public school?' 'You not tough.' We never took it serious, they were our friends. It was little shots they took because we had that higher education they couldn't get. It never really bothered either one of us. We knew we were blessed to have higher education, and we didn't take it for granted."

The biggest talker on the team was a talented pitcher from South Richmond's notorious Easter Hill projects named Terry.

Josh Harvey: "Terry thought he was better than everybody, we used to always get into it man. We'd go back and forth, 'I'm way better than you boy,' 'I'm a grown man.' ''

Paul Webster, Jr: "Terry made a lot of people mad. We all thought we was the best and that we was better than one another. But Terry, he would go on and on. 'Boy you suck,' that was his favorite thing to say. He did it to everybody. He thought he was the greatest ever. But that's how we rolled, that's how we motivated each other."

The problems between Terry and one of TK's teammates, James, were rooted in something much deeper – a bloody, longstanding feud between their families.

Multiple court opinions shed light on the violent rivalry between the boys' fathers to control the sale of crack cocaine in the Easter Hill projects. Terry's father Joe was addicted to crack and possessed a quick temper. He had a reputation for violence and a history of committing home invasions and robberies of other drug dealers.

James' father and uncle controlled the crack trade in the Easter Hill projects in the mid-1980's. Around the time James and Terry were born in 1986, the two families were in a turf war.

Terry's father Joe conceived a plan to rob James' mother Pam because she stored money for James' Sr. at her home.

On July 1, 1986, around 10 p.m., two men knocked on the door of Pam's house. Pam took the chain off the door and opened it. On the porch were two men carrying a 22-inch rifle and a 12-gauge shotgun. She tried to close the door, but they pushed it in. The impact from the door knocked her onto the living room floor.

Chaos ensued. During the robbery, Pam's mother Tina ran into the room and hit one of the men. One of the assailants demanded money, then fired a warning shot into the ceiling with the shotgun. After a second warning shotgun blast into the ceiling, the assailant pointed the shotgun down and fired into the back of Tina's head. He then fired a second shot at Tina before aiming at Pam and shooting her in the back as 16-month-year-old James watched. The two men closed the door and fled.

Pam crawled to the front door, but could not open it. James pulled the door open for her and she screamed for help.

Pam survived the attack and testified that Joe's brother Victor was the triggerman.

There was conflicting evidence as to whether Terry's father Joe or Uncle Victor committed the crime. The brothers resembled each other closely. Victor argued in subsequent appeals that his defense was incomplete because potential witnesses in Richmond adhered to a code of silence, and failed to testify due to fear of retaliation or antagonism with Richmond police.

Terry's father Joe was later killed in a drive-by shooting in 1989, when Terry was just 3. His Uncle Victor's subsequent appeals have been denied.

Landrin Kelly: "Terry was a good-ass player, he was raw. He was a good kid, but he played too much and liked to charge – he had a mouth. We had the whole team over at my mom's house and Terry was talking shit to James. James was about to whup his ass. Terry was scared and wanted to go home. I let 'em go and James whupped Terry's ass."

Paul Webster Jr.: "Between TK and Terry, it was a normal catcher-pitcher relationship, except that TK was an easy target. Terry would throw the ball in the dirt, and TK would say 'Throw the ball in the glove.' Terry would say, 'Catch the ball boy!' Landrin sent TK the signals, TK gave Terry the signal, and Terry would throw something else."

Despite the animosity, Landrin's Richmond all-star team advanced to the California Little League World Series tournament 10 miles north of Richmond in Rodeo. In the championship game, Richmond played a team from Orangevale, outside of Sacramento. It was a contrast in skin color and culture. Orangevale's all-white team was from a semi-rural, modest, suburban community. Richmond's team was all-black, loud and scrappy from the rough inner city.

Landrin Kelly: "I had the boys march onto the field in a straight line doing a chant, 'Ready or not, here we come, you can't hide, we gonna fiiiind you, and take your troppphy.' When we got to the dugout we chanted, 'I'm fired up, you fired up, YEAH. I'm fired up, you fired up, YEAH.' During the game, they had pitching, we had pitching. It was tough. A nail-biter."

Landrin's team went on to claim the title. It was a big moment and a concrete example of Landrin's dedication and work ethic paying off. He now had won a Little League World Series title as both a player and a coach. More important, Landrin was beginning to realize his passion for working with kids. For TK, it would be the first of many opportunities to handle pressure in big moments.

TK, bottom left, Landrin, top right

CHAPTER EIGHT

The Way Out

TK'S WAY OUT of the ghetto and Landrin's plan for remaining out of prison were the same – stay busy. Landrin and Bevelyn made it a priority that TK had something to every day, whether he was at school, baseball practice or working one-on-one with a tutor.

Bevelyn hired her neighbor, a retired Catholic school teacher, to tutor TK at least once a week beginning in the first grade. She also obtained partial financial aid so that TK could attend private schools in Richmond – St. Cornelius followed by St. David's.

Landrin covered the rest of TK's tuition with the proceeds from his two jobs. He had been promoted to dietary assistant at Vale Care Convalescent Hospital, calling in tray orders to the kitchen based on the specific needs of elderly patients.

Landrin Kelly: "Some people needed their food blended or ground up because they had no teeth. Some people were diabetic. These people were sick and had special needs with their food. Elderly people were dying every day in there. I'd smoke cigarettes outside, listen and talk with them – get some wisdom and knowledge, because they done been there, and done that."

Meanwhile, management at Home Base recognized Landrin's aggressive, street-level business mentality and work ethic, and promoted him from night crew to Department Head of Garden. In the new position, Landrin was responsible for ordering inventory, managing employees and anything else that needed to be done on a day-to-day basis to run the department.

With promotions came more money, which Landrin spent on his kids. Christmas morning became a big affair for TK and the other grandchildren. Some of TK's friends didn't have basic food and shelter. They survived through the help of neighborhood friends, theft, older street figures or their own ingenuity. They certainly didn't have a pile of presents to open on Christmas morning. TK had two piles of presents. Every year, TK, Tra'Meka and Lajada first opened up presents at Landrin and Mary's apartment in their pajamas.

Tra'Meka Kelly: "We got everything we put on our lists, plus other things. We had all the latest gadgets you can think of, that kids where we lived did not have – basketball hoops, arcade games, Nintendo, the latest shoes – Jordans, Ken Griffey Juniors, Scottie Pippens, Grant Hills – I got them too even if I didn't want them. That's how my dad was. Terrance would tell me, 'You're wearing them wrong,' and he'd lace them up different. So I'd have to wear my shoes how he wore his shoes."

After the first tree was cleared, Landrin and Mary brought the kids to Bevelyn's house, where a huge Christmas tree overshadowed a pile of presents.

Tra'Meka Kelly: "It was like Christmas you see on a magazine at Grandma Bev's. We each had ornaments with our picture on it. None of that is normal in Richmond."

After the grandchildren tore through their second set of presents, Bevelyn lined up fine china on the kitchen table and a feast was served.

Later, Landrin and Mary drove to their aunt's house in Berkeley where the kids received hundreds of dollars worth of checks from Landrin's Grandma Brown and the other aunts on Lanny Sr.'s side of the family. Finally, Landrin always saved to buy TK at least one 'big-ticket' gift per year. Everyone remembered one in particular.

Paul Webster Jr.: "We were all excited because if TK had something, we had something. We was all brothers. When he got the go kart, we all knew, 'OK *we* got a go kart now.' TK wasn't stingy, he was far from selfish. He was just like, 'OK, you can drive it, just don't break it.' "

Jamie Richards Jr.: "It was crazy having that thing, especially in Richmond. It was like, 'Wow, now we've got a go kart? Shoot. Normally we'd go to a place to do that and now we've got it at home?' We took that thing everywhere. We was in Berkeley with it. That thing was dope."

Josh Harvey: "We were driving that thing around Nichol Park one time. We were out in a dirt field. Everybody got a turn. I got a turn myself before Danerio got in there."

Paul Webster Jr.: "So our friend Danerio Brown turns it over a bunch of times and smacks into a telephone pole. He only had a few scrapes, but the go kart was trashed and TK was upset. He said, 'Man, look what you did to my go kart!' Landrin told him, 'Look at Danerio, he scraped up!' TK was like, 'So what? I don't care about his scrapes! I don't got a go kart no more! Now what am I supposed to do for fun?' So I say, 'TK we can fix the go kart. Only thing wrong is like the engine, and you're gonna need a new steering wheel…' "

Landrin Kelly: "I fixed the steering wheel and gave him a new rule. 'Nobody drives the go kart except me and you.' "

Tra'Meka Kelly: "Our childhood, even though we did grow up in Richmond, we were still able to be kids. Terrance and I hung out at the house and watched *Coming to America* on repeat. We'd play in the front yard, walk to the store or build clubhouses in the trees blocks away. We'd steal snacks from Grandma Bev's house and bring them to Nicholl Park. We liked to climb this big tower. When I got to the top, Terrance shook it and yelled, 'I'm gonna shake it so hard your glasses fall off.' I'd scream back at him, 'I'm tellin' dad, Terrance, I'm tellin' dad!' I wore big thick glasses until I got to high school. TK had all the jokes about my glasses. He'd say, 'Your glasses so thick you can see people waving on a map.' There was nothing wrong with him so I had no comeback. We weren't worried about shootings. We had no worries."

Mary Kelly: "We did a lot with the kids, whether it was camping, excursions up to the snow or trips to Chico for family reunions. We kept 'em busy. When we wasn't going as a whole family, Landrin and I took the kids to San Francisco. We stayed on the go so they wouldn't want to hang in the streets. They knew where I was born and raised, North Richmond, but they never had to experience it themselves. Whereas Landrin and I experienced things up and close and personal growing up."

TK had more than most of his friends in Richmond, but to not repeat his father's mistakes, Landrin had to teach him what he had experienced and how to survive in a place where the odds are stacked against you.

Landrin Kelly: "Gunshots, police and ambulance sirens – all the time. There was a lot of commotion from the trains – the tracks were right around the corner behind my mom's house. Then there was also an Amtrak train in front of our house going to Oakland that came at 6 a.m. every morning."

Richmond is an industrial city plagued by pollution and the threat of chemical spills, and children growing up in the city have a higher likelihood of developing asthma. The Chevron Oil Refinery was built in 1902 and is one of the biggest and most productive refineries in the country. It's also the largest employer in the city. The refinery had numerous toxic chemical spills and fires in the 1980's and 1990's. In 1993, a General Chemical rail tanker exploded in the city, releasing poisonous gas and landing 25,000 in the hospital. Officials in Richmond responded by implementing a system of emergency warning sirens tested every Wednesday in case of a toxic chemical release.

Landrin did not hide any of the realities of Richmond from TK. The effects of the drug scourge during the 1980's and 1990's were evident all around the city.

Landrin Kelly: "I'd point things out to him. 'Look at these guys doing drugs. I used to do that. I used to be a crackhead. Anybody tell you that, you ask them – well where your daddy at? My dad out here taking care of you!'

"I let him know what was going on, and what to be aware of, and what could happen. I showed him the outcome of drugs and alcohol, what it could do to you. I didn't hold nothing back from him. I showed him where I used to hang out and some of the guys who stayed out there. We saw one of my old friends who I'd grown up with on the corner begging for money. I gave him a dollar so he could get something to eat or whatever:

"Daddy how do you know him? He look toe-up."

"This guy used to be one of the rawest shortstops around."

"Damn, he the same age as you?"

"Some jealous guys tricked him. Told him to hit a joint, but they had laced it with sherm [PCP]. He hit it one time, went crate, and was *gone*. *Out*. Talkin' to himself. Hallucinating. And he never came back."

Paul Webster Sr.: "These kids were just as smart as us because we were tellin' them stuff. We ain't perfect. We ain't the type of parents that go in the back and drink. We'd drink right in front of them. And we told what to do and what not to do. We told them our war stories and how we was growing up. You might as well tell your kids rather than somebody else, because then they'll be hurt."

Louis Montgomery's house on 33rd Street was a typical meeting place for the neighborhood kids and dads after games. Louis' father, Gerald Montgomery, was a fellow coach and head umpire in the boys' baseball league, and his mother, Shannon Montgomery, was the president of the league. Their middle class home in South Richmond was similar to the warm environment that the kids could find at Bevelyn's house down the street on Florida Avenue.

Landrin Kelly: "Shannon was like the boys' mama, TK called her mama, too. We went to Gerald's house a lot after games – we'd play dominoes, cook, drink beers and talk smack. We were all friends, but we coached different teams. We'd break down the game from that day, especially if it was a loss. 'This guy should have played third.' 'Your pitching rotation was all fucked up.' We'd adjust accordingly and beat that team up the next time we played 'em."

As a neighborhood gathering place, the Montgomery house was also a place where Landrin and Paul Webster Sr. frequently embarrassed the boys.

Paul Webster Jr.: "TK and I saw too much. Our dads would fight. Car accidents. Some of the stories we heard… we were just like, 'If we can refrain from being like our dads… that'll be good,' because our dads is a lot alike. My dad's favorite was Strawberry Hill, and Landrin's favorite

47

was King Cobra. There was a lot of nights where Gerald had to kick our dads out of his house, a lot of embarrassing moments. Alcohol was they poison. There were nights where we had to tuck our dads into bed and take their shoes off when we were young. Plenty of nights."

Landrin Kelly: "After long nights at Gerald's house, Terrance used to tell me, 'Dad, you can't embarrass me like that.' Or he'd confide in my older brother, and my brother would let me know later that I need to tone it down."

Late nights out on the weekends were also affecting Landrin's relationship with Mary.

Landrin Kelly: "On the weekends, it was too much of me making up for lost time during the week. Staying out late, partying. Mary worked full-time and was the more business-like one. She took care of everything at home. Around that time I was driving around on a suspended license and the police issued a warrant. I had Terrance's equipment in the car with me but he had gone home earlier. I left at 3 a.m. to go home and change for work. It was foggy out. The police got behind me and that was it. They towed my car, put a 30-day hold on it and took me down to the station where I called my wife.

"They impounded the car, so I couldn't get Terrance's baseball equipment out of the back. He didn't have his cleats or his bat for our game the next day. My wife and my momma told him what happened, and he was just out of it. I only missed two games his whole life and that was one of them. He had one of his worst games."

Paul Webster Sr.: "I was with TK in the dugout that day. You'd hear other people talking about what happened with Landrin. TK heard that, and *that* affected him. We around some gossipy-ass people in Richmond. Landrin doing such a good job, people wait for that situation so they can gossip, 'Well apparently he ain't doing that good.' But out of all the people gossiping, Landrin's the parent out there with the kids. They don't come out like Landrin and me. We're picking up their kids and coaching their kids. It was easy to pick on Landrin, and TK heard all that. Hearing all that stuff, TK might have felt down because he got feelings man. TK love his daddy, and *he* could talk about his daddy, but you better not."

Landrin Kelly: "When I got out, I told him, 'Man, I fucked up. Sorry about that man.' 'Dad, I needed you there. I needed to hear your voice.' "

*   *   *

TK's two families formed a permanent bond in 1996 when Landrin and Mary married at a church in Oakland. Landrin stood at the altar with his best men: older brother Lanny Kelly Jr., Uncle Billy Dempsey Sr. and Paul Webster Sr.

Paul Webster Jr.: "Landrin was crying up there like a big ol' baby. He always used to get on us for being crybabies. He was happy, smiling and crying…a lot. I remember thinking, 'You talk about us crying on the field, look who the big crybaby now?' "

Mary Kelly: "He shed enough tears for both of us. That was the longest walk of my life. I was shaking and when I got up there and saw him crying. I fixed my mouth stone-faced because I didn't want to break down and cry myself.

"We went to the Martin Luther King Jr. Center for the reception afterwards. My mother-in-law told me, 'Mary Lou I didn't know if you were gonna say I do or I don't!' "

TK was junior groom and Tra'Meka the junior bride. Brother and sister walked up the aisle together and right before the vows, there was a mini-wedding. TK presented Tra'Meka with a small ring to symbolize the two families coming together as one. Then, he gave her a spin.

Mary Kelly: "That was the 'aww' moment of our wedding."

CHAPTER NINE

The Ramp

"EASIER TO STAY IN SHAPE than it is to get in shape," Landrin grunted between drags off a cigarette. "If you stayed in shape over the summer you wouldn't be going through this right now. Stay in shape, keep your muscles tight and you won't feel the soreness once the season comes."

Landrin's eyes shifted to the long covered crosswalk that elevated over the Bay Area Rapid Transit [BART] tracks. The ramp is three blocks from Globetown and connects Nichol Park to the neighborhood. TK and his teammates came to know the covered crosswalk simply as, 'The Ramp.'

TK knew what lay ahead on this scorching-hot day. He was 10 years old now, dressed in shorts and running shoes.

"Over-and-back is one," Landrin barked. "You do five-to-10 runnin' hard. Let's go."

Landrin saw the potential in TK before anyone else. He'd forge his son into the star athlete he never had the discipline or resources to be. Landrin started at fullback and linebacker for Berkeley High School and later Kennedy High School in South Richmond, but his mind was elsewhere. He had never honed his craft or done serious conditioning during his prep career.

TK played Pop Warner Football beginning at the age of eight. He had a big-boned frame and slow, clumsy feet. He was athletic, but not yet a standout.

After sprinting 10 laps over and back, TK doubled over in front of Landrin, covered in sweat. Then he threw up. Unfazed, Landrin handed him a water bottle:

"No pain, no gain. The more you put in, the more you get out."

The young athlete making a name in Richmond at this time was a boy named Quinton Ganther. Quinton was the biggest, baddest kid on the block and later played in the NFL.

Quinton Ganther: "I first met TK when he was five and I was seven. TK was that big clumsy kid with baby fat. He didn't know how to control his body yet. You knew that once he grew into his body, he would be good."

Landrin Kelly: "Quinton was very competitive. He was the stud of the Pop Warner Leagues in Berkeley. He played quarterback, and people were scared to run at him. And on defense, he laid people *out*. He was way better than Terrance, talent-wise, coming up."

Louis Montgomery: "Quinton had kids tying his shoelaces for him. He was a bully, a grown man. My dad had to talk to him and tell him that bullying stuff is not OK."

Louis and Quinton grew up and lived together as brothers after Gerald and Shannon Montgomery unofficially adopted Quinton, who had no choice but to be tough growing up. His parents struggled when he was a child, and Quinton had to fend for himself and his younger sister on the streets at the age of seven.

Quinton Ganther: "Everyone in the neighborhood had a part in raising me. My road was different. My godparents, they gave me a chance at life. They showed me the love that I wanted so bad as a child. My godmother Shannon told me, 'I just want to give you the same opportunity as everyone else.' That meant everything to me.

"We all played together at Nicholl Park. Everyone in the neighborhood was close-knit. The love that Miss Bev and Landrin gave TK, that was the kind of love I wanted from my father and my mother because I didn't have it. Bevelyn was a part of raising all us kids. Landrin wasn't my coach directly, but he *was* my coach at the same time.

"Landrin cut TK no slack. He demanded excellence from him. He was on him, 24-7. Sometimes you'd feel bad for TK. If you could imagine Landrin's facial expressions – he was so serious. He was like that on all the kids, but TK was his baby, his love, his everything. But if I didn't deliver? Oh, he'd rip me too."

Paul Webster Jr.: "Landrin wanted the best out of TK. He was there at every key moment. Whether good or bad, he was there. You don't see that a lot with black kids and fathers. He worked hard to make sure TK had everything he could possibly wish for."

Quinton Ganther: "Landrin might have been hard on TK, but he didn't disappear on him and didn't abandon him. I was envious of that. I really didn't appreciate what Landrin was doing until I got older."

Jeremy Williams also knew TK, Landrin and Bevelyn from their childhood days in South Richmond.

Jeremy Williams: "TK and I didn't play sports together but we bumped into each other a lot when we were younger. Richmond is very small – so if you're around the same age brackets, you're bound to run into each other. When I was younger, I remember that all the kids that played around Nicholl Park used to hang out at TK's grandma's house or his dad's house.

"Landrin and Bevelyn – they were just cool people. Bevelyn could cook and kept TK in line. Some people who live with their grandparents – the grandparents let the kids feel their own way. But TK's grandmother kept it strict. That was her heart.

"I'd come to Landrin's house and wait for TK to get home from practice or whatever he had goin' on. Landrin and I would get a few games of dominoes in while we waited for TK. It's rare in Richmond to have a father who will step up and take care of a son full time. I can assure you that it almost never happens. The only people I know in that situation is because their mom died – that's it."

On the football field, TK initially played offensive and defensive line due to his big body and slow feet. He grew up wanting to play linebacker like his dad and older cousins Johnny Dempsey and Malik Carr. Dempsey had played linebacker for Skyline High School in Oakland and had a reputation as a hard hitter.

Johnny Dempsey: "Growing up, I looked up to my older cousin Landrin. He was five years older than me, so I wanted to be like him. He played Pop Warner football, and that's why I got into football. He played linebacker in high school so that's why I wanted to play linebacker at Skyline."

Determined to build up the speed to play linebacker, TK now prodded Landrin off the couch for workouts at the park. Father-son drills became a daily occurrence as Landrin ratcheted up the intensity.

Landrin Kelly: "Terrance had them big feet for a kid his age. His shoe size was bigger than his age until he was 12. He had size 10 feet when he was eight, and he'd sometimes trip over his feet. So the first thing I wanted to work on after football season was his footwork.

"I put him through drills at the park – jump rope, twisting his hips, how to turn and take angles. I'd take a ball and have him get set. Then we'd do the shuttle drill – 'Ball this way, ball that way.' He slides his feet laterally with the ball as quick as he can.

"Backpedaling drills. I'd stand as quarterback. 'GO' – he starts running – 'RUN' – he steps up –'PASS' – he pedals backwards. When I throw, he's gotta flip his hips and get to the ball.

"Sideline-to-sideline drills and angle drills. You put a cone here, start there and you got to run to that angle. And he got closer to the ball every time because he learned how to take his angle."

The drills reinforced the coordination and balance TK learned from taking ballet as a child. He may have started slow, but TK developed quick feet to match his hands.

After football season, it was back to training for baseball in the Mustang league, where Landrin's team was now known as the Pirates.

Mary Kelly: "As Terrance got older, it seemed like Landrin got meaner and meaner; and he yelled more."

But TK was older and bigger now, too. On what would have otherwise been a routine practice on a nice day at Nicholl Park, TK did something unexpected.

Paul Webster Jr.: "So we run to the ramp and back like we did at every practice. Then I hear Landrin yell, 'RUN! TK! RUN!' TK must have been fed up, because he just walked the final lap in."

Landrin Kelly: "I tell him, 'OK. You can walk home.' He said, 'Alright,' and turned around and walked."

Paul Webster Jr.: "I said, 'TK you want me to walk with you?' Landrin says, 'No, he can walk home by himself.'"

Landrin Kelly: "TK shouts back, 'I ain't got no problem walkin', I'll walk home!' 'Well go then! You always wanna talk back and have an attitude? Walk your ass home!' 'Fine I'll go! Ain't that far anyway!'

Paul Webster Jr.: "He didn't pack none of his equipment. He just turned around and walked. Everybody on the team looked at each other like, 'Did this really just happen?' That was the first time TK had stood up for himself as far as his dad yelling at him.

"Usually, my dad would go to bat for TK, and Landrin would go to bat for me. So the next game, TK and Landrin are going through one of their moments. Landrin had benched him after sending him home from practice, and TK is once again crying before the game.

Landrin Kelly: "I see Terrance strapping on his catcher's gear. I tell him, 'Boy I told you you're not playing, sit your ass down!' He starts crying. 'Keep crying! You're gonna sit the bench until I say.' "

Paul Webster Sr.: "I'm like, 'No. We one game from the championship. We not sittin' TK on the bench because his bat is hot right now. He's rippin'. I need him.'"

Landrin Kelly: "Yes I am sittin' him on the bench. You gonna go against my word? And I didn't do that shit with you last time you sat Lil Paul on the bench for no reason at all?' "

Paul Webster Sr.: "Well that's my son.' 'OK. This my son.' 'Fuck that! You can't just be on him! He wanna play? Let him play!' 'He's disrespecting his team, we all 'posed to be one!' "

Paul Webster Jr.: "So now our dads is face-to-face. They push each other, curse each other out. 'Fuck you!' 'No, Fuck you!' This was all before the game with the other team watching. It made us look so un-unified. They did that all the time. They still do it today."

Paul Webster Sr.: "When the game comes, we gotta put everything down and leave everything at home. We need TK. If you got an issue with your son, then after the game he can do some more running. But right now, he's playing. At the same time, I realize I did the same thing with my son."

After games, the dads regrouped back at Landrin's, Paul's or Gerald's house.

Paul Webster Jr.: "Like brothers, they kissed and made up without no apology, no talking it over. No, 'You wrong.' No, 'My bad for that.' After each time, they said what they wanted to say. Then it's back to business."

*   *   *

On the football field, TK had always played in older age brackets because of his weight. Around the age of 11, he hit a major growth spurt. After the spurt, he was longer, leaner and taller than his peers – far from the chubby kid who was once the focal point of 'talk about' sessions. Landrin's nephew elaborates.

Lanny Kelly III: "Terrance loved to eat. As he got taller, he kept weight on him and didn't lose his power. He never really got too slim. Whenever Terrance came over, my dad made potatoes of some kind for him because he loved potatoes. One time, everyone's eating and I'm struggling with my plate. I had some potatoes left. Terrance looked at me and told me, 'You not gonna eat your potatoes,' and he just grabbed them and ate them all. Then he looked at my dad, and said, 'Hey Unc, you gonna eat your potatoes?' And he ate all of those potatoes. Then there was potatoes in the pot and he finishes all of those too. It gave new meaning to his nickname, Potato Head. After that he was just Potato Man.

57

"My dad is Big Lan, he's the oldest brother – he helped take care of Landrin when Landrin was growing up. When Terrance was around, there was never a point where my dad wouldn't listen to him. He taught me and Terrance the same values – the values he also taught Landrin as a kid. He told us, 'Don't get caught up in the streets of Richmond.' 'Do your thing. Don't worry about people talking about you.' Because we was in Catholic school our whole life, we got talked about a lot. My dad always said we had the best of both worlds – because we got the higher education, but we also hung out in the streets – so we got to see both sides as we grew up. We couldn't control where we lived, but we could control who we hung out with. We could control our decision making. My dad preached being yourself heavily. 'Don't follow the crowd. Never hesitate to do something you want to do because other people aren't doing it.' 'If you're not comfortable with it, don't do it. Go with your first instinct. Your best instinct is your initial instinct.' "

*   *   *

Back on the field, Landrin's intense drilling and pressure had its intended effect.

Landrin Kelly: "TK started hitting balls out of the park, 320 feet, when he was 11 years old. They nicknamed him, 'Bastion TK.' And he got humble. He'd jog around the bases after a home run. When kids asked him, 'Why you not excited?' He'd tell 'em, 'Man, I 'posed to do that.' Then he'd put his catcher's gear on and get ready to catch."

Paul Webster Sr.: "TK wasn't that rah-rah guy. He didn't really like the spotlight. He never went off keel. When I coached him, he'd be the same person when I got mad and hollered at him that he was after he hit a home run, rounded the bases and came back to the dugout. You ain't gon' get nothing different out of him. As a human being – you've got to love that. Sometimes people get self-righteous with accomplishments. None of that with him."

Paul Webster Jr.: "It reminded me of Josh Gibson. They say Josh Gibson hit a home run one-handed. Well, TK hit a grand slam one-handed. When it came time to hit and we started dropping bombs, everybody stopped talking."

TK's play had been noticed. Jarvis Brown, the vice president of Richmond's Little League and a fellow coach, had a connection with Eric Johnson, who coached an all-star team based out of Danville, an affluent East Bay suburb.

Eric Johnson asked Jarvis for a list of the best youth baseball players in Richmond. Jarvis recommended TK, Kevin Webster and Maurice Butler. Johnson selected TK to try out in Danville for a team that would play in Beijing, China. TK made the team and Johnson found sponsors to pay for his trip.

The family then raised money to finance Landrin and Lanny III's $1,200 all-inclusive package in China by selling sweet potato pies, slabs of ribs and barbecue dinners at Little League games and various job sites.

Landrin Kelly: "We sold them on Fridays for parents who came home from work and didn't have time to cook or were too tired. My mom spent $50 to make sweet potato pies and we sold 20 of them for $10 each – make a quick $200. Then go back to the store and repeat the process.

"It was a 21-hour flight to get to China. I never experienced anything like that. Ten? OK. But not no 21-hours. We was on a real big plane, everybody watching movies all day, getting to know each other. You had kids from all over California – L.A., Richmond, Fairfield, Sacramento, Danville – everywhere."

One of these players was Dave Purpura, from the majority white suburban community of Pleasanton, 40 miles southeast of Richmond.

Dave Purpura: "Terrance hit the ball with authority, you definitely felt his presence when he was at the plate. As good an athlete as he was, I was more impressed with how he was as a person. TK and Landrin were from a very different background than I was and we were coming from different walks of life, but I felt like there was absolutely no difference between us. They were both quality people. TK was positive and upbeat, always smiling. He felt like a brother, another guy, another teammate."

Landrin Kelly: "Once we landed, we were jet-lagged for a while. The package got us three meals a day. We did guided tours and saw the Great Wall of China. TK and Baby Lanny [Lanny Kelly III] went all the way up to the top of the wall. We watched acrobatic shows, and went to the Beijing Zoo. He seen the different culture – how they live, how they eat. He was like, 'Damn dad...' The Beijing team ended up winning it all. We took second in the tournament."

The China trip was further evidence of Landrin's success since giving up 'The Life' and also showed potential doors opening due to TK's blossoming athletic prowess. But back home, nothing was guaranteed. Landrin doubled down to keep himself on track and shelter his son in an increasingly dangerous environment.

TK at the airport before China

TK, Landrin and Lanny III on the Great Wall

CHAPTER 10

Ghosts and Legends

THE CHINA TRIP offered a glimpse into endless possibilities and different worlds – life beyond the ghetto, beyond California and even beyond the USA. But in Richmond, reality was blunt.

Louis Montgomery: "TK and I went back to my house after a game. TK was 12, I was 13. We changed out of our baseball clothes, showered and got dressed. We were on our way back over the ramp to hang out at Nichol Park.

"There were two older dudes sittin' down at the top the ramp – in the middle of it. We noticed them but didn't pay no attention. As we passed by them in the middle, they came at us. They pushed me, shoved TK and said, 'Give me your chain.'

"These guys were in their early twenties. We pushed back for a minute. We were both thinking, 'Naw, we not giving you no chain.' Then the other guy reached for a gun and pushed us back, 'You think I'm playin wit'chu? You think I'm playin wit'chu?' We said, 'Naw, man, we ain't trippin.'

"We handed them the chain. It was basically like, 'Our life ain't worth no chain.' They ran off. A lot of people at the park heard what happened. People chased them, but they got away."

Landrin Kelly: "I pulled up and TK says, 'Dad, they took my chain!' They ran through the park. I drove around to the other side and chased them but they got away."

Louis Montgomery: "When we played basketball late at night in front of my house, we'd leave the door cracked open because we'd hear gunshots and have to run inside. We had good times, but we were aware of where we were growing up at."

Landrin Kelly: "You hear gunshots every night. That's why Terrance used to wear headphones while he did homework. I'd say, 'How can you concentrate listening to that music?' 'Dad, every time a gunshot or a police siren goes off, it distracts me. If I got the headphones on, I can get my work done.' "

With so many pitfalls in their immediate environment, Landrin re-dedicated himself to TK's sports career. He took over as coach of TK's Richmond Steelers Pop Warner football team and fashioned his work schedule around TK's games. Landrin had three jobs during this time, two part-time jobs and a full-time job. He still worked at Vale Care Convalescent Hospital and Home Base and picked up a part-time job at Price Club, a warehouse gig on the Richmond docks. For his new job he drove trucks to different Price Club locations around the Bay Area and operated a forklift.

Meanwhile, now possessed the speed and conditioning to play linebacker. Landrin's work on the ramp had paid off.

Paul Webster Jr.: "Linebacker was our favorite position growing up. I can remember the grin on TK's face when he got to play. He said,

'Paul you comin' to my game? I'm finally playin' linebacker!' He was like a coach on the field."

Landrin Kelly: "TK would be in the defensive huddle. I'd give him the defensive calls via hand signals – '5-2', 'Man-to-man,' 'Linebackers criss-cross and blitz.' He'd step out of the huddle, read my signal, go back and tell them what I call. If someone was out of position, he'd direct them and put them where they supposed to be. If the other team scored, I'd yell at him and we'd go back and forth. 'Man, where you at! What the fuck is you doin' out there? You ain't in position!' 'I was! I was! They wasn't in position!' 'Well, then get them in position!' "

Josh Dozier: "TK and I were playing for the Richmond Steelers and Landrin was coaching. We were playing the Oakland Dynamites. Landrin got a 15-yard flag for yelling at TK on the sideline. I remember him telling the ref, 'But I'm yellin' at my own kid!' "

Landrin Kelly: "The refs didn't understand that between Terrance and me, it was actually two coaches yelling at each other on that field. We studied plays. One of the team moms taped the games. I'd go to one of the coach's house and we'd all break down last week's game. I'd get the tape after, take it home and show Terrance what happened.

"At linebacker, I taught him to watch the hips. You can't move nowhere without the hips. Your head can go anywhere and if you watch the head, they can juke you. Back then, everybody was all about the Barry Sanders. So I told him, 'Stop watching people's eyes.' Over time he started watching the hips. And when people tried to fake, he'd fake with them before he made the tackle."

In his final Pop Warner years, TK began to separate from his peers and flash star potential.

Paul Webster Jr.: "We were all like, where did this come from?' He started being a heck of a linebacker. Landrin had him hitting that ramp. He was faster and taller than everybody."

Josh Dozier: "On the football field, TK hit hard and was one of the best conditioned guys out there. Great teammate. He always made sure we were on the same page on the field. He was *extremely* smart, even at that young age, on what plays they were running and how to dissect plays. He was ahead of his time as far as thinking on the field, not just pure athleticism. He was never the most physically-gifted. He knew how to use what he had to be successful. When I realized this guy was really good at multiple sports, I was like, 'This dude could be something.' "

Louis Montgomery: "I played defense with TK in football when we were Midgets. It was in an all-star game. Man, it was his energy, just to be out there with him. That's when I knew, I was like, 'This boy dangerous. This boy bad. He raw. He gonna make it.' "

Johnny Dempsey: "We were at McClymonds High School in Oakland, and Terrance was playing in a Pop Warner game. He was wearing my old number, 32. I grew up watching a lot of linebackers play and I watched a lot of football. From the second I saw him play, I was so impressed. Not in a sense of, 'This is the greatest thing I ever saw,' but more because of his technique and the way he went about his business on the field at such a young age. He was so fundamentally sound. The way he scraped all the way down in his stance. All his reads were correct. I gave him something to follow. At one time, I looked at myself as the great player in the family. Then Terrance came up and just crushed everything I'd ever done."

Paul Webster Sr.: "When he played football and baseball, Landrin had that intangible. He wasn't the biggest guy out there or the best athlete, but he was tough as nails. His attitude was, 'Let's play all day.' You wanted Landrin on your side – that never let you down. That grit. That Dennis Rodman. He'll fight you. He'll bite you. He'll scratch you. He's been an underdog his entire life. Now TK wanted to be better than his dad, better than that legend at Nicholl Park. He was just like Landrin, but in a smarter, nicer way – he'd been educated more and he went to class more than Landrin. The whole village raised TK – you had grandparents, you had fathers, you had uncles and aunts raising TK."

Robert Turner, Landrin's old defensive coordinator at Kennedy High School, also watched both Landrin and TK play.

Robert Turner: "As an athlete, Landrin was like a lot of guys from Richmond – he had that heart – that *pitbull in a chihuahua's body* mentality. His mentality was, 'I don't care how big you are, I'm gonna go against you.' Landrin could have been a really good athlete, but he didn't use half his potential. His mind was somewhere else. He was a jerk. I can still remember him giving some of our coaches the finger. He thought he should have been playing a lot more, but he wasn't putting in the work to be out there.

"I saw a lot of me in Landrin because he was a wannabe hoodie. With the peer pressure and the different influences around him back then in the late 80's, I could see Landrin heading in that direction. I grew up in North Richmond, which was the worst of the worst. But I played football and got a scholarship to San Diego State where I played safety. It helped me to get out of Richmond and meet people from different walks of life. Landrin never got that opportunity.

"TK was roughly 12 when I met him. I saw him play a couple times just going around the football fields in Richmond. He was a man among boys out there. I've met a few kids like that over the years, and he was one of them. I was really proud of Landrin because instead of the streets, he was involved in his family. I've been coaching for 30-something years and you're always seeing moms. So many black fathers aren't around. You don't see a lot of fathers around unless their son make it – then you hear 'em say, 'That's my boy.' I was really happy to see Landrin so involved in his son's life."

Pastor K.R. Woods: "I first met the family around 1999. The youngest of Bevelyn's children, Latonya, came to our church first, and then Bevelyn and the rest of the family started coming. I met TK about the same time. Outstanding young man. Charismatic, gregarious and very mannerable. In control of his emotions. He always drew a crowd with him – he would bring a whole row of teammates and guys from the neighborhood. Many of the young people that we have in the church today came because of him. He was always in church with his grandmother, every Sunday."

Lanny Kelly III: "TK didn't talk me into playing football. He said, 'You're going to play football.' I wanted to play because he played. The first day we got our pads, Landrin put me in the backyard with Terrance. I was eight and he was 12. Landrin handed Terrance a football and told me I had to tackle him, and that I wasn't going in the house until I did. I'm thinking with the relationship Terrance and I had, he would let me tackle him after the first time so we go could inside. Was I wrong. He ran me over, over and over again. After about an hour, he seen the beatin' I was taking, so he finally let me tackle him.

"Before every game, Terrance told me, 'Always play hard whistle-to-whistle, and never let 'em see you cry. He'd say, 'Yeah, I'll be at your game.' And I couldn't wait for him to get there so I could show him what I learned from watching him. Whenever he came, I'd be into the game but I could sense that he was there. We'd make eye contact, and he'd give me some sort of gesture, whether it was a thumbs up, a fist, any little thing.

"Having him there watching, knowing I'm usually the one trying to go watch him, that motivated me. I wanted to play harder when he was there. I didn't want to mess up because I knew I would hear from him, 'Aww you struck out.' He would tease me, but not to the point where I felt bad about it. It was motivational teasing."

As TK's final year in Pop Warner came to a close, he and Paul Webster Jr. were anxious to prove themselves at the next level.

Paul Webster Jr.: "Like my dad said, from Little League sports to high school sports, that's when you separate the men from the boys. As far as talent went, TK, myself, Josh Harvey, Terry and a few others had separated in terms of who was elite – who could actually make it."

As for where TK would prove himself, Bevelyn's private tutoring and selection of schools meant that he had the grades and the options to choose. Most of TK's friends from St. David's were going to St. Mary's College High School in Albany or Salesian High School in Richmond. Both were private schools with strong academic reputations. TK had grown up in Richmond and Berkeley and would be comfortable at either school.

TK was ultimately accepted to St. Mary's, Salesian and Bishop O'Dowd, another reputable private high school in Oakland. TK's choice was to go with the majority of his friends, but Bevelyn had other ideas:

"No. *Wait.* De La Salle gon' take him. I already know."

Landrin's niece Krystal was a cheerleader at Carondelet, the all-girl school across the street from De La Salle in Concord. TK commuted to Concord with her several times to watch games during middle school.

At De La Salle's Owen Owens Field, TK watched De La Salle standout D.J. Williams, a future NFL linebacker, rip through opposing defenses as a running back and lay devastating hits from the linebacker position. The De La Salle varsity football team was riding a national record 100-game win streak playing in the highest division in the North Coast Section.

Landrin Kelly: "Terrance and my momma enlightened me to De La Salle. He had watched their games and was likin' the atmosphere. He was like, 'Dad I wanna play for them. They raw.' The kids in the neighborhood ragged on him when he was thinking about going out

68

there. They told him, 'You ain't gonna make it at De La Salle. De La Salle too hard for you.' "

The problem with De La Salle was distance. Concord was 40 minutes away from South Richmond driving one way with no traffic. It was also a different world than inner city Richmond, Berkeley and Oakland.

Then, Bevelyn got the call that De La Salle accepted TK. Landrin's older sister Lona filled out paperwork applying for financial aid, which was approved.

Landrin Kelly: "My mama made the decision for where he was gonna go. And that's what we did."

Like it or not, TK would be pushed out of his comfort zone.

Bevelyn Kelly, high school graduation

Left to right, clockwise: Bevelyn, Lanny Sr., TK, Lanny III

Landrin and TK, Richmond Steelers football

Top middle - Landrin; top right - Paul Webster Sr.
Below Landrin, right - TK; next to TK, right - Paul Webster Jr.

TK, Tra'Meka, Lanny III, Tahira (Lanny III's sister)

CHAPTER 11

De La Salle

THE BUZZ OF AN ALARM CLOCK. TK groaned and peered at the device –
5 a.m. – then smashed the snooze button.

"Terrance, get up!" Lanny Sr.'s yelled from kitchen while cooking
his grandson's breakfast.

"Boy, get up and get your shower," Bevelyn hollered.

TK, 14, stumbled out of bed like a zombie. This was the picture
of TK in the classroom, in the halls and at home for the next four years –
exhausted.

In the Bay Area, De La Salle is known for many things. It's known
as a great school academically. It's known as prestigious and expensive.
The Spartans are known for great sports programs, especially football. To
surrounding public schools, it's the butt of 'all-guy campus' jokes.

But De La Salle's football success is also a point of pride in
Northern California, especially in its dominance over Southern California
teams. Alumni proudly wear the colors. Sports at De La Salle are highly

competitive and require greater commitment than other schools. Year-round practices and early morning workouts are the expected routine.

TK was a three-sport athlete at De La Salle as a freshman. To make 7 a.m. workouts prior to school with a long commute, he had to be up earlier than most, if not all, of his classmates. Lanny Sr. drove him out of Richmond every morning no later than 6 a.m.

TK slept in his grandfather's ancient Honda as the surroundings changed from inner city blight to greenery and space and finally to middle class suburb with shopping malls and ranch-style homes as they arrived in Concord.

Deans Joe Aliotti and Bob Gould welcomed the new class in De La Salle's theater for orientation. Aliotti, a former college quarterback, also worked as an assistant coach on the varsity football team with the informal title of 'Coach In Charge Of Yelling At The Refs.' Gould, a mountain, was a former De La Salle linebacker.

"I'm looking out at a bunch of YOUNG MEN," Aliotti stressed as he pointed out clothes that failed to abide by the school's uniform requirement. "That means I expect you to DRESS like YOUNG MEN. What does it mean to dress like a YOUNG MAN? Collared SHIRTS. Wearing a BELT. Wearing SHOES. That means you don't wear HATS while indoors."

De La Salle is a religious school. Prayers are held and reiterated before every class. Students and teams attend chapel. Faculty and some students perform daily prayers in a periphery courtyard.

But De La Salle is also a culture of sports. Headlines often revolve around championships and athletic accomplishments. Intramural sports like basketball and quad hockey draw a crowd and hold bragging rights. During March Madness, the quad and cafeteria are abuzz with bracketology as OOOOHHHHs and AWWWS echo through the halls with the latest buzzer-beater.

As TK walked into De La Salle's gym for the first sports rally of the year, the freshman class received a roaring BOOOOO from the upperclassmen surrounding them in the gym's stands. There is a hierarchy at De La Salle that the faculty, teachers and coaches support. Upperclassmen are allowed various privileges denied to freshman and sophomores. Freshmen are the butt of jokes, pranks and rituals. Freshman year at De La Salle is an initiation period.

If a student, usually an unsuspecting freshman, gets tossed out of lunch line for cutting or dropped a soda on the floor, everyone points and yells, 'OOOOOOOOOHHHHHHHHH', which grows louder from the scene of the incident until much of the campus is in on it.

De La Salle is an all-boys school that offers co-ed classes for upperclassmen in partnership with Carondelet. The result is that freshman and sophomore classrooms become arenas of no-holds-barred discussions, depending on the class.

The teachers at De La Salle are special. Many coach the school's powerhouse sports teams – baseball, basketball, soccer, water polo, swimming, track, cross country, golf.

Two of the longest-tenured teachers at De La Salle are football coaches Bob Ladouceur and Terry Eidson. They established the culture with the football program, and the team's success spread to everything else in the school. The program dominated headlines outside and influenced the school inside.

A former Division 1 college running back, Ladouceur was an intimidating presence. He roamed the halls stone-faced in a leather jacket and sunglasses, usually by himself.

TK's first class began with what would become a ritual. The teacher at the front of the room asked, "Are there any intentions?" After a pause:

Teacher: "St. John Baptist De La Salle."

All: "PRAY FOR US."

Teacher: "Live Jesus in our hearts"

All: "FOREVER."

TK was unlike many of his teammates at De La Salle, who had older brothers go through the school and knew what to expect. Everything at De La Salle was new for him – especially the new demographics. De La Salle was majority Caucasian with small Hispanic and Filipino minorities and a tiny African-American population. Wealthy kids drove to school in shiny new cars. Night and day from Richmond.

Mary Kelly: "TK told me, 'It's a trip.' Everything was different, and he had to adapt to it, but he did like it. It was stressful, but it wasn't nothing he couldn't handle."

Paul Webster Jr.: "He talked about how different the people were as far as them being fortunate and lifestyles. He said it was no jealousy, no enemies. Like in the high school movies where kids is having fun and it's all cool. The nobody kid is taking the popular kid's girlfriend – like that. Just all happiness."

Lanny Kelly III: "He had fun hanging with his De La Salle friends as opposed to his Richmond friends, where you never know if someone's gonna be jealous or a fight might happen."

Tra'Meka Kelly: "He just commented on the life that they lived. He was like, 'Those kids drive to school in Benzes, Escalades. The food in the cafeteria…you know, it's cool over there. They come from nice backgrounds like us.' Our parents had provided us with nice things so we never felt like where we lived. So when he got there, he fit right in. He didn't feel out of place. He felt right at home at De La Salle."

Jamie Richards Jr.: "He liked it but he felt like most people going to new schools or new communities – a little uncomfortable. It's a new place, a new area. Even how people talk is different. But TK was good. He knew how to adapt."

TK found comfort in sports, which facilitated his transition in Concord.

Jackie Bates: "T.J. Ward and I had played our last year of Pop Warner football together. At the beginning of freshman year at De La Salle, we sat in the locker room one day and waited for practice to start. This tall guy walks in. Long arms. I'm looking at this dude like, 'Who is he? A linebacker? Tight end? This dude is huge!' He had this spark about him. He was a happy dude. Real joyful. He had this real inner connection with God, you could just feel it. We clicked right away. After that day, we were always together."

At lunch, TK sat at an all-black table that included some of the best athletic talent in the San Francisco Bay Area. Future NFL all-Pro safety T.J. Ward was part of this group, known as the 'Amigos.'

T.J. Ward: "TK and I knew a lot of the same people away from De La Salle, so we naturally clicked and always hung out together. We were all pretty much one big group."

The Amigos consisted of TK from Richmond, Ward and Maurice Drew from Antioch, Damon Jenkins and Johnny Tucker from Oakland, Demontae Fitzgerald from Walnut Creek, Willie Glasper, Eric Love and Cameron Colvin from Pittsburg, Nate Kenion from Vallejo, Jackie Bates from Benicia, Alijah and Aaron Bradley from Hercules, Demetrius

Williams from Concord and dominant senior linebacker Kevin Simon from Pinole.

After lunch, TK struggled to keep his eyes open through afternoon classes until, *SNAP*, piercing bells jolted him awake at 2:20 p.m., which marked the end of school and the beginning of football practice. His grandfather picked him up 6:30 p.m. for a long ride home before he ate, showered, washed his equipment and did homework.

Landrin Kelly: "It takes a village to raise a child. My family was my backbone in raising Terrance and helping him make the transition to De La Salle. My dad drove TK and cooked his breakfast every morning. I worked two jobs and provided his income. My younger sister Latonya was his personal shopper and stylist. Either my older sister Lona or I would give her a credit card to get TK's clothes. She'd go out and shop for him and get an outfit or two out of the arrangement for herself. We got him about 20 collared shirts and 10 pairs of pants. He could match it up and fix it up however he wanted to look. So we had him looking professional whenever he stepped out."

Lona Kelly, Bevelyn's oldest child, was the most business-like of the siblings. Ten years older than Landrin, she graduated from San Francisco State and worked for Kaiser. Lona and Bevelyn helped TK with homework, class projects, and any paperwork required from De La Salle.

Sondra Dempsey: "As a family, everybody participated in raising Terrance. He never took a bus to school. There wasn't nothing held back from him. They gave him their best in every way they could. It was about trying to mold him and shape him into the best individual he could be. It was about giving him the foundation."

The village may have put him in position to succeed, but at the end of the day, TK had to step up and do the actual work.

Louis Montgomery: "As far as studies go, I wasn't as disciplined as TK. You had to be disciplined as a student to succeed in that type of environment. Our parents were hard on us as far as school goes. I got whuppings because of grades. Coming from Richmond, I wasn't the greatest student in our group and I *definitely* wasn't the worst student. My younger siblings, TK and his little cousin Lanny, they were all more disciplined in school. My sister graduated with a 4.0. I just wasn't that type of cat. TK was."

*   *   *

On the football field during his first practices at De La Salle, TK felt comfortable despite intense competition. De La Salle's freshman class of 2000 was the most talented in the history of the school. Athletes came from all over the Bay Area.

T.J. Ward: "We all coming from different parts of the Bay Area where we was, 'The Guy.' TK was the guy from Richmond, Jackie from Vallejo, Cam and Willie from Pittsburg, me from Antioch. When we all came to De La Salle it was, 'OK, we gonna see who's the best.' It was a challenge. Every practice, every workout, every game. It was competition – who was gonna be the best."

Jackie Bates: "We were all very competitive. We knew we were blessed to be in that situation – having some the best players in Northern California all on one team. We felt unstoppable."

Wide receiver Drew Curto, from Danville, recalls meeting TK as a freshman.

Curto: "Terrance was a bigger, taller freshman. Already about 175 pounds. He had a natural talent, a nose for the game, and he hit harder than anyone else. He had long arms and a huge wingspan. He was a playmaker on the field. He had instincts. He knew where to be. He was one of a handful of guys like that.

"Off the field, nice kid. Treated everyone fairly. There were some kids that went around trying to prove they were tough. TK was never a punk. He never tried to intimidate you. He was tough, but he never tried to show it. He let his play on the field talk for him. Outside of that, he was happy-go-lucky, smiling."

Jackie Bates, from Benicia, had the quickest feet on the field and raw speed that would eventually take him to the NFL.

Bates: "TK was nasty. Rangy. Like a big ol' corner or something. Athletic, but also big."

Chris Biller, from Concord, was a stocky man-child as a freshman. Already built like a senior, he strutted around confidently like a sumo wrestler with his chest puffed out and a perpetual grin spread across his face.

Biller: "Terrance and I were the linebackers freshman year. He was big, but still lean. You knew who were gonna be the gamers or not, and he was one of them. All we tried to do was learn how to read the pulling guards, and it took all year. Off the field, Terrance was quiet. We weren't great that year."

Drew Curto: "TK and Biller were the Mike [middle] and Will [weakside] linebackers. It seemed like they were inseparable freshman year. Those were two of the toughest kids I had ever met. Biller hit so hard, and TK was right there with him. It was not a place you wanted to go as a wide receiver."

Parker Hanks, from Alamo, was a blond-haired, blue-eyed, all-American looking kid who was soft spoken and nice off the field, but hard-hitting on the field.

Hanks: "Freshman year I handed the ball off to TK. TK ran the ball hard and he knew the plays. He was athletic and instinctual. He smelled out holes and cuts. He ran over kids when he needed to."

82

By December 2001, TK had established himself as a talented, play-making freshman at De La Salle, and was named the freshman team's defensive player-of-the-year. Even if he had not yet fully embraced De La Salle, TK's first year had been a success. Back home, some unexpected changes were taking place.

Freshman football, 2000

CHAPTER 12

Separation

BY THE EARLY 2000'S, violence in Richmond involved an increasing number of young victims and 'wrong place, wrong time' deaths. Landrin's generation had been protected by an unwritten street code, which gave kids a 'free pass' by those involved in the drug economy and street level crimes.

Mary Kelly: "In the 70's, murders were happening, but it didn't involve young children. It was older people, dope fiends or people who had robbed someone. They were doing things to cause people to want to hurt them, so it wasn't unexpected when it happened. When I was growing up, if I was to get too close to those situations where people in your front yard overdose with needles in their arm or sell dope, they'd say, 'Get back in the house.' I wasn't able to be a part of that lifestyle. Even drug addicts tried to encourage kids to do right or do better."

This code eroded over time, thanks in no small part to the crack cocaine scourge of the 1980's that hit Richmond and other inner cities across the country especially hard and led to the first parentless generation of children in America – the crack generation. The children of many crack users were raised by their associations on the street.

Black fathers were the first to go, a process which started well before the crack era and was due in large part to discrimination and drug abuse.

In post-World War II Richmond, blacks were confined to menial employment when well-paying wartime positions dried up. Black children attended segregated, overcrowded public schools. "Negro patrons not wanted" signs hung outside shops in downtown Richmond, and blacks were not served at many white restaurants.[1] Blacks also could not use public hospitals [Bevelyn Kelly was born by a midwife in North Richmond], purchase houses or commercial office space. Moreover, racially restrictive housing covenants restricted blacks from living in white neighborhoods until well into the 1960s.[2]

Even after passage of the Civil Rights Act in 1964 and the Voting Rights Act of 1965, segregation in businesses, city services and schools persisted. This eroded victories in the civil rights era. Disillusionment with the Vietnam War and the national emergence of a drug culture contributed to the downturn.

Black leaders in America were also targeted and eliminated. In 1963, a white supremacist assassinated civil rights activist Medgar Evers in Jackson, Mississippi. In 1965, radical member of the Nation of Islam assassinated Malcolm X in New York City. In 1967, the government

---

[1] Moore, Shirley Ann Wilson, *To Place Our Deeds*, University of California Press, 2001. Kindle. Loc. 1455.

[2] *Id.* Kindle. Loc. 1564. Blacks were first permitted to purchase homes in Richmond's Parchester Village development in 1949. Parchester residents had to lobby to obtain lighting, sewage, telephone and transportation services for the subdivision.

targeted Muhammad Ali after he refused to be drafted into the United State Army and stripped him of the world heavyweight title. In 1968, a white supremacist assassinated Dr. Martin Luther King Jr., which sparked a week of social unrest nationally and race riots at Richmond High school.

Police abuse was yet another problem. In Richmond, a group of white police officers known as the 'Cowboys' earned a reputation for ruthless beatings and arbitrary use of police power in the black community.

Landrin Kelly: "The Richmond Cowboys was racist cops. There's more black and Hispanic cops today, but back then they were all white. They'd stereotype, beat and kill black males. If you got pulled over for a traffic ticket and complained that you didn't do anything, they'd take you up to the station and beat you. They got away with it all the time."

Paul Webster Sr.: "The Cowboys came out when the drug era came. Back then, it was older black people selling drugs. So when they started seeing these older people having money without jobs – if you was black and had a chain on, or if you was in a new car, they'd pull you over. Later, the Cowboys found out who the main drug dealers was. Two of the captains of the police got involved with one of the head dope dealers, this guy named Q. He was a ruthless drug lord, and his backing was the police. For a time, you had two of the Cowboys working with the main dope dealer. It was all corrupt. That's how the drugs got pushed into black neighborhoods in Richmond."

Robert Turner: "A lot of the black men in my generation or in Landrin's father's generation wasn't around because they were *taken away*. As a black person you didn't have a lot of privileges back then. If you wasn't a great athlete and didn't catch a break, your best opportunity was to get on the corner, sell drugs and make some money. So with a lot of guys, the only thing these fathers knew how to do to make money for their families was something illegal. If they get arrested or killed, all of a sudden they're gone."

President Reagan's Anti-Drug Abuse Act of 1988 amended the Anti-Drug Abuse Act of 1986 and mandated that convicted drug offenders serve at least 85 percent of their jail sentences. The amendment also created new drug enforcement units to patrol inner city streets. A year later, in September 1989, President George H.W. Bush allotted $50 million to target crime in public housing projects. The new laws resulted in a massive rise in the incarceration of black males while drug abuse eliminated many black mothers.

Robert Turner: "I started working for the Richmond school district in the 80's and saw firsthand what happened in the crack era. You had babies having babies. 35-year-old grandmothers. I had kids coming to school addicted to crack because their parents were on crack. I had *mothers* buying crack from their kids. I had one kid at Kennedy who sold crack to his mom. She didn't pay him, so he beat her up. She called the police. When they questioned him, he said, 'She owed me money, so I had to do what I had to do.' After that, the police take the son to jail and the mother decides to go to her son's house to find his crack. The police go to the son's house to look for evidence and find the mother. She broke into her son's house and was smoking his crack."

Mary Kelly: "The crack generation started using the younger kids in the 90's and early 2000's. They'd say, 'You hold the drugs. You stay here and watch for police. You run the drugs to customers.' In return, they'd give the kids shoes or money or whatever else, so that the younger kids become married to the older person who influences them. They know the younger kids will only get juvenile hall time if they get caught. And because these older guys' parents were dope fiends themselves, or prostitutes, this is normal for them. They don't know anything different. So you have crack babies having babies, and this is the result – there is no moral code anymore. Anything goes."

Landrin and Mary responded by moving the family to Vallejo, 15 miles north of Richmond.

Tra'Meka Kelly: "By the time Richmond really started to change, we lived in Vallejo and Terrance was away at school in Concord. We were actively involved in school and sports, so we didn't know what was going on. For Terrance, by the time he got home, he barely had enough time to shower and go to sleep. Our parents always protected us from those types of things."

After the move to Vallejo, Landrin and Mary's relationship deteriorated. Both worked demanding full-time schedules. Price Club promoted Landrin to head foreman of the docks in Richmond and gave him responsibility for distribution to 25 Price Club locations around the Bay Area. His crew received and shipped out 25 trucks a day and used forklifts to load freight from the docks and trucks.

Price Club merged with Costco and the company officially changed its name to Costco Wholesale in the late 1990's. Costco eventually closed its warehouse in Richmond and transferred Landrin to the Costco warehouse in Tracy, 65 miles east of Richmond in California's Central Valley. The commute to Tracy took at least an hour, one way, with no traffic.

Landrin Kelly: "After I got transferred, I went back to getting up at 4 a.m. again because we had to be at the Tracy location at 6 a.m. My morning shift ended at 1 p.m. I'd do errands, call my mom and we'd talk about Terrance. She'd tell me, 'Your son need to this, this and that. He needs money for this.' I'd say, 'Go grab a check out of my drawer,' and she'd sign. She had my signature down to a T. It was all about the things Terrance had to do.

"I bought him a cell phone, and I'd call him a few times a day. I'd ask, 'What'chu doing, what'chu got?' 'OK, where you at?' We had to stay in communication at all times, because that first year at De La Salle over in Concord was rough."

Landrin drove to Concord in the afternoons to watch Terrance's freshman football practices at De La Salle. Then, either he or Lanny Sr. took TK home after practice. In the evenings, Landrin went to his second job at Home Base, now called Home Depot, from 7-11 p.m.

Landrin got every Thursday night off so he could watch Terrance's games at De La Salle. With the added commute, the new schedule left little free time to spend with Mary, especially during the work week. On weekends, he wanted time for himself.

Landrin Kelly: "I was hanging out too much. I took care of business Monday through Friday, but Friday night through Sunday night was my time. A lot of the conflict was about me not coming home and staying out late on the weekends."

Mary Kelly: "Landrin and I – we had to go and grow. We couldn't see eye-to-eye. Things happen. We never divorced, but we decided to separate."

Landrin Kelly: "I left everything in Vallejo. I told her, 'Just give me my clothes, I don't want nothing.' I went and stayed with my mom. We still had communication. It was hard. We was accustomed to a lifestyle that had been broken."

Mary Kelly: "We had to be mature enough to have a conversation and say, 'It's not just about us, it's about these kids too.' We let them know, 'This had nothing to do with you guys. You didn't cause this.' We made sure our kids knew this wasn't their separation. They were still brother and sisters. TK would go hang out with Tra'Meka and Lajada at my house in Vallejo, and Tra'Meka would still go stay with her dad, Landrin, in Richmond. We may have been separated, but we didn't separate from our kids. Everyone still came together over the holidays and Terrance could still call on me for anything – whether it was a ride, money or whatever else he needed."

Landrin Kelly: "Mary and Terrance still had their relationship, and I still took care of Tra'Meka during breaks and holidays or whenever she wanted to come hang out. About a year after Mary and I had separated, I moved out of my parents' house to live in Modesto because it was closer to my morning job at Costco in Tracy. Then I met someone, Nicole. Modesto was too far out in the valley with all of Terrance's stuff going on in Concord, so I moved in with Nicole back in Richmond.

"Nicole and I went out together and had a lot of parties at our house. She had a son, Brian James. Brian was one year older than Baby Lanny [Lanny Kelly III], and I had coached them since they were 6. We won the California Little League World Series twice with those younger teams. Terrance and Brian became like brothers – they'd wrestle, play and run around the house together. Brian looked up to him."

Lanny Kelly III: "Brian and I grew up playing together. He was very playful. He liked to joke a lot and go back and forth, talking about people."

Paul Webster Jr.: "Brian was short, and everything that come with a short man having something to prove. He was dark-skinned, ran his mouth a lot, talked a lot, joked around a lot. And then he'd get mad and be quick to fight. He had a chip on his shoulder."

After moving in with Nicole, Landrin's life took another turn after an altercation at work.

Landrin Kelly: "I was working at the big Costco warehouse out in Tracy. This white guy called me a nigga, so I slapped his ass and we had a fight. The company investigated the incident. They said he was wrong for saying it, but I was wrong for hitting him. So they fired both of us.

"I still had my job at Home Depot but I needed that second job so I sent out a ton of applications. I got a job at a wine distribution center."

*   *   *

The chaos in Landrin's life should have affected TK. His parents had separated. His father moved several times and was fired from one of his jobs. He commuted an hour and a half each day to go to school – away from the friends he grew up with and the familiarity of home. Nevertheless, Bevelyn's influence remained the anchor. No matter where TK was on Saturday night, he had to be dressed and ready for church with his grandmother on Sunday.

Landrin Kelly: "She really started pushing church when he got into high school. If he was at my house on Saturday night hanging out, she'd call me in the morning and say, 'You gotta get that boy up for church.' I worked two jobs all week, so Sunday was my day. I'm not getting out of bed. But he had to go. I went on special occasions – Mother's Day, Christmas, Easter.

"Everybody used to like to spend the night at my momma's house. She cooked and let them do what they wanted, as long as they were respectful and followed the rules. But if they spent the night, they had to be ready to leave at 8:30 for 9 a.m. service in Berkeley at Covenant Worship Center."

Louis Montgomery: "TK got me and my little brother to go to church with him a lot. He'd actually wake me up at my house, 'C'mon, c'mon. Come with me.' 'Naw I'm not goin'. Who let you in the house this early to wake me up and make me go to church?' After he got his license, he made us go to church with him. He'd bribe us with Jack In The Box breakfast if we'd go."

The influence of Lanny Kelly Sr., or 'Pops,' also kept TK grounded. TK still slept in a twin bed next to his grandfather in Landrin's tiny old room.

Landrin Kelly: "Growing up, TK and my dad liked to rassle [wrestle]. My dad was a boxer in the army. He taught Terrance the proper stance and how to throw a jab. Terrance was like an old soul, because he was raised by my mom and dad. When you raised by grandparents, you get that real foundation. With these young hip hop parents, you don't get that. Terrance was totally different than some of these other kids from the ghetto because he had the respect and he had the foundation. He had the fear of God and he believed in God. He had a dad that was there and grandparents that were there. These other kids' mothers was on drugs, or were single parent.

"My dad taught him about the streets and about girls. They'd bond together in my old room, watch *Perry Mason* or cowboys on TV. He had Pops wrapped around his finger. They never had problems."

Lanny Kelly III: "I used to share a bed with Terrance at Grandma Bev's. He was a loud sleeper...some nights I'd wake up on the floor. So I started sleeping with my grandfather. He told us jokes and old stories about his childhood. But after every laugh he always gave us a lesson – how we could make things easier for ourselves. If I told him, 'Hey Pops, guess what I did in my game today?' He'd listen, but as soon as the story was over, he'd say, 'OK, well how your grades lookin?' It was always about education. He'd tell us, 'If you the smartest one in the classroom, you can be the smartest one on the field. If you don't do good in school, you won't do good on the field. If you can study your playbook, you can study your schoolwork.' "

Tra'Meka Kelly: "Terrance and Pops sharing a room, it went on for so long that I thought it was normal. Looking back, I think about that room being so small, with all of the kids piled in there with Pops. It made us bond. We watched boxing and Pops talked to us about school.

"Pops was the man. He had this stick, we called it the 'Mean-Old-Man-Stick.' He wouldn't hit us with the stick, but he would always say, 'Imma go get the Mean-Old-Man-Stick.' We would joke with him while

he watched TV. 'Pops, where your stick at?' He'd say, 'Alright now, alright.'
"

Lanny Kelly Sr. had beaten throat cancer and suffered from a pulmonary disease. He carried an oxygen tank and mask with him at all times. He slept with a sleeping mask connected to an oxygen machine that extended into the hallway and emitted a shrill noise.

Johnny Dempsey: "Terrance was so laid-back and nonchalant about everything, and I think he got it from his grandfather. With TK and Pops, it was more like they were buddies, like they were brothers. Pops never showed anger, he was cool with everything. TK was the same."

CHAPTER 13

Dark Clouds

ALERTS from incoming text message interrupted the constant hiss of Pops' oxygen machine and the low hum of a passing BART train outside.

Pops' raspy voice called out:

"Boy get up. Check that phone.

"Terrance, get up!

"Get up boy!"

TK reached down groggily and opened his flip phone. 10 missed calls. Eight new text messages.

His eyes popped open.

*   *   *

Paul Webster Jr.: "It was the week of Christmas vacation at Kennedy High School in Richmond. I seen Terry at his locker."

Terry was the talented pitcher that TK battled with on all-star teams growing up. He played freshman baseball with Paul Jr. at Kennedy and showed a lot of potential.

Paul Webster Jr.: "I told Terry, 'Boy when we get back, you know we start on that baseball field.' He said, 'Yeah fa'sho.' Later that week, me and Josh was chillin' at my dad house. We watching TV, and we get a call. 'Terry got shot and was in critical condition.' Later, he passed."

A vehicle approached and opened fire as Terry sat in the backseat of a station wagon in South Richmond's Easter Hill projects. His only fault was being in the wrong place at the wrong time.

Paul Webster Jr.: "I thought, 'Dude I just seen him four days ago. For him to be the first person gone…he was so full of life. It was our first close friend, one of our brothers – dying. It hit all of us extremely hard. Not having him and his loud-mouth, obnoxious self around. We missed it a lot."

Landrin Kelly: "TK and I didn't go to Terry's funeral because that was turf shit. I wasn't about to jeopardize my son's life and bring him to the funeral in case any funk happened. We put Terry's number on our jerseys later that summer to remember him."

Quinton Ganther: "As kids we played baseball at Nicholl Park and in the back lot of the projects, all day and all night. It was like we had an unwritten pass. It's like, 'I don't care what happens – these kids are hands off.' After Terry died, it became, 'Anyone can get it.' Now they'll gun down kids to make a point. Terry was a damn good player. It's sad man."

Paul Webster Sr.: "That was the start of them dark clouds. Everything from then on changed. We had kept the kids so that nothing could happen. Doubt creeps in. The shit we doin', this good system we had, it ain't working. Terry was our boy, he was like my son. We all went through a lot because of that, and we all grew closer. The boys really turned into men after that. They saw what we had told them – verification that the shit is real out there. They started coming home early without us yelling at 'em.

"Now, we wondering whether we did the right thing with how we raised them. Ain't nothing you can do to prepare for the death of a friend or a kid. Terry was a good kid, a fun kid. He'd be on a different team and come back and spend the night at our house. He liked jokin' and laughin'. He'd help me with the dishes. After he was gone, I started drinking more, changing practice times, second guessing myself. Looking back, we probably should have all got some counseling or something. Life is never the same after that. After that, it was, 'Watch who you be around.'

"We had to talk to our kids about conflict resolution. They'd come back after a night out and say, 'This dude was looking at me funny.' I'd say, 'Yeah, well, stuff like that happen, you need to walk away.' And they'd say, 'Well I ain't no punk.' I'd say, 'Ain't nobody no punk but you got something to do the next day.'

"See, our boys is cocky. They ain't no punks and they from Richmond. I'd tell 'em, 'You get up at five in the morning the next day and run five miles, they don't. What's getting you up in the morning, that's got to make you walk away.'"

After returning from the holiday break, Paul Jr., Josh Harvey and other old teammates struggled with the loss of their friend. TK also took time off to remember Terry before De La Salle's demanding freshman basketball program began.

Drew Curto: "At the end of the break, we started basketball practice. TK was gone for a week. He didn't tell anybody. Nobody could get in touch with him. The coaches didn't know what's going on. So after a week he's suddenly back in the morning before practice. Its 5:45 a.m. in the De La Salle parking lot and TK's wearing street clothes and a beanie, eating a Burger King breakfast. Later, we warm up on the court before

96

conditioning. TK gets the ball, dribbles and shoots a free throw. It goes straight up – air ball. We're all dying laughing. He looks over at us and says, 'I stiiiill got it!' ''

De La Salle's varsity basketball team was a perennial contender in the California Interscholastic Federation playoffs and had won the 1999 CIF Division I state championship the year before. As TK and Landrin approached a ticket kiosk for a varsity playoff game, an older parent asked TK, "So you brought your uncle with you?"

"Naw, that's my dad," he said.

At just 31, Landrin was one of the youngest parents in TK's freshman class. Many were in the late stages of their careers or retired.

*   *   *

In the spring, TK played on De La Salle's freshman baseball team. Steve Fujimoto, from Walnut Creek, describes his first interaction with TK.

Fujimoto: "I first met TK at baseball camp in the eighth grade before De La Salle. The funny thing about TK when I played baseball with him was that he never wore a cup, and TK played catcher. We couldn't understand not wearing a cup, especially when you played that position. But he just didn't give a shit."

Fujimoto also played football with TK. Like Biller, he was a powerfully-built freshman with the frame of a gorilla. On the baseball field, he was known for bulldozing catchers in spectacular home plate collisions. In the classroom, he liked to karate chop people.

Steve Fujimoto: "TK's grandma Bevelyn was always around and came to every game. She was like his mom. After games we'd barbeque and she brought this potato salad that everybody fuckin' died for. Landrin was the same. He wanted to meet everyone that was around TK. You could tell that was his entire life – Terrance. He was always joked and laughed with us."

After TK's freshman year at De La Salle, he played summer baseball back in Richmond and spent free time meeting girls.

Anthony "Ace" Brown: "I played on the same teams with TK's little cousin Lanny III since T-ball, and my older cousin Danerio Brown played on all of TK's teams. So we were always together. We were the Browns and TK and Lanny were the Kellys. TK was like my big cousin. De La Salle was a different world for TK in a lot of ways. But a big difference for him was that it was an all-boys school and you couldn't ever see no girls."

Paul Webster Jr.: "It was freshman year summer after a baseball game. Josh Harvey, TK and I walked from my house to my girlfriend Ebony's house. I thought Josh was gonna start talking to Ebony's friend Chastity. When we got to Ebony's house, we were all hangin' on the couch, and TK was kind of awkward around Chas. Then we walked to the store and I seen TK in the lead actually talkin' to Chas.

"After that, TK was like, 'Yeah I got her number,' and they started talking. I was like, 'Whoa.' Me and Chas was the oldest, and TK and Ebony was the youngest. We had a basketball game. Me and Chas versus TK and Ebony. Ebony and TK both actually played organized basketball, but we beat 'em."

Chastity Harper: "I met Terrance through Ebony and Paul. When we played that basketball game, at that point Terrance and I weren't dating. But that was where I really started to like him. My mom was against me going to meet Terrance's family because she didn't know them. But my mom knew Landrin's girlfriend Nicole from growing up – so when she found out Nicole was dating Landrin, she called Nicole to get information about the family. Nicole actually drove me to Bevelyn's house in South Richmond to meet the family for the first time. My mom trusted

Nicole's opinion and felt comfortable with me going to the family's house with her."

Paul Webster Jr.: "Next thing you know, it was cool. My best friend and my girl at the time's best friend is together – that's cool, that's a lot of good times."

Chastity Harper: "We couldn't drive at that time so we walked everywhere. We weren't telling our parents where we were going. We'd walk from Ebony's house to Paul's house, or they came to Ebony's. They'd pick up Portumex burritos on the way a lot. It must have been like a three-mile walk.

"TK was a little awkward at first. His friends teased him about being a virgin still, even though we were only freshman. I went to a private school, too, so we had that connection. He had really tough friends and grew up in a tough neighborhood, but through it all, his family protected him. With his friends from Richmond being the way they were, you would assume he behaved a certain way, but he didn't. There were a lot of things that he would act like he was into, but in reality, he wasn't. He was different.

"He was hardly ever serious. Him and his friends talked about each other a lot, but in a joking way. Those relationships meant a lot to him. They picked on each other, but it was all love. He laughed a lot and had this infectious laugh. He was really easygoing. He didn't take himself too serious."

Mary Kelly: "When I first met Chastity, I thought, 'This is a classy young lady.' I liked her style. She was very mature. She had her standards, and she wasn't going to lower those standards."

Lanny Kelly III: "TK was a gentleman as far as opening the door for Chastity and taking care of her. It gave me a good look and model for my upcoming relationships. He didn't mind having her around the homeboys and family events. Chastity always looked out for me and treated me as if I was a little brother."

Tra'Meka Kelly: "My brother was prince charming in my eyes. When he was gonna go to my Grandma Bev's house, I'd say, 'Terrance just stay home one more day!' I wanted to be with him 24/7. So when Terrance tried to tell me he had a girlfriend, I was like, 'You don't have no girlfriend.' 'I do have a girlfriend, she's nice!' 'I don't care. I don't like no girl you date.' So when he introduced me to her, he said, 'Chastity this my sister Tra'Meka, Tra'Meka this my girlfriend Chastity.' 'Hi.'

"I was so mad my brother had a girlfriend. I was young and I was just like, 'Oh *no*. You in *my* space, this is *my* brother. Who are you?' But she wasn't some girl trying to date him for the moment. So I had no choice but to get to know her. After I got to know her, I gave her a pass.

"Over time I realized I couldn't ask for a better girlfriend for him. Chastity had her head on straight. She was going to school. She wanted to get a degree and be something. She wasn't one of the girls that we grew up with that's known for sleeping around or whatever. I love Chastity. That's my sister."

Landrin Kelly: "They was best friends. They'd come to my house, do their homework and chill out together. They had a real solid connection. When he didn't have practice or nothing, he hung out with Chastity.

"When Terrance first got involved in sex, he wouldn't talk to me about it. I used to tell him, 'I know you fuckin' boy. I know you fuckin'.' 'Naw, dad, we ain't even doing nothing.' 'Boy, I ain't stupid. If you have a baby, everything that come to you go to that baby, because that baby ain't ask to be here and you ain't got no job or nothing else.'

"Terrance confided in my brother. During the week, Terrance and Lanny III were at my mom's house. On the weekends, the boys went to my house or my brother's house in Berkeley. My brother taught Terrance the basics when it came to that stuff."

Chastity Harper: "Terrance's world at De La Salle and his world outside school were very different. The people, the demographics were totally different. But he always remained the same. He didn't stay with a particular crowd. He fit in in both areas and it wasn't a big deal to him. He grew up in the private school system too, so he was used to it. I admired his ability to connect with different types of people."

CHAPTER 14

It's In The Water

A PARTY LATER THAT SUMMER made the vast differences between TK's two worlds all too clear. The party was at Lefty Gomez Recreation Center in Rodeo, 15 miles north of Richmond – where TK and Paul Jr. had won the California Little League World Series title years before.

Paul Webster Jr.: "A big group of us went out. TK was there. I don't know why, but everybody decided to wear Avirex leather jackets to the party that night. When I got to Lefty Gomez, I was like, 'This is stupid, it's gonna be hot in here and we got on these big leather Avirex coats. Other people wore FUBU and Air Force Ones. The white t-shirt was big back then.

"So we paid our five dollars, got patted down and walked in. People dancing in different groups, bumping and grindin'. Music blasting. Some people drinking hard liquor, fifths of Hennessey and gin. Everything was going fine, and then I remember a song came on that changed the tides of everything. It was *What You Gon' Do* by Lil Jon. Next thing you know, I had got into it with a fella. We had an argument and everybody says, 'It's a fight! It's a fight! Take that outside!'

"So everybody about to go outside. Then everyone says, 'Oh my God, they got guns!' There was a totally different fight outside, and everybody stampedes back inside to get out through the back door.

"Dudes came in with guns. There was only one exit besides the windows and it was in the back. As everybody runs back in, I turn around and BAM – the dude that I got into it with before sucker punches me. I get up and see another dude coming inside with a gun.

"I hear gunshots. I see a window and jump head-first through the window. A kid followed me through the window and got caught. I grabbed his belt buckle and threw him down to the ground with me. After that it was just gunfire. You don't know where your brother at, you don't know where your friends at. You with people you don't know trying to hide.

"TK was in the back. He ran all the way across the baseball field, hopped a fence and just kept running. We met up after. I was just happy that everybody I went to the party with got home how they came.

"Something happened at every hall party. I don't know what it is; we say it's in the water in Richmond. You never run from nothing and you stand up for everything. The mentality is, 'One minute I can be your best friend, the next second I'm your worst enemy.' "

Jeremy Williams: "Growing up in Richmond, things can happen at any time. If we're hanging out at a party – we could be having fun – our minds are somewhere totally different. But when we hear them shots, we're reminded exactly where we are.

"We all used to party at the Lefty Gomez Center, it was the place to go. But shit was always happening there. About 12, 12:30, the party's over. One time, these people from North Richmond had some guns and

103

they were *in* the party. They shot the whole place up. That was the last time I ever went there.

"We were so young and silly. As an adult, right now, there's no way in hell I'd go to no shit like that. We didn't have no problem with nobody, so we figured it wouldn't happen to us. But there was always shootings. People jumping out windows. One time I ran out of there and I fell. So if they had tried to shoot me, I would have been gone.

"TK and I used to go to Wendy's in Richmond a lot. If I'm in line at the drive-thru, TK would get out of his car and surprise me. He'd knock on my window and say, 'Look at'chu slippin' – you know, like I'm not paying attention to my surroundings. He scared the shit out of me one time doing that; I spilled soda all over myself."

Paul Webster Jr.: "Richmond is nothing like L.A. We didn't bang colors. You always had the Southside of Richmond versus Central versus North. After that, you rep your block, your hood, your street, your set. You got Parchester, you got Central, you got North, you got Southside-Maine, you got the 26 or the Hill, the Temples, Crescent Park, the Townhouses, Carlson and Chanslor, the Tens, the Thirties, the Forties, the One-Way – you got all these different parts that rep they hood."

An understanding of how the division began requires another look into history. Prior to World War II, Richmond was a tiny suburb with a population around 20,000. After the Japanese bombed Pearl Harbor in 1941, America threw the full weight of its industrial capacity into the creation of planes, ships, vehicles and armaments as it officially entered the war.

Poor workers from across the South, eager for an opportunity to make a wage in the new wartime factories and shipyards, boarded crowded buses and trains destined for northern cities and the West Coast. This massive shift in population, known as the Second Great Migration, brought millions of newcomers of all colors to Los Angeles and the San

104

Francisco Bay Area. In Richmond alone, the population swelled to over 100,000 virtually overnight.[3]

The creation and mobilization of naval shipyards in San Francisco, Marin County, Oakland and Richmond transformed the region into the greatest shipbuilding center in the United States.[4] In San Francisco, new migrant workers flocked to Hunters Point Naval Shipyard. In Oakland, the Moore Dry Dock Company expanded its operation and began hiring black workers for the first time. In Richmond, black workers found jobs in the massive Kaiser Shipyards, which produced 747 vessels during the war, making it one of the most efficient wartime production facilities in history.[5]

Before the war, black workers were restricted from the shipyards, and only 20,000 blacks lived in the entire Bay Area. After the war, that number swelled to 120,000, with 14,000 in Richmond alone.[6] While low income housing was built to accommodate these workers per the U.S. Housing Act of 1937, it was temporary, overcrowded, barracks-style housing. These areas became known as, 'shipyard ghettos.'[7] Many of these same barracks-style homes remain in Richmond today.

The original residents of industrial wartime cities such as Richmond were less than thrilled to share job opportunities, schools and public services with the newly arrived poor migrants, especially black migrants. The Ku Klux Klan marched openly in Richmond before the onset of the war. Black migrants arriving in Richmond therefore began

---

[3] Archibald, Katherine, *Wartime Shipyards*, University of Illinois Press, 2006. Pg. xvi
[4] *Id*. Pg. xxvi

[5] National Park Service. *World War II in the San Francisco Bay Area*.
    http://www.cr.nps.gov/nr/travel/wwIIbayarea/ric.htm

[6] Archibald, Katherine, *Wartime Shipyards*, University of Illinois Press, 2006. Pg. 1ix

[7] *Id*. Pg. xxvii

their new lives in shipyard ghettos or in unincorporated North Richmond, where blacks in Richmond had been traditionally confined.

The end of the war in 1945 abruptly halted the supply of good jobs in the shipyards and a reality check – if you were black, you would not be hired for the majority of the remaining jobs. If you were hired, it was for a job that paid less. Richmond's economic bulwark Standard Oil, now known as Chevron, did not begin full scale hiring of blacks in Richmond until the late 1960's.[8]

Blacks in the post-war San Francisco Bay Area could find employment in government positions, such as those at Alameda Air Station, Oakland Naval Supply Center, Oakland Army Base and Mare Island, but there was fierce competition and the requirement of a high school diploma and prior experience working in either the shipyards or in the Army. This was a rare combination because many blacks had dropped out of high school to work and raise families from an early age.

The Kelly family's Pastor, K.R. Woods, grew up in South Richmond's Deliverance Temples Apartments. His maternal and paternal grandfathers migrated from the South to work in Richmond's wartime shipyards during World War II.

Pastor K.R. Woods: "In Richmond, blacks could only live in certain areas. First, it was North Richmond. Then, they moved down into Central and South Richmond. But the crime really accelerated when the people in my parents' generation – the children of the migrants, couldn't get jobs. So they turned to the street economy – drugs, clubs and gangs – to make money. People started going to jail for drug charges and robberies. The result was the absence of the black father from the family.

---

[8] Moore, Shirley Ann Wilson, *To Place Our Deeds*, University of California Press, 2001. Print. Pg. 600. Note that there were exceptions where a few black workers were hired at Standard Oil before this period.

The mothers raise the children and the kids' guidance is coming from the streets. Richmond was a microcosm of what was going on all around the country in this respect."

Without higher-paying jobs, many single black mothers in the generation after the migrants could not afford to live in the few middle class neighborhoods that did not restrict blacks, such as Laurel Park in South Richmond or Parchester Village to the north.

Pastor K.R. Woods: "You couldn't move into Laurel Park unless you had a pretty good job. Most of those people worked with the government."

Bevelyn Kelly was like many other single black mothers in the 1960's supporting large families – her only option was to live in or near the 20 public housing projects built in Richmond before and during World War II where blacks were not restricted. While some of Richmond's housing projects, such as Atchison Village, were successful, others turned into prison-like enclaves such as Globetown or Southside Richmond's infamous Easter Hill projects.

Pastor K.R. Woods: "Landrin and I's generation was one that grew up in these projects in the 70's and 80's, where our dads weren't around because they were out on the streets. It was all about what project you lived in, because they're designed to keep you in. You got all these poor kids in there with no dads, or with dads coming around every now and then. So you had an automatic divide with the neighborhoods or streets that we were restricted from. It became, 'Us against them.'

"When I was growing up, the Richmond Townhouses disliked the Easter Hill Projects. Easter Hill disliked First Street. Parchester Village disliked Kennedy Manor. Then you've got the beginning of Section 8 vouchers and cheap rent, so the incentive for some people goes away. When the single mother in this situation has multiple children, each child diminishes her ability to be gainfully employed and take care of her family."

Paul Webster Jr. "In TK and I's generation, it turned from, 'Who was ya'll brawling with' or, 'They got into a fight again?' into 'Who got shot?' 'Who got killed?' "

Paul Webster Sr.: "When Landrin and I grew up, worst thing – you get your ass whupped. We fought with knuckles instead of guns. We sold drugs, but we ain't killing nobody. Landrin and I had plenty of fights. When we mad, we'd put socks on our hands, go outside and fight. Probably be mad for a couple of days but that's it. With these young kids, the value of life went down. And when you live in Richmond, that's scary as hell."

A flare at the Chevron refinery in Richmond

CHAPTER 15

The Jump

TK'S SOPHOMORE YEAR at De La Salle began the same as his freshman year but with the added difficulty of more advanced classes. He struggled with 5 a.m. alarms, long lectures, commutes and workouts. He played on the junior varsity football team coached by Vic Galli, a former De La Salle player who utilized the speed and athleticism of his players in a spread offense rather than the Spartans traditional run-heavy veer offense.

Drew Curto: "Vic Galli was a run-n-gun type of coach. We had a lot of athletes on our team. On varsity, the system is, 'Pound 'em with the run to open up the pass.' JV that year was, 'Let's spread it out because our guys are much better athletes.' TK came into his own that year. He laid hat on defense as a linebacker and ran the ball on offense."

Johnny Dempsey: "I remember watching my little cousin play that JV year at De La Salle. I told Landrin, 'He's a Division 1 player.' I seen the way he flowed. He had hips. The way he opened up – his lateral movement. He was a sound football player and he knew how to get to the ball. He had great feet."

T.J. Ward: "TK and I rarely snapped on each other out on the field, whereas Jackie Bates and I snapped on each other all the time because we'd been going at it since we were 8 years old. TK and I just joked around about stuff – like him being sloppy, or me being hella little. But TK was never the type to embarrass anybody. He would only joke on you if you joked on him."

Jackie Bates: "TK and I were inseparable that year. We were always in competition with each other, and that drove us to be better players. If I didn't play up to par, he let me know. And I did the same to him. We were on each other hard and pushed each other every day. It was all in good nature. We came from good families. We knew the type of abilities we had, and we wanted to be the best. We competed in everything, whether it was running gassers – whatever – we competed, and it really paid dividends for us. But when we got off the field, we left it all there. Off the field, we were brothers.

"When I went over to Landrin's house in Richmond, they treated me like a son and welcomed me with open arms. It was a real loving family. They wanted you to succeed. We ate good over there – steak, baked potatoes – some of the best meals I ever had."

The biggest moments of the season came in early October as the team traveled to Southern California to face off against Long Beach-Poly. The junior varsity teams played at Long Beach Polytechnic High School on Friday night.

Drew Curto: "People drove around in low-riders and yelled at us from the other side of the fence. We played on a baseball field with chalk lines and barely any grass. Nothing was painted. That game was a wakeup call because of their speed. They returned the opening kickoff to the house on us. We had done that to plenty of people, but that had never happened to us. Then they kickoff to us and Jackie takes it to the house."

Jackie Bates: "We gave them a good spanking. After the first half, those dudes were done. They'd had enough."

Landrin Kelly: "They was crying at half time ready to quit. Jackie ran two kickoffs back. Terrance had like three touchdown running the ball. We whupped 'em."

The main event, played between the two program's varsity teams at Veterans Stadium in Long Beach, changed the landscape of high school football. Called, "The Game of the Century" by national media, much attention has been devoted to the matchup between Long Beach-Poly, ranked No. 1 in the nation, and second-ranked De La Salle. The Spartans had a 116-game win streak going into the game, which featured nine future NFL players and a hoard of others who would receive Division 1 scholarships.

On the field, it was Maurice Drew's coming out party with a four-touchdown performance in De La Salle's 29-15 victory. Before the game, Drew was a talented backup to senior running back Alijah Bradley, itching for an opportunity to shine. After the game, he took the spotlight and never gave it up. The 'Game of the Century' spawned a book, *One Great Game*, by Don Wallace, and was featured in another, *When the Game Stands Tall*, by Neil Hayes.

*   *   *

TK had another big year on the field and split the junior varsity MVP award with Jackie Bates. But this became an afterthought after he got called up to the varsity team for the North Coast Section 4A playoffs.

Bob Ladouceur, then De La Salle's varsity head coach, describes TK as a tall, thin, rangy kid when he first met him.

Ladouceur: "He was athletic and ran well. He was quiet and did everything we asked him to do. He had a lot of courage. He was very determined and smart in what he was doing on the field. He understood the game well. You could tell he'd played it for a lot of years. There was an upside to him for sure.

"When we bring underclassmen up to varsity, we usually put those guys on scout team to see how they'll engage varsity players. Most of them are very gun-shy. They come up and they're a little scared. They just don't want to mix it up with the other kids. Terrance had no problem with that. He'd stick his head in there and just go – take his collisions and deliver 'em too.

"I knew then that this kid was gonna be a good player. He wasn't shying away from anybody. He had the courage to do it even though his body couldn't hold up because he wasn't up to the physical aspects of the game yet. He was over-matched physically and hurt his shoulder a bit, which wasn't surprising given his physical stature. He really wasn't invested in the weights yet at that time because he was still playing other sports."

Assistant coach Justin Alumbaugh kept a close watch on TK after he got called up to varsity. Alumbaugh was a De La Salle linebacker during the 1990's. In 2001, he coached the varsity team's linebackers and tight ends. Today, he is the team's head coach.

Justin Alumbaugh: "Sophomores endear themselves when they get pulled up if they don't run their mouth and they're not chicken...when they're not afraid to stick their nose in there. Terrance wasn't afraid. He wasn't physically ready to dominate or anything, but he wasn't scared. Those linemen would hit him and drive him back. He'd take some, but he hit them back too. He didn't run his mouth because he was never a mouthy guy. He liked being out there and was a fun guy to be around. That has a way of endearing yourself to older guys."

Erik Sandie, from Danville, was the team's top lineman heading into the 2002 season.

Sandie: "I was a junior at the time starting at left guard next to Derek Landri. TK came up late in the season and had a locker across from us. He was new on the roster, so we gave him a hard time just like anyone else."

Sandie and Landri's football careers continued at the college level at Colorado State and Notre Dame, respectively, while Landri later played in the NFL.

Erik Sandie: "It was hard to say anything mean to TK or do anything to him because he was a genuinely nice guy. Landri gave him a hard time about how small his chest was, of all things. Physically, TK was a lengthy guy. He hadn't grown into his body all the way – he definitely needed to hit the weights. On the field, you knew he was gonna be good. There are very few sophomores that are brought up and actually play when the game matters, and he did."

Parker Hanks: "It was a playoff game at DVC [Diablo Valley College], and they put TK on special teams after he got called up. TK *lit* some dude up and made an insane tackle on kick-off. I still remember all the seniors on the sideline yelling and going crazy after that. I already knew TK could hit from my freshman year, but those older guys were like, 'Holy shit this guy can hit!' That hit opened everyone's eyes up."

Junior Cole Smith started at linebacker on the 2001 team and grew up in Crockett, five miles north of Richmond.

Smith: "My dad worked construction and my mom taught at Canterbury, a private school near Hilltop Mall in Richmond. She was part of the first graduating class at Kennedy High School in South Richmond, which was predominantly black even back then. I went to Canterbury until eighth grade, so I spent a lot of time in Richmond.

"In Richmond, there's a lot of awful stuff going on – yes. But I also knew a lot of good people from there as a kid. Most of the people I knew from Richmond tried to serve the community, coach the kids, things like that. That being said, things happened. Recess got canceled because there's gangs in the parking lot. Or our teachers sometimes said, 'No one wear Starter Jackets,' because kids got jacked for Starter Jackets.

"I played baseball for Rodeo and we played against TK's Richmond team in all-stars – they were always the team with a ton of speed. In football, I played for the West County Spartans. My football and baseball teams were always majority black. That was what I knew and it was OK for me being a white guy around a lot of black guys because I was good at sports. I didn't know that was different until I got to De La Salle.

"Terrance was a freak athlete. It's hard not to notice a guy doing what he was doing as a freshman, on JV – on the basketball court, on the baseball field – so when he came up and made plays on varsity it didn't surprise me. You knew he was such a stud already. No one thought TK was gonna come up and sit the bench on varsity.

"Terrance was a charismatic guy, but he wasn't arrogant. With West County Youth Football – anyone who was good and had that charismatic quality was also cocky or boisterous or arrogant. Trying to make a name. It always drove me nuts because I was never really like that. Terrance was kind of a unique guy in that way. He had the talent and the charisma, but he wasn't loud or cocky."

Landrin Kelly: "Terrance didn't like the commitment of De La Salle at first. It's not for everyone. Gettin' up at 5 and not getting home until 8 at night. And after that he had to eat, do his homework, wash his stuff and get ready for the next day. But he maintained a 3.0, and he was happy to get a taste of what it was all about on varsity. They won another national championship that year.

"After that sophomore season, he told me, 'Forget basketball, forget baseball. I'll just play in the summertime with my friends. I'm gonna play football dad.' I told him, 'Go for it then.' And that's exactly what he did.''

*   *   *

Paul Webster Jr. was 6-foot-2, 280 pounds as a sophomore. As a starter for the varsity football team at defensive tackle, he had a much different experience than TK at Kennedy High School in South Richmond.

Kennedy had been a good school, widely-known for athletics and state-of-the-art academic programs when Landrin and Paul Webster Sr. attended in the 1980's. By the late 1990's, however, Richmond's crack epidemic, violence, lack of funding and bankruptcy of the school district had irreparably damaged Kennedy's programs and reputation. By the 2000's, Kennedy's long, rectangular, windowless frame resembled a prison more than a school. The nickname for JFK at school became 'Jail for Kids.'

Paul Webster Jr.: "De La Salle got cameras and the news coming to their school for good things. We got cameras and the news at our school for bad things. We're talking about 75 seniors graduating out of a senior class of over 200. I did an interview with a local news channel about how our baseball field and facilities were bad. How we didn't have uniforms and how there was violence at our school. I played third so I showed them the lift on the field I played with. I told them how I hadn't worn a cup my whole career. They asked me how I felt about them taking sports away from kids at Kennedy. I told them if you take sports away, there'll be even more drugs and violence."

Louis Montgomery: "I was the quarterback for Kennedy my senior year. We played against Piedmont High School for the Bay Shore Athletic League Championship. Piedmont had Drew Olson – good quarterback who later played at UCLA. It was the first time Kennedy had been to the championship in a long time. The game started at 3:30 p.m., but it got dark fast. We lost the championship game because we didn't have no damn lights.

"Even after telling you that story, I think the difference between De La Salle's program and our program was the coaches. That's not to say we didn't have good coaches. But our coaches didn't do what they needed to do as far as getting kids to school. We had talented kids – it wasn't like all our kids flunked out. I just don't think they knew how to implement things as far as film and motivation. At De La Salle, they know how to motivate kids, and not just the stars. They know how to push the other kids that aren't getting all the publicity."

Paul Webster Jr.: "I went out to Concord and practiced with De La Salle a few times to see how they operate. Just being around TK's teammates – hanging out with them and going to a team dinner before their games – seeing all that and how different it was compared to what I seen and been through in Richmond. Their team was together 100 percent. They had faith in each and every one on the team. At Kennedy, I just had faith in myself in what I was gonna do. It was amazing how different it was.

"Terrance didn't have any of his hometown friends pressuring him to cut class or do stupid stuff – get into fights and all that. Everybody was friends with everybody over there – there were no enemies. The atmosphere was so different, so uplifting. It made you want to be better. It made you want to be a part of something. It made you look forward to getting up and going to school and going to practice. There was a togetherness about the whole thing instead of separation. There was no jealousy.

"In Richmond, anything can happen at any given moment. We can all be having fun, then two seconds later, it's over – riot, fights, gunshots, windows busted – the whole nine. After Terry died, everything escalated. I was never out to hurt nobody. If I'm gon' hurt you, I'll fight you. I don't need a gun to prove that I'm a badass.

117

"But then my life got threatened. My friends picked on some cat and he told some older dude. Here I am walking to school by myself because I was late – dude tells me to come to the car, and he's got a gun in his lap. Once that happened, that's when I started carrying a gun to school. I kept it in my locker. I couldn't get caught slippin' coming home from school.

"Every party we went to, there was fights. People who didn't know how to fight, they was quick to have a gun. That's when gun violence escalated and the chaos started. My parents and my grandma told us before we went out at night, 'Don't ya'll be fighting. Learn how to walk away.' But that's what we did – we fought. You can't mess with Richmond. It's something we grew up on; something we attest to.

"Now TK wasn't a big fighter. I don't remember him fighting one time until we got a little older – and that one time he did lay a guy out. But before that he was off in Concord. The rest of us, we'd go to Oakland, San Francisco, wherever. Different songs come on and they tell you to, 'Rep yo hood' or whatever – and then it escalates. When you go to four parties, and each of those four parties get shot up, you bring a gun – not because you plan on shooting anybody, but just in case you get into a corner and need to shoot yourself out to live. That's a risk a lot of us were willing to take.

"Something happened at every hall party – like at Lefty Gomez. There was always gunfire. My mom and aunties started bribing me to stay home. They'd say, 'I'll buy pizza. Ya'll can have some girls come over, play some music and have a lil house function. We won't bug ya'll.' They tried to influence us not to go out."

Louis Montgomery: "You knew your friends hanging in the streets versus your friends trying to go to school and play sports. It's crazy how things change growing up. As kids, we all played sports with each other, hung out together and competed with one another. Now, these same guys could be out there killing each other."

118

After winning another national championship, the De La Salle varsity football team got its only break of the year.

T.J. Ward: "We were at a party at Andy Briner's house and after it ended we're all about to go to sleep. It was me, Maurice Drew, Nate Kenion, Demontae Fitzgerald and Jackie Bates. TK's asleep on the couch. So TK gets up to go to the bathroom. After TK leaves Jackie hops on the couch like he's gonna sleep there. None of us say anything – we just watch to see what happens. So TK comes back in the room. He says, 'Hey I'm sleeping there.' Now, Jackie isn't gonna back down. He's gonna test you to the max just to see what you gonna do."

Jackie Bates: "Terrance got up and was gone for a minute, so I got on the couch. He came back and said, 'I'm sleeping there.' 'No you not.' 'Jackie. I'm trying to be cool. I'm sleeping there.' 'Bruh do what you gotta do. I told you, you got up. Too bad.' "

T.J. Ward: "TK says to Jackie, 'Boy get off the couch I told you I was sleeping there.' We're all sitting back laughing, snickering at this point. Jackie says, 'You ain't gonna move me, come move me off the couch.' We're all like, 'Ooooooooooooo!' So TK grabs Jackie by the leg and pulls him off the couch. They wrestle and TK gets Jackie in a headlock. Then TK jumps up and down on top of Jackie with him still in a headlock."

Jackie Bates: "You know – TK was a big ol' dude."

T.J. Ward: "So they stand up and Jackie pushes TK. TK rushes him and they knock over Briner's lamp – the lamp breaks and the light shuts off. So at that point we break it up. TK's pissed and goes in the other room. Jack's sittin' there mad. No less than 20 minutes later, they go get TK and he comes back in the room. We all asleep in the room without a problem."

Jackie Bates: "It was a brotherly altercation. There was nothing negative about it. You know, I guess I like to try people, and he let me know he wasn't having it. He kind of put me in my place to be honest about it. We always had a better understanding for each other after that."

T.J. Ward: "TK wouldn't go out of his way to hurt anybody. He was a nice guy, cool, gets along with everybody. But don't test him. He's not about that. No one ever touched him because they had so much respect for him. People respected him because he was such a good person, but at the same time, they respected him because they knew he didn't take no trash from anybody.

"Later that night, Briner walks in the room and tries to turn his lamp on. 'Man who the fuck broke my lamp!' "

*   *   *

Chastity Harper: "After Terrance's season was over we went over to Steve Fujimoto's house in Walnut Creek. There was a bunch of white kids there listening to music. So we're hanging out, then me and Terrance go in a room and start messing around or whatever."

Steve Fujimoto: "Everyone was over at my house because my parents weren't home. We all just tried to hook up with our dates. There were people in every single room in my house, it was like a brothel. I lost my virginity in my room that night. A bunch of people were out in the main room. When I came out – everyone called me out by the look on my face – they knew what just happened. TK is next door in my parents' room with Chastity.

"My parents got home right when I came out. My dad walks into his bedroom and I hear him say, 'Hey! What's going on?' "

Chastity Harper: "Fuji's *dad* comes in the room. I was so embarrassed."

Steve Fujimoto: "TK jumped up and ran out of the room to the other side of the house. Everyone was dying laughing, making fun of him because he got caught by my dad."

*   *   *

Parker Hanks: "Sophomore year for history class we had to make an ancient Roman history play and videotape it. We chose the assassination of Julius Caesar. Our friend lived on a country club so we filmed the play out on the golf course. We wrote the script on whiteboards and had a guy sit behind the camera with the whiteboards as we filmed. We did that for hours and hours. It was Biller, Sean Wilhelmy, Fuji, Lou Wolf and TK.

"TK had a few small parts. He played a servant and one of the assassins. He drove around on a golf cart and messed with Biller the whole time. By the end of the video we're all doing donuts in the golf kart and wrestling around."

Steve Fujimoto: "Lou was mad at me all day. TK drop-kicked Wilhelmy on camera and Biller tackled me. The video actually turned out alright. So we finish the report by the time its dark and drive over to Cal-Berkeley to watch a De La Salle playoff basketball game at Haas Pavilion."

Chris Biller: "So after the game at Cal, Terrance is like, 'Hey can I get a lift home?' 'Is Richmond near Berkeley?' 'Yeah, it's close.' I was just pumped that I had my license. So Lou, Parker and I get some Jack In The Box and take Terrance home. Well, Richmond was not so close to Berkeley."

Parker Hanks: "We take him home through I-80 north and drop him off at his grandma's house in Richmond. It was a really small place. We just hung out in the kitchen with TK's little siblings or cousins because his grandma was asleep. TK tells us we should probably leave before it gets too late. As we left, to be honest, I was scared shitless. There were

121

people on the streets. I thought to myself, 'I need to get back on the freeway ASAP.' "

*   *   *

Before he got called up to varsity, TK hadn't adapted to De La Salle and the 'other side.' That changed as he worked out with teammates at the highest level.

Louis Montgomery: "After those first two years over there in Concord, I saw TK get more disciplined and shape himself into what he wanted to be – a football star. You could tell he had made that decision and was preparing himself to become special. You could see the mind frame he was in with the way he was building his body. After that, every time I saw him, he just got bigger and bigger."

Paul Webster Jr.: "From the program that I was in at Kennedy versus how they ran things at De La Salle, I see why he got so good. Now, he had it in him and put in the work, but it was a whole different ballgame over there. It was like me being at a junior college and him being at a Division 1."

Drew Curto: "This is what De La Salle football does. It turns an average player into a good player, a good player into a great player, a great player into a star. TK could go from a great player as a kid to a star at De La Salle."

After varsity workouts at the end of his sophomore year, TK began to fill out his long, lanky frame. He grew stronger and more explosive.

Chris Biller: "Sophomore year you start puttin' it on. You turn into more of a man of an athlete in a sense. You ever seen an athletic instance of someone where you watch and say to yourself, 'Whoa….'?

"It was spring semester sophomore year. Raining outside. People are shootin' hoops at break. Terrance had on lugz, jeans, a collared shirt, a big sweatshirt and a backpack. The ball rolls to him. He grabs the ball, jumps up and dunks it with two hands. Keep in mind he's 5-10 or 5-11 at that point. I was like, 'I see where this guy is going…' "

CHAPTER 16

License

TK WAS THE FIRST to get something amongst his friends – whether it was a toy, a go kart or a new pair of shoes. This trend continued when TK turned 16 in April 2002.

Paul Webster Jr.: "It was the second round of a baseball tournament in San Jose. We ragged on TK because he went to take his driver's license test before one of the games. So he shows up a little late that day. We're all stretching and warming up and he comes running in. When we see him, no one is focused on the game anymore. We're all excited because now he can be our chaperon and drive us. Everyone asks him, 'Did you get your license? Did you get your license?' He says, 'Man I don't wanna talk about it.' I didn't say nothing to him.

"After warmups I go sit down next to him in the dugout. I ask him quiet, 'So bro, you get your license?' He smiles and says, 'Yeeaaah dawg, we can drive now.' After the game he finally tells everybody."

Jeremy Williams: "We had a master plan. We had a list of people we'd call to try and use their cars. TK would say, 'OK, I'm gonna ask my grandma, my daddy, my aunty, my uncle, Nicole.' Somebody just had to say yes. Once we got a car, we'd round everybody up and go all over the Bay Area to find a party. We'd go to parties at Milpitas Skating rink in the South Bay or drive all the way out to Sacramento."

Louis Montgomery: "I remember Terrance driving us to a lot of Black Friday and Black Saturday parties – it was a little teen movement that had parties all over the Bay Area – Martinez, Vacaville, Fairfield, El Cerrito. It was fun because you were in there with kids from all over. It wasn't just kids from Richmond, you'd get kids in there from Concord and even the Danville crowd depending on where the party at."

Paul Webster Jr.: "That's when it all started. His life drastically changed. He was the only one with a license. You seen how fast people changed from talking about TK to riding on his dick. 'Oh, TK got a license? Now I'm TK's best friend.' A lot of people wanted to hang out with him, be around him, get a piece of him after he got his license. They tried to use TK for what he had – because not only can TK drive, but now he a big De La Salle football player.

"I had other responsibilities at the time – I helped my mom take care of my brothers and sisters and I played two sports. I was like TK – I always had something to do, whether it was practices, games or the batting cages. I wanted to go pro and I took my craft serious in football and baseball. We were the only ones besides Josh trying to take our athletic career somewhere. TK was my competition as far as being the best out of our group. Some of these other guys had quit sports and had a lot of free time. They made themselves available to TK because he could take them places. His name was buzzing and he had girls wanting to be with him. TK could take them to do adventurous things like Concord mall or Marine World or whatever else.

"I had to tell TK, 'These guys don't get spoiled with the love and the time of their parents like we do.' We spoiled with the time, the gifts, the love, the whuppings, the arguments. We got our whole parents. They get a few dollars from their parents and then it's, 'OK go do what you want to do.' With our parents it was, 'Call us when you get there. Call when you on your way home.' They parents wasn't like that.

"And TK was a good person. He shared everything. He'd give people rides to parties, take you to school or pick you up from school. He'd pack his car full of people and take everybody. If you wanted to wear his clothes, he'd let you wear his clothes."

Landrin Kelly: "Lil Paul used to be on Terrance a lot. A lot these ghetto kids was trying to hang around Terrance because he could drive. Paul would keep it real with Terrance. Keep him down to earth, keep him grounded. They'd talk shit back and forth. Paul would tell him, 'You ain't all that, I remember when you was pissin' in your cot. I'm still better than you.' They had that camaraderie and that competitiveness just like me and Big Paul."

Paul Webster Jr.: "When TK got his license, that's when he started being influenced by the people he was around. I didn't hang out with those guys as much as TK did because I had an opinion. It was like a mother or a big brother's opinion – 'You know I don't think we should be doing this.'

"He was getting a lot of that – from me, from Landrin, from Granny Bev. He probably thought I was jealous or he just got tired of hearing it because I sounded like a parent. I was never jealous of TK, I was proud of my brother and I'm gonna hang out with him whether he a nobody or a somebody. I thought, 'If you doing better than me – great, in the long run its gon' come back to me anyway because we best friends. Whatever happen to you happen to me.' "

TK was very much a child of the San Francisco Bay Area, with friends and family spread out across the region. Landrin, Bevelyn and his childhood friends lived in Richmond. His Aunt Lona and Uncle Lanny Jr. lived in Berkeley. His biological mother, sister and brothers on her side of the family lived in San Francisco. He had other family and friends that lived in Oakland, Vallejo, Pinole, Benicia, Fairfield, Antioch, Pittsburg, Concord, Clayton, Walnut Creek, Lafayette, Alamo, Danville, Blackhawk, Livermore and Pleasanton.

Landrin Kelly: "He knew how to work the system when it came to food. When he got his license, he'd drive back from Concord and stop at my brother Lanny's house in Berkeley to see what he cook. Eat over there, then go to my sister Lona's house in Berkeley to do homework. See what she cook. Then drive to my house in Richmond. See what I cook and make a lunch. Then drive home to my momma's house and eat whatever she cook.

"He did the same thing with money. He'd say, 'Dad, lemme get some money, lemme get some money!' When he did good, I'd give him $60 after games and tell him to go have fun. But other times I'd tell him, 'Check it out, I don't have it right now. Imma get it for you, but you have to wait. I got bills.' And sometimes he'd get mad and say, 'Alright *Landrin*.' So if he was disrespectful, talking back or had an attitude, I didn't give him no money. He'd get money to get back and forth to school, but all that extra activity is out if you wanna talk back. 'No, you don't get no $50 for the weekend. No movie, no dates, no extra gas money, no nothing.'

"Terrance knew how to manipulate the situation. He'd go to my mom and my little sister Latonya who stayed with my mom. 'Momma, daddy trippin.' 'Huh boy,' and she'd give him a little money. Then he'd go to Lona's house in Berkeley and do the same thing because she was always the most financially stable."

Paul Webster Jr.: "They spoiled him like that. He did get besides himself sometimes. I'd say, 'Dude, he said no.' 'Cuz, he can't give me $20?

It's to get to school!' 'Bruh, do you really need it or do just want extra money?' But that's just TK growing up, becoming a man. We all went through that."

Chastity Harper: "Terrance definitely got upset with Landrin and his aunts Lona and Latonya. They tried as best as they could to protect him and treated him like a baby. They wanted him to do certain things and be with certain people. Lona was the aunt where, she didn't take anything. Of course as a kid it's natural to think, 'They're too strict.' There were plenty of times where, if he didn't get his way, he got upset. He had so much respect for those people that he wouldn't talk about it to me. It was something I saw in the way he was acting. There was a time where him and Landrin weren't talking even though they lived together. I told him, 'You can't avoid your dad. You live with him. Or, you'll see him at Bevelyn's.' "

Mary Kelly: "He got everybody for money. Even though Landrin and I were separated, Terrance and I had our own bond. He'd call me and say, 'Mookie you out here?' 'W'sup Mr. T.'

"I lived in Vallejo at the time and he'd drive out to visit me. We'd eat or shop and he'd hang out with his sisters. He'd ask for me for what he wanted, $20 or whatever it was, and I'd just laugh and make sure he got it. He knew he could get anything from me. But the thing was, he wasn't just gettin' it from me, he was gettin' it from his daddy, his momma, his Aunty Lona, from everybody. And his pocket stayed fat."

Mobility for TK meant visiting friends from De La Salle in different areas – Jackie Bates in Benicia, T.J. Ward in Antioch and Cameron Colvin or Willie Glasper in Pittsburg.

Paul Webster Jr.: "Grandma Bev trusted us with her car right after he got his license. We told her that we were going to the movies and that we'd be at my house in Richmond. We were actually with Jackie Bates and some other people at his house in Benicia. I get a call later from my mom:

'Where ya'll at?' 'Oh we're in Benicia at Jackie's house, one of TK's friends.' 'Well, tell Terrance to call Granny Bev.'

"I go inside and tell TK, 'I think Granny Bev is on to us. I just talked to mom, she saying to call Granny Bev – she's been trying to call your phone. You been ignoring phone calls?' 'Yeah.' So Granny Bev end up calling *my* phone.

"I'm like, 'Dude, Granny's calling *me* now.' 'So what! Don't answer, don't answer.' Granny Bev drives to my mom's house to get her car, but we're not there. My mom calls me and says, 'I don't know what ya'll doing, but Granny Bev just came over here. So apparently ya'll lied?' So now I'm in trouble.

"I walk back in the house and tell TK, 'WE HAVE TO GO. My mom keeps calling me.' 'What are you talking about man!? We ain't got to go nowhere!' 'OK, since you don't want to come outside and talk to me, I'll tell it in front of everybody. Granny has got up out of her bed and came to my house to get the car, and guess who's not there? We have to go. We're in trouble.'

"So now we're embarrassed because everybody else hanging out without a problem. As we drive home TK says, 'What we gonna' do?' 'I'm done with lying, I'm tellin' the truth when she asks.'

"When we get back Granny Bev says, 'Give me the keys. You can't use the car for a week.' I'm like, 'Great, now what we gonna do?' "

With or without a license, church remained non-negotiable.

Chastity Harper: "I went to church quite a few times with Terrance. Sometimes we were late and snuck in the back. His grandmother sat at the front with all the other first ladies of the church.

Everyone looked up to Bevelyn and respected Terrance as well because that was his grandmother."

Pastor K.R. Woods: "Bevelyn was a church mother that oversaw some of the younger ladies. She was one of the sweetest ladies I'd ever met. She called me 'Lil Pastor' because Landrin and I were around the same age and went to school around the same time.

"She was very kind to me and my family. She took me in as a Pastor as well as a son – as an extended-family member. As a church mother, Mother Bevelyn helped out with prayer and Communion. The church mothers wore white on First Sundays, which was Communion Sundays. It's a special position in the church. Anytime anyone lost a loved one or was sick, they visited those people, prepared and delivered meals, and comforted the family. They encouraged those people and were mentors for our young women in the church.

"There were many times where Mother Bevelyn talked with our younger ladies about some of the things she had been through as a young woman. She was very much respected and honored in our church – she was a pillar. I could always count on her to be there and for her support. Her home was open to everyone. Sometimes I try to figure out how she had time to do it all – raise the kids, be at the games, run the day care, be at church. She was just an amazing woman."

Mobility meant that TK could drive to San Francisco to visit his biological mother, who lived in the Sunnydale Housing Projects – the largest in the city.

Chastity Harper: "It was Easter Sunday. He didn't talk about his mom at all, so I didn't know much about her before that day – I was just oblivious to it. So we drive to San Francisco, and we head into a really bad part of the city. I was shocked by the place we ended up. It looks worse than Richmond, at least visually, to me – it was projects.

"We pull up, and his mom and little sister are there. I didn't even know at that point TK had a little sister – she just lit up when she saw him. She was crazy about him. We sat there and talked and reminisced. I could tell his mom was very proud of him. Terrance's relationship with his mom seemed awkward compared to what I saw between him and his dad, his aunts and his grandma. With his mom, it was her trying to build a relationship, and Terrance resisting it. His older brothers and cousins came up and we all talked. They were all so happy to see him. After that, I just kind of found out things as I listened – that he was around his mom a little bit earlier in his life before he moved in with Bevelyn."

Mobility meant trips to wealthy teammates' houses in Lafayette, Concord, Clayton, Walnut Creek, Alamo, Danville, Livermore and Pleasanton. Hanging out with teammates on 'the other side' was nothing new to TK – he had played with teammates that in lived wealthy neighborhoods as a kid.

Landrin Kelly: "I was in touch with Terrance before he'd stay the night over there on the other side. I made sure he was being respectful and not being a problem. I'd tell him, 'Be polite. Be thankful.' He knew how to respect other people's houses.

"He was likin' it over there and he loved to bring his friends. Some of these guys had massive houses – mansions – money clips with $1,000 in 'em. Rolex watches and diamond rings out in the open. Tennis courts, swimming pools, elevators. There were only certain people Terrance could bring over there. He was scared to bring his other friends – some people get sticky fingers when they not used to being around all that. But he loved it, and that's why he was so determined to make it and be somebody – because he wanted the finer things that he saw over there for his family and for himself."

Jeremy Williams: "I went out there with TK a couple times. It was different over there – a different life. Parents said, 'OK you guys have a good time, we're gonna go upstairs. You guys want us to order pizza?'

131

They didn't have no worries. If you not family, you can't come to nobody's house in Richmond and be all good like that. That ain't happening. They gonna say, 'Who the fuck is you? What you doing here?' Unless you come to somebody grandma's house. In Richmond, grandparents cook because they from the South. That's how they are. But if you go to somebody's mom's house? They not with that."

Lanny Kelly III: "Being in those houses out there, Terrance was never jealous or felt like he didn't have what they had. He never told me, 'Oh I was in this house,' or 'I seen this,' or, 'They had this amount of money.' It just motivated him. He always said, 'Lil cuz, we gon' make it. We gon' be alright. We gon' be straight. We not gon' have to worry about nothing. We gon' get Granny Bev a big house.' "

CHAPTER 17

Step Up

TK HAD THE MOTIVATION, but he was still just a lanky athletic kid with potential. He'd need to log an extraordinary amount of work to transform his body and get on college radars. After winter break in January 2002, he dove into his first real offseason as a De La Salle varsity football player.

De La Salle's voluntary conditioning program begins every January. Players enforce attendance. Much of the team's edge on the field is due to its work in the weight room during the offseason.

Johnny Dempsey: "Terrance took me into De La Salle's weight room once. I don't know if it's still there – but it said, 'How do you want to be remembered?' That always stood out to me. That's the way they carried themselves at De La Salle. I refer back to that with my own son – he's in high school now. 'How do you want to be remembered?' "

De La Salle's weight room is a testament to the program and to the school. Two box rooms filled with squat racks, benches and iron weights. No mirrors. Chalk everywhere. A few inspirational quotes adorn the walls. Anything but state-of-the-art.

Parker Hanks: "We got after it in the weight room. We're there by 6:30 a.m. before school. It's quiet and everyone's tired, but the intensity is there, you can feel it. We wear wooden weightlifting shoes and have grease from the bars all over our shirts. Superficial bruises from the bar and clean grip marks on our thighs and shoulders. You had some intense guys in there."

Everyone recognized TK's talent as a sophomore, but he had to bulk up to capitalize on it. Commitment is central to De La Salle. Players on the team hold each other accountable, sometimes in a not-so-loving way.

John Chan: "I had been on varsity since I was a sophomore. Before that season I wanted to take over the reins and be the captain as a senior. So I was kind of an uptight asshole when it came to football. Terrance in the weight room that year was pretty lazy. He was strong, no doubt he was strong. But he also liked to mess around."

Cole Smith: "As the guys who were gonna be the leaders in the upcoming season we had to ride Terrance a little bit. It's easy to rest on your laurels when you've been the stud athlete as a freshman and on JV. Until you get a dose of, 'Maybe that's not all I can rely on,' it may take a little something to switch that mindset. Terrance also had his hands in other sports – the basketball thing, the baseball thing. So he always had an excuse – he's doing something else. He feels like he's doing more than other people because he plays other sports. That happens a lot. It takes a special person to stay focused in all three sports at De La Salle and take on all that pressure as a 16 year old, especially when you commute in from Richmond every day."

Chris Biller: "He was just uninterested in there."

Steve Fujimoto: "He wasn't lifting like we all were. He was getting away with his talent."

Terry Eidson was the team's defensive coordinator and special teams coach, an equal partner to head coach Bob Ladouceur.

Terry Eidson: "When Terrance first started with us, we thought he wasn't playing up to his potential. His work ethic wasn't all that it could be."

Justin Alumbaugh: "I first met TK when he was a sophomore working out with the varsity team. He was skinny, weak. Athletically gifted, but kind of rested on his laurels a bit."

Chris Biller: "To show up in that program as a 15, 16-year-old kid, they asked a lot out of you. A lot of the stuff we did, it wasn't about going out and playing the game. They asked you to change your lifestyle, to change how you behave. They wanted you to go in and lift weights and practice 12 months out of the year.

"The other thing is – a lot of us grew up around De La Salle. I had an older brother there who was my idol. He lifted weights, he listened to Lad. I'm like, 'I'm doing that.' The Fujis? Same way. Parker Hanks? He had older brothers at De La Salle – same thing. All that same culture."

John Chan: "At one point or another, we'd all met each other at De La Salle football games in middle school. We'd play football games on the practice fields behind the track. This is what we grew up around. Terrance didn't grow up around that culture."

Chris Biller: "So it's kind of unfair to say, 'Listen, you need to drink this Kool-Aid more.' Because that's it. That's De La Salle – you gotta buy in.

"TK drives in from Richmond, so he's got a 40-minute one-way commute ahead of him. We practiced 'till 5:30 or six at night, if not later. He's gettin' up at five in the morning. He's probably thinking, 'Where am I?' He's in Concord and all of a sudden he's on varsity. Now he's got Lad, Eidson – he's got all these honchos yelling at him. Maybe he didn't really understand the potential he had at that point either. The thing is, until you

135

spend a lot of time around De La Salle and really understand the magnitude of what it's all about – it is more than football. What they asked out of us – it was a lot work, man.

"Then at De La Salle you also get so much of, 'OK honey, I'm gonna drive you to practice, here's your nice big thermos filled with ice water or whatever.' You get all these privileged kids that are like, 'Aww, mom got me the Cyto.' That's why it's different when you think about De La Salle – some of these kids just had it laid out. They had rides; they had gas in the car – all these things you don't think about. But sometimes you just can't make it. 'I don't have a ride, my mom's at work. What do you want me to do?' And the coach is like, 'Figure it out, kid.'

"At the same time, that's why it's great. It's a great lesson – 'The world doesn't wait for you, kid.' With Terrance, OK, his JV year he missed a couple practices and workouts. He's like, 'Dude I don't have a ride.' The guy lives far away. So he might miss some conditioning, but he'll throw the helmet on and be the best player out there."

If TK hadn't fully bought in yet, he nevertheless made an impression with his play on the field and through his sense of humor and charisma off it.

The movie *When the Game Stands Tall* portrays the varsity coaches at De La Salle as jovial, gentle peace-makers. One former two-way starter explains what the movie's portrayal lacked:

"The coaches were mean. Relentlessly mean. If they saw weakness, they attacked. They weeded out the weak through mind games. If you weren't mentally tough, they slowly weeded you out of any playing time."

Mary Kelly: "All that stuff that I argued with Landrin about when Terrance was younger, I realized how much it helped when he got up to varsity because they couldn't break him down. His dad had him in tears when he was younger. He wasn't going to let these coaches see him cry."

Chris Biller: "That summer, it was our first couple days in pads. We're seeing whose gonna start. The wide receivers go do their work, and the linemen line up against the linebackers. Alumbaugh puts Terrance in – he's gonna get a run at linebacker. No passing, just banging. Oklahoma drill-type thing."

Cole Smith: "I had been a linebacker – that was my deal through my first three years at De La Salle. So I was apprehensive about switching to lineman as a senior. But we needed linemen and we had two really good linebackers in these two young guys – Parker and Terrance. That's what makes De La Salle special. Everyone takes their role and does what's best for the team."

To test TK's mettle at linebacker, the coaches put him up against Erik Sandie in the drill, which required TK to shed Sandie's block and tackle the running back trailing behind. With the departure of seniors Derek Landri, Andy Briner and Javier Carlos, Sandie was now the team's biggest, strongest player and a bulwark on both sides of the line.

John Chan: "Sandie was a crazy-big white guy from Danville. Shoes untied, duck-footed. A disgusting individual."

Chris Biller: "Sandie was a huge-strong guy. I don't think he even talked in high school. So Sandie saunters out to try and block Terrance. It's a big step from beating up on JV kids to, 'Here's the show...'

"The coaches blow the whistle and Terrance *lights him up*, puts his helmet right in Sandie's chin – **BOOM**. It was a big collision. So Coach Lad is right into Sandie after that yelling at him.

"So what happens is, they're just gonna run the same play. You get lit up, that's what they do – 'Run it again.' We all watch. 'Alright, here we go...'

"So Sandie runs out visibly angry, like he's just gonna kill Terrance. I'm thinking, 'Man, Sandie coming full speed…that's hard.' Sandie charges full speed at Terrance and Terrance just moves out of the way. Sandie eats it and Terrance makes the tackle. He was in Sandie's dome so bad."

Terrance and Sandie became good friends during the 2002 offseason.

John Chan: "Terrance loved Sandie, he made him laugh. It was just how disgusting he was."

Chris Biller: "Think about the dichotomy. They're two completely different people. You have TK from Richmond. Then you have Sandie from Danville, the rich suburb. Sandie always has a bag lunch with the most scrumptious snacks – huge sandwiches, protein shakes."

John Chan: "When Terrance said hi to Sandie, he'd always say, 'What up Sandnuts.' To this day, I still call Erik Sandie, 'Sandnuts.' "

Cole Smith: "Sandie was known as being a stud and Terrance hadn't played a snap on varsity yet. It takes a lot of confidence to come into that situation – whether it was the hit on Sandie or the nickname – it takes a special kid to step in there and have the balls to do something like that."

Scott Hugo: "I was a sophomore on varsity for the first time that summer. You're bottom of the totem pole at that point, trying to get the foundation – what's going on, what are the expectations. I'll never forget TK and Cole Smith – they pull me aside. TK chuckles and says, 'Hugo, watch this.'

"So TK and Cole go up to the row of urinals in the locker room. There's no barrier between the urinals in there. These two tiny young freshmen are at the urinals peeing. You could see their eyes go wide as TK and Cole – these two stud varsity football players – go up to the urinals next to them.

"TK and Cole take one look at each other and drop their pants down to their knees – the, 'Pants-Down-Piss.' You can see the freshmen as their eyes go wide with this look on their face like, 'What the hell is happening.' TK and Cole just have this sly little smile on their faces. That was one of Terrance's defining traits. He had a great sense of humor."

Cole Smith: "TK had the same perspective I had. There's a way you can mess around with kids to make them feel uncomfortable, and then there's a way you can do it to endear yourself to them. With TK, people could be intimidated by him – he's a good athlete and everyone knows him. So it was a way for him to show that he's just a normal guy that fucks around. It helped put people at ease around him. For Terrance, that was important – to have people feel comfortable around him.

"Because TK was comfortable in his skin. His mentality with girls was different – he didn't feel the need to act tough. He could be friendly and joke around. My wife Jenn had classes with TK. He called her, 'Cole's Broad' or 'CB.' In history class, when the teacher did roll call, TK would say, 'CB' after her name was called."

Turn on the news or read a comment section online and you'd think races in America are at war with one another. But flip over to a football game and you see white and black fans cheering for teams mixed with white and black players. You see players of different races embrace after a big win. You see color disappear.

But that doesn't mean there isn't awkwardness and tension when worlds collide for the first time. The brotherhood in those moments is built after months and years of hard work.

John Chan: "When I was a sophomore, we had a basketball game after team dinners. It was white versus black. I thought, 'What team am I on…' You're talking about 15- and 16-year-old kids, from a ton of different backgrounds, coming together on one team and dealing with it for the first time. The things we said to each other may have been horrible and we may have beaten up on each other, but as soon as it wasn't internal, we all had each other's back."

Chris Biller: "We had people from all walks of the Bay Area coming together and we disagreed about things. You had kids that were rich, poor and everything in between. Some of the black kids were from really tough neighborhoods. You had some Danville kids that were flat-out scared of the brothers. But then you had some guys where – whether they were from a dangerous area or not – they weren't gonna back down regardless of where they were from. That made us tougher as a team. When we all messed with each other, it was a reason to mess around, for banter, for bravado. It was about toughness. It was all one locker room despite the differences, like a family at the end of the day. We had huge brawls. It didn't come to blows, just headlocks, shoving, good solid roughhousing or whatever. Right after, we'd go out on the field and stretch."

Jackie Bates: "We tried each other. But if someone from outside the team did something, before I could blink my eye, Chan, Fuji, Biller, Wilhelmy or whoever, they'd all be there ready. We had each other's back like that."

Drew Curto: "People got called out. If there was a problem, you'd go out on the field and squash it. Yeah, people would talk shit – but that was part of us being around each other 350 days out of the year – it comes with the territory. We were like brothers. Being on that team, I've never had anything close to that feeling outside of my immediate family."

Steve Fujimoto: "During my sophomore-junior year, after our team dinners and basically any time throughout the season – at school, after practice, before practice – we had big wrestling matches. A lot of the times you had white guys going against black guys, or the 'Amigos' as they

140

were known at De La Salle. On campus, if we saw TK, or TJ or any of the other Amigos, we'd shove 'em into lockers or whatever. It turned into massive wrestling matches. They were hard, but no one was ever throwing punches. I got into it with TK pretty good a couple times. It was pretty equal.

"Any time you'd see TK, he was asleep. I'd stick pencils in his nose or whatever in class. One time, we're out in the hallway. I shove TK, so he turns around and head-butts me right in the crown of my nose. My eyes watered up after that one.

"Another time I'm talking in front of the team. No coaches around. TK runs up and sticks me in my chest. Didn't see it coming. I fall on my back, down for the count; he completely knocked the wind out of me. Everybody died laughing. I was pissed, but when I went to get him back, I whiffed. He could move well – he wouldn't let you get your hands on him. That's the thing about TK – he was quiet, but he was rough."

Erik Sandie: "The De La Salle locker room was very territorial. Different rows had different meanings. We'd always joke around. It was, 'You can't come down this row.' So if you wanted to mess with the other row or disrespect their row, you'd walk down their aisle."

John Chan: "I remember from my freshman year – the closer you were to the weight room and the training room, the more status you had. So my freshman year – D.J. Williams, Tosh Lupoi, Demetrius Williams, Matt Gutierrez – all the good players, they were all in that row.

"My junior year, that row became, 'The Block.' It turned into the black dudes and the people who had enough playing clout to say, 'I'm taking that locker.' So my senior year, it was me, Demontae Fitzgerald, Maurice Drew, Aaron Bradley, Jackie Bates, T.J. Ward, TK, Willie Glasper and Damon Jenkins. It got to the point where people said, 'Don't walk through here.' "

Jackie Bates: "It was predominantly black players in there. But there was some other players that weren't black in there as well that were just tough guys. It was a fun thing, about building confidence and camaraderie. It was, 'We got heart and we're protecting this streak.' If you were on that team, you felt like the toughest dude on earth. You weren't gonna take no crap from nobody. Sometimes we tested people, sometimes people tested us. Fuji and Biller, those were some of the strongest guys I've ever met in my life. They'd come over there and wrestle three or four of us at once, even if it's just one of them."

T.J. Ward: "We had a rule. You couldn't walk through our aisle without permission. Or you had to be a VIP member to walk through. So Fuji and Biller and them, they were like, 'Fuck that shit.' And they'd run through. Right before practice, people got their shirts ripped off, slammed on benches. When you think back, somebody really could have got hurt."

Steve Fujimoto: "So the aisle on the other side of The Block – that was us – all the lineman and linebackers besides Terrance. We were like, 'OK, fine. You motherfuckers can't walk through our aisle either.' Before school, we'd take their shoulder pads and pants and put it in the middle of our row. Then we'd get our gear on and guard their pads. One of them would have to fight in there to get their stuff. But Terrance was rough, he didn't care. He'd go right in there, get his shit and fight us all off."

Parker Hanks: "We'd throw equipment, tape balls, trash and food between the aisles. If someone got hit too hard – say someone got hit in the head or something, it got heated and turned into a brawl. When it got heated, TK was the guy in the middle breaking it up; the mediator."

Cole Smith: "Terrance never felt the need to act tough when the situation escalated. With some of the other guys, it got to the point where we were all about to get in a real fight. But you always had a level-headed guy like Terrance who got everyone to chill out. And that was important, because everyone – white or black – listened to Terrance."

Erik Sandie: "TK was so even-keeled in the midst of all that. He was kind of wise beyond his years. He didn't let anything get to him. He had the ability to let things roll of his shoulders. I never saw him mad once. On the football field, it was almost a problem – trying to get him pissed and motivated because he was so much the opposite."

*　　　*　　　*

As the summer wore on, TK earned a starting position next to Parker Hanks at both linebacker and tight end.

Hanks: "We had high expectations from the coaches. They'd been in our ear all summer. 'We're expecting you to lead the defense. You're the anchors.' "

Justin Alumbaugh: "Terrance was one of our more athletic players, but he was weaker and slower than a lot of guys. He struggled with that and he struggled with the minutiae of the game at first. Studying film. Knowing the ins and outs of our defense. Knowing opponents. He knew what he was supposed to do, but he didn't know what everyone else was supposed to do, which is a requirement for a top-level player. He just wasn't as committed at that point."

Parker Hanks: "We'd run gassers at the end of practice. 10-to-12 on Monday and it slowly got cut down throughout the week. TK and I were required to run the lowest time because we were starting both ways for the two most conditioned positions on the offensive line. We were required to run sideline to sideline in 40 seconds. The lineman had to run it in 42-45 seconds.

"If you missed your time, you had to do it again at the end. TK missed his times when he started and was out of shape. But then, he started pickin' it up. For a while, we competed. Then, by the middle of that junior year, he was in condition, and he was beating my ass.

"Practices started with warmup and special teams. Then we'd break off into position drills. There'd be six or seven of us linebackers. Every week we worked on certain skills – one week, its shedding blockers. Another week, it's working on our drops. Then, it's developing the young guys and their reads.

"Then we get quizzed on the scouting report – our reads, tendencies and what not. So we're sittin' on a knee in a half circle, brainstorming, doing mental reps. There were only so many tendencies that every team had. Our scouting reports were so good that we had a percentage breakdown on a majority of the plays the other team ran. A lot of times we got it down to two plays if they were in a certain formation.

"It was like Socratic Method in law school – you had to know your shit. Alumbaugh would say, 'Parker when they line up double-tight and motion their receiver short motion – what do they run?' I'd have to know that it's, 'Screen right or bubble screen.' Those tendencies really helped in calling the defense.

"TK wasn't as prepared as he should have been at the beginning, and Alumbaugh got on his case. Alumbaugh as a coach – he's straightforward, gritty and intense. He doesn't hold anything back. It's all about discipline, motivation, hard work and self-accountability. It's not acceptable to him to have to tell you twice. He was very vocal and a great motivator. Lad was the final say if it got that far. When it came to Alumbaugh getting on TK, he learned his lesson quick.

"Between TK and I, it was about picking each other up if a bad play happened in practice. TK hit hard. That's all we wanted to do was just hit people as hard as we could. Some days were just about crazy hitting, 'Bring your shit, earn your keep' type days. Other days were more walk-through, depending on how we developed during the week.

"There was one week where the coaches were trying to see what we could bring to the table as far as hitting people right before the season

144

started. So you had this drill where you set up as a linebacker. Then you have two linemen in front of you in pads – a guard and a tackle. Then there was a running back behind them. So, what you had to do was shed both blocks – but you had to do it correct – off your outside shoulder.

"So they set up four linemen across from us, and TK and I as the starters are the first linebackers in. TK hits a guy full speed so hard that he falls over and has to rest on one knee – he gave him a concussion on the spot.

"By the end of it, we had knocked out three linemen. They had to bring in reserve linemen for that drill as we knocked people out – it was probably only 10-minutes long."

Sophomore quarterback Kevin Lopina, from Pleasanton, recalls his first interactions with TK.

Lopina: "When I got moved up to varsity, I ran the scout team offense at quarterback. Terrance and all those guys let me have it – a 'welcome to varsity' thing. Competing against TK – he was everywhere. I would drop back to pass and he's there in coverage. When I run the option, he's there to hit me. He was always in the right place and sideline-to-sideline fast. I run one way, turn around, and there he is. He was very hard to beat, very hard to get a successful play on."

By the end of the summer, first-time varsity players such as TK and Jackie Bates were ready to roll.

Jackie Bates: "That summer was about long workouts in the sun getting black as heck. Hard workouts. Pulling sleds. Deep squats. Running. Countless hours of film. Passing league games. After a while, you get accustomed to it. When you work that hard, you don't feel the pressure because you're prepared. You're ready to go do it."

On the Thursday night before the season opener, the team met at one of the player's houses. It's a weekly ritual during the season that every De La Salle football team performs.

Landrin Kelly: "Parents were required to come to four of the Thursday night meetings. My mom and I helped set up the food and make sure the boys get served. There was a lot of camaraderie with the other parents and coaches. It came to be like a big family.

"After we ate, the coaches took the team into the garage while the parents and mothers stayed in the house. I'd go outside, smoke a cigarette, and listen to the coaches talk shit to 'em and everything. Going to those team dinners in some of those big houses – that really boosted Terrance's determination, because that's what he wanted. He said, 'Dad, I'm gonna get a house like this for you.' "

Kevin Lopina: "Terrance may have dressed differently, but he was always polite when he came to my house – whether it was for team dinners or just to hang. Sometimes, Terrance brought his friends from Richmond out and we'd go out together in Pleasanton. Everything was different – the way people dressed, the culture, the way people looked at them. Terrance understood that and embraced it. He was the leader – he was so intuitive when it came to things like that."

*   *   *

The 2002 home opener was against Archbishop Mitty High School of San Jose at De La Salle's Owen Owens Field. For the team's reputation and record, the field is unassuming. Tucked away at the back of campus and seating just 5,000, it's a far cry from Texas high school football stadiums that seat 30,000 and above.

As the Spartans home stands filled, Landrin arrived with a big group of supporters from Richmond dressed in dirty combat boots, jeans and an old Starter Jacket.

146

Landrin Kelly: "It was a big group, maybe 30 of us that drove out to Concord for his games. My brother and I, we worked two jobs. We didn't care how we looked. We were like, 'Don't look at me, look how good my kid look!' "

Landrin and the men in the family made sure Bevelyn, Chastity, all of the aunts, younger siblings and cousins had good seats in the middle of the home stands. Then, they went to the top of the baseball field's bleachers, which had a bird's-eye view of the football field and where they could smoke cigarettes. Landrin's younger cousin Johnny Dempsey stayed with the women to record every game in center of the stands.

The results of the season opener against Mitty were unsurprising for the No. 1-ranked team in the nation. The Spartans defense smothered another over-matched Northern California foe. On offense, Maurice Drew performed as expected with 131 rushing yards, including a 51-yard touchdown run, and a 55-yard punt return for a touchdown.

Parker Hanks: "After every game, Bevelyn gave me a big bear hug. She was really short, so she'd put her arms straight up to the sky to hug you. Landrin was always with about six guys in Starter jackets, who were all cool. He'd bear hug you and loved the hitting. He'd come over so excited and tell each of us, 'Parker nice hit on No. 30! TK you laid No. 41 *out* on that play! Nice jobs, guys!' My dad would come over, give Landrin a high-five and TK's grandma a hug. We'd all shoot the shit for a little bit. We got along like brothers."

John Chan: "Landrin was at every game in a green De La Salle hat and knew everybody on the team. He knew if you were a captain. He knew how you were doing and how you had played."

Chris Biller: "Landrin took a real interest in all of the players. He'd ask, 'Are you getting letters? Are they giving you a look? I heard this college was looking at you. You're looking good out there.' "

147

Cole Smith: "You could tell TK was Landrin's life and that he'd invested everything in him; that it was why he got up in the morning. It was like he was living his life through TK. It seemed like Landrin didn't necessarily want to be known by Landrin. He wanted to be known by TK."

Landrin Kelly: "I told Terrance I was proud of him and that I loved him every day. He didn't like me kissing him in front of everybody. I told him, 'No matter how big you get, you'll always be my baby.' He didn't have no problem with it when it was just me and him. When people were around, he got embarrassed."

Paul Webster Jr.: "That's how Landrin show his affection, his emotion. Growing up, he'd hug TK and kiss him on the cheek after every game. He'd tell him, 'Love you, boy,' whether he did good or he didn't do good. He did it to me too. And TK was like, 'C'mon man, beer breath.' But Landrin was lettin' him know – 'Even though I ride you, I still love.'"

Lanny Kelly III: "Landrin plants these big, wet, sloppy kisses on your cheek. So nasty, I'd hate it when he'd do it me. I wasn't half as big as Terrance, so he wouldn't have to wrestle me to do it. He could just grab me."

After the game, Landrin drove from Concord to Johnny Dempsey's house in Oakland to get the freshly-recorded game tape.

Landrin Kelly: "TK got home after games at about midnight. We'd sit back and watch the film from that night. I'd pick out his mistakes and ride him before the coaches could get on him when they reviewed tape as a team the next morning. I was his worst critic and his biggest fan – I critiqued every little thing. He didn't have any major faults, so I got him about the little things and tried to correct those – the way he ran; the way he held the ball.

"He had a bad habit of ducking his head during tackles. I told him, 'You gonna get a stinger and break your neck. Gotta keep your head up, can't go in there head-first with your head down.' I'm looking at his technique because that's what the coaches look for – how well you move your feet, how you tackle, how you hit. I told him, 'Stay on your block. Stay on your man until the whistle blow.' And we'd go back-and-forth until he got too tired."

Saturday morning, TK had to get up at 7 a.m. to be in Concord for practice at 8:30. After warmups, sprints and drills, the team reviewed film in the cafeteria and evaluated performances from the night before.

Parker Hanks: "It was a pretty big, open space. Around 55 of us in there, so you could hide if you sat in the right place. TK sat in the back with his chin tucked into his chest. He'd doze off, drooling and snoring. He never got caught."

*   *   *

TK focused 100 percent on football throughout the following week at school. At lunch, the football team split into offensive and defensive groups to scout the upcoming opponent, nationally-ranked power St. Louis of Honolulu, Hawaii.

Not everything had gone to plan against Mitty. Maurice Drew sprained his ankle in the game, which left De La Salle potentially without its best player against St. Louis. The Honolulu powerhouse, ranked 17th in the nation by USA Today, had at one stretch won 14 consecutive state titles on the island and had a big, physical roster in 2002. The Spartans flew 2,500 miles west to Hawaii to take them on.

Landrin Kelly: "We flew out there with the whole family for the week, about 10-deep. Me, my mom, my sister, my girlfriend and her kids, my niece Tahira and Lanny III. It was a family thing."

Jackie Bates: "My mom and Bevelyn were sightseeing and enjoying the weather. Landrin was at every practice taking pictures. It was an exciting thing to go and play an elite school in Hawaii where the Pro Bowl is played."

It was a fun trip for family and friends, but all business for players and coaches facing a tough, nationally-ranked opponent with a 126-game win streak on the line.

Landrin Kelly: "As soon as we got off the plane from the five-hour flight, Terrance was off to practice. Coach Lad made it clear that they were in Hawaii to take care of business. The team took a tour of Pearl Harbor. I went with them. Long Beach-Poly was also there on a tour. They stared us down and talked smack."

De La Salle's game with St. Louis was part of a double-header at Aloha Stadium. Long Beach-Poly, rated No. 2 in the nation, would take on two-time defending Hawaii state champion Kahuku.

That night, the players went to their hotel rooms early.

Parker Hanks: "TK and I roomed together on every trip. We'd talk about the game and write out our commitment cards. TK was always on the other side of his bed talking to his girlfriend real quiet. He loved to sleep – he always went to bed early. And he snored."

After an intense week of practice, it was time.

Landrin Kelly: "30,000 in the crowd and they was fired up that night. TK went up against a guy that was 6-5, 310 pounds."

Jackie Bates: "We were built on speed, toughness and outworking people. But those guys were big and physical. We were way outmatched in terms of size. Some of those defensive linemen were like NFL players."

Despite St. Louis' size advantage, De La Salle's special teams, execution and overall team speed were too much as the Spartans jumped out to a 21-0 lead. Despite the injury, Maurice Drew rushed for 125 yards and a touchdown and senior defensive back Damon Jenkins ran for big yardage on special teams returns. Junior receiver Cameron Colvin had a breakout game with two bombs, including a spectacular 46-yard Lynn Swann-like catch to set up De La Salle's opening score. St. Louis fought back, but it was too little, too late, with a final score of 31-21.

John Chan: "I was so impressed by our linebackers in Hawaii, TK and Parker were both huge in that game. It was the first time we had played a four-wide team. Coach Eidson had implemented this new scheme over the summer. It was a quarter-quarter-half coverage, and we used it against their offense that had a lot of dink and dunk passes. They used a shotgun formation and it was an easy read. If the fullback was on the right side, they'd throw to the right. If the fullback was on the left, he'd go to the left. You could see Parker tapping his helmet in the game indicating which side they were going to. We shut their high-powered offense down with that scheme."

Landrin Kelly: "After that game he was so excited.

'Dad I'm about to get it. I'm about to get it dad.' "

*   *   *

The following week, De La Salle traveled an hour south to take on the St. Francis Lancers of Mountain View. St. Francis was another Catholic school with a storied history, including 13 titles in the Central Coast Section.

After the emotional win versus St. Louis and five-hour flight home, the team lacked intensity against the Lancers. Maurice Drew sat out due to his lingering ankle injury.

Jackie Bates: "It was a rainy game and that slowed us down. Maurice was injured so I had to step up at running back. Terrance had like 13 tackles or something crazy and he caught a touchdown pass. We really snuck by those guys."

De La Salle beat St. Francis by the thin margin of 14-0.

The biggest game of the season was next – a rematch of 2001's 'Game of the Century.' This time, De La Salle was ranked No. 1 and Poly No. 2 as they prepared to play at Memorial Stadium on the campus of the University of California, Berkeley.

As in the St. Louis game, Long Beach-Poly was much bigger than De La Salle. Poly's defensive line, rated No. 1 in the country, included 6-5, 250-pound Junior Lemau'u, who had committed to USC. Lemau'u was 5-9 Chris Biller's assignment at right guard.

Poly's line also featured 6-4, 275-pound Josh Tauanuu, rated the top defensive lineman in the country, and 6-2, 300-pound Kevin Brown. The defense was anchored by Mark Washington, a 6-3, 240-pound hard-hitting linebacker who would go on to play at Arizona State and in the NFL.

Unlike the St. Louis game, Poly had more overall team speed than De La Salle. Poly's blazing-fast receiving corps featured USC-bound Derrick Jones and NFL-bound sophomore DeSean Jackson. Lorenzo Bursey's 4.4-second speed complemented Poly's attack out of the backfield.

Landrin Kelly: "I was devastated because I couldn't make the game – it was only the second time in Terrance's life I missed a game, and it was a big one. I had been offered a distribution job at Zep Cleaning Products. It was better hours and pay than my Home Depot job in the store, so I went back to part-time at Home Depot and took the job with Zep.

"I eventually became a District Manager for Zep. I had 25 stores that I ordered for. I had five guys, and each guy was responsible for five stores. I checked inventory and made sure they were fully-supplied and that the right orders had been put in. We had a corporate meeting in Atlanta that weekend and I had to be there."

The game was played on a picturesque sunny Saturday afternoon in Berkeley. Massive tailgates were held outside of the stadium by families and alumni on both sides before kickoff. The helmets of Poly linemen towered over their De La Salle counterparts as they streamed onto the field. At 6-1, 255 pounds, Erik Sandie was De La Salle's biggest, strongest player.

Sandie: "I had so much energy because it was a day game. It was the first day game any of us had ever played in."

Jackie Bates: "There had been a lot of talk that we wouldn't be able to beat 'em this year. In the locker room before the game, Landrin called TK. He put him on speaker phone and Landrin got us all pumped up.

"We get out on the field and Freddie Parish has, 'Drew Who' written across his back plate. He was talking a lot of crap about what he was gonna do to Maurice Drew."

Parish, a hard-hitting safety, had committed to play at Notre Dame.

Despite all the talk, the game opened with a methodical drive featuring a heavy dose of Maurice Drew. De La Salle never let up in what turned into a 28-7 rout. The Spartans simply out-executed Poly in all facets of the game, and its defense completely neutralized Poly's speed.

Drew finished the game with 161 rushing yards. De La Salle's unheralded senior quarterback Britt Cecil threw three touchdown passes, including a final, long touchdown pass to TK on a tight end drag that sealed the game.

Cole Smith: "The year before against Poly, we beat them and executed well, but we didn't physically dominate them by any means. We were physically over-matched and we just played the game of our lives. Whereas in 2002, we handled them."

This De La Salle team was small and hadn't practiced well over the summer. The team had a number of juniors such as TK move into starting positions for the first time. Poly was once again big, athletic and fast across the board. In the papers, Ladouceur called the win his greatest victory.

Jamie Richards Jr.: "I seen when De La Salle played against Long Beach-Poly at Cal-Berkeley. I called TK right after the game. I was like, 'Bruh, I'm proud of you!' He was so humble about it – 'I appreciate it, bro.' That's how we were raised since the day care days – to be humble."

The Spartans rode momentum through the rest of the regular season, steamrolling the rest of their Northern California opponents. The playoffs were no different.

John Chan: "We destroyed teams in the playoffs. Our line really improved throughout the year. It was me at left tackle, Fuji at left guard, Cole Smith at center, Sandie at right guard, Biller at right tackle. Then you had either Terrance or Parker at tight end.

"They'd overload me as the tackle. Then it would be me, Biller and Sandie on the right crashing that whole side of the line. Then Fuji and Terrance would pull and lead up into the hole. So Terrance was basically a pulling tackle or a fullback leading into those holes."

Cole Smith: "To start the year, people thought Parker was the better-blocking tight end. But by the end of the year, TK was the better blocker. It was like having another offensive tackle in there with us. We didn't need to pass the ball — we just steamrolled teams."

Jackie Bates: "Against Hayward, Maurice ran the opening kickoff back and it was basically over after that. We all felt like we could score at any moment. It was really almost unfair. But with the preparation we put in, that was the outcome."

It was a devastating running attack. With his raw power and low center of gravity, Maurice Drew was the most difficult high school running back in the country to tackle. Later in his career, Jackie Bates clocked at 4.23 seconds in the 40-yard dash.

Landrin Kelly: "They was thunder and lightning. Drew was thunder, Jackie was lightning. You had Terrance at tight end. Demontae on one side and Cameron on the other side at wide receiver. Playmakers all over the field and any one of them can make it happen."

The Spartans blew through Antioch and Hayward and faced an undefeated San Leandro team, rated No. 24 in the country, for the North Coast Section 4A Championship. San Leandro was led by 6-4 senior quarterback Dennis Dixon.

Maurice Drew intercepted Dixon's first pass and returned it to the 1-yard line. He added 142 rushing yards and two touchdowns in a 42-14 rout.

Chris Biller: "San Leandro, they were a physical ball club. They had some crazy, tough dudes. And we just ran right at them. We just ran power."

After the celebration and another crown as the nation's No. 1 high school football team, the graduating seniors cleared their pads and moved out of their respective aisles in the locker room. TK and the rest of the juniors moved in with the weight of a 138-game win streak on their shoulders.

Amigos - 2002

CHAPTER 18

The Element

TK SPENT WINTER BREAK with friends and family back in Richmond after the big win against San Leandro, which was a cause of anxiety for Landrin and Bevelyn. As he drove around Richmond, Landrin noticed an increase in the number of make-shift memorials to slain young black men on street corners. Helium balloons, teddy bears, and a few bottles of liquor were all that remained of some victims; many had done nothing wrong. The street element had been in Richmond from the time when Landrin and Paul Sr. were boys. But cases involving gun violence and young children increased as TK and Paul Jr. reached 16.

The 'Nut Case' group in Oakland was a prime example of the desensitized, ultra-violent world of the Bay Area's poorest neighborhoods. Police records did not classify the group as a gang, but instead as "a group of young men who engaged in random violence."

In late 2002, members of the group – in their late teens and twenties – embarked on an indiscriminate spree of robberies, shootings and killings in Berkeley, Oakland and San Francisco.

By day, the group played Grand Theft Auto on PlayStation and smoked marijuana. By night, they smoked more marijuana and drove around with military-grade assault rifles looking for victims to rob, beat and shoot.

During an interview with police, a member of the group said that "all the Nut Cases do is kill people." Sometimes they killed "just to be doing stuff," even if there was no money to be found on their victims.

In late November 2002, members of the group approached four Hispanic men socializing outside their apartment in West Oakland and demanded money. The men did not cooperate and fought back. Three of the four men were shot with a shotgun. One was shot in the face. Another lost an eye. A third victim was shot in the stomach and suffered major trauma.

In December 2002, the Nut Cases drove up to a group of 15-20 people standing around an intersection in West Oakland. Several members of the group jumped out of the car and shot into the crowd. One victim suffered a gunshot to the back and died.

Two days after Christmas, members of the group drove up to a crowded house and opened fire on the holiday party inside with an "M-16-type" assault rifle.

A guest at the party had made a fatal mistake by inviting his female neighbor into the apartment. The neighbor was dating one of the Nut Cases, who overheard the interaction.

Two people, including a 14-year-old boy, were killed in the subsequent shooting. A witness said she saw two victims lying on the floor after the shooting. One was bleeding profusely and had an internal organ emerge from a stomach wound. Another lay motionless on the floor with a head wound. Still another was shot but survived. Twenty shell casings from a .223-caliber assault rifle were found at the scene.

One of the shooters later told police they went to the house to "spank" everyone inside and that they were "handling business."

Shortly after, in January 2003, the Nut Cases went out at night planning to commit a robbery. They spotted a young Asian couple carrying laundry from a car to their apartment. After a brief scuffle with the Nut Cases, the man begged for his life as his wife and toddler watched from the doorway. The man was shot in the head. His family ducked and avoided gunfire. The Nut Cases walked away with $31.

In February 2003, members of the gang drove around in Oakland and smoked marijuana. They realized they needed gas and decided to rob someone to obtain the money. The group passed two random people on the street. They shot and killed both people and used a credit card from one of the victims to purchase gas.

Later that night, the Nut Cases committed another robbery and shooting, leaving a victim gravely injured. Members of the group subsequently drove to San Francisco where they shot and killed another victim.

Court records for one of the Nut Case defendants show how killers are created in some of the poorest neighborhoods in America. The defendant was born to a mother in jail and raised by a grandmother, who beat him. His mother was addicted to drugs and moved frequently. He attended a variety of schools but never learned to read or write and dropped out in the ninth grade. His role model and older brother was a vicious killer. He was arrested several times before his indictment for the Nut Case crime spree at the age of 17.

By the end of the Nut Cases' reign of terror in February 2003, seven people were dead, 12 shot and more than 30 robbed or assaulted.

Such 'Nut Case'-esque violence was also occurring in nearby Richmond.

Louis Montgomery: "It was 2003, right after I graduated from Kennedy High School. My friend Jordan and I were driving to see some female friends before I left Richmond for St. Paul's college in Virginia. Being in Richmond late at night – somebody happened to shoot up my car. Luckily I didn't get hit, I dang near could have died. But our friend Jordan got shot up.

"I rushed him to the hospital. I couldn't get a hold of nobody. My parents didn't answer. The next person I called – I called Miss Bev's house. TK and Miss Bev were right there, they were the first people on the scene."

Lanny Kelly III: "TK and I would be at Grandma Bev's house chilling, doing our homework, watching TV. We'd hear gunshots. We'd mute the TV and listen. Then we'd try and guess what type of gun they was using based on the type of bang we heard.

"We'd say, 'Oh that's a .45. That's a .22. Oh that's a machine gun.' It was that close where you could tell the difference. It was so natural for us to hear that – we never tried to duck or anything for stray bullets. We figured that was part of Richmond, that's part of where we live at. There's nothing we can really do about it. We'd just continue on with whatever we were doing as if it didn't happen."

Mary Kelly: "As Terrance got older it was free game for anybody out on the streets of Richmond, like the whole city had gone buck-wild; like they opened the floodgates and everything bad that could happen in the city – drugs, prostitution, killings – it all started happening."

Landrin Kelly: "I bought a house in Hilltop Richmond TK's junior year after football season. Hilltop was out of the flatlands and a better area than where I grew up at because there was less street traffic. It was harder for them down in the flatlands to get up to Hilltop. They'd come up there sometimes, but they needed a ride. I felt Terrance would be safer up there. My mama wanted me to do it because she could feel what was

160

happening too. She didn't want her baby to be around everything going on down there and planned on selling her house in South Richmond.

"Nicole and I was moving out of our apartment when her baby daddy came over with an attitude, calling Nicole all type of bitches and stuff. So I had to come out there as the man of the house. I popped his ass upside the head. Then Nicole's son Brian comes running out the house and tries to swing at me, so I chase his ass down the street. Baby daddy steady talking shit, 'Oh you don't need to run from him!'

"So then TK comes around the corner and gets into it with Brian, 'Why you swinging at my dad? He take of care you, he feed you, and ya'll about to move into our house!' Brian was like, 'He ain't about to hit my daddy.'

"Time went by and we all eventually moved into the new house up in Hilltop. TK and Brian was cool, but it was moments like that – where me and Brian got into it – where those two had problems.

"Our Hilltop house was a four-bedroom with a big den. I sealed the garage and converted it into TK's room. He had a big flat screen TV in there, a regular bed and a futon bed. We had all the pictures where he was doing his thang framed on the wall with the help of my friend who worked at Kinkos – he blew up the articles and pictures for me."

After a solid junior season on the football field, the family knew TK had a shot at a scholarship. To capitalize on the opportunity, he'd need his grades and test scores up as well.

Landrin Kelly: "My mom paid an instructor from The Princeton Review to help Terrance prepare for the SAT and ACT. He also did a lot of practice problems with Lona. We had him take the SAT three times. The last time he took it, he scored an 1,132. He maintained a B-average at De La Salle."

Chastity Harper: "Lona was the aunt that held the family together. She went overboard when it came to Terrance and Baby Lanny and making sure all the business got done. When Terrance wasn't buckling down to write his personal statement for college applications – it was Lona who made sure he sat down and did it.

"As we got older, Terrance stayed at his dad's house more because he had more freedom there. He was at the age where it's natural to be rebellious. He was driving and he was like, 'I'm grown.' At his grandmother's house in South Richmond, Latonya lived there so of course she was gonna be in everything he did. Pops was also his roommate there and Lona came over almost every day. Plus you had the day care kids."

Landrin Kelly: "Somebody was at my mama's house all the time. Lona and my brother – they lived elsewhere – but all of my siblings' mail came to that house. So everybody came there after work. There was somebody running in and out all the time – there was never a lonely moment over there."

Chastity Harper: "Everyone being over at Bevelyn's got on Terrance's nerves sometimes. If he wasn't listening or being disrespectful, Latonya would twist his hair or tell him she's not gonna buy his school clothes anymore. So you had all these different people telling him what to do and trying to protect him from different influences. He wanted to be away from that as he got older."

CHAPTER 19

He Had Totally Changed

TK HAD A SOLID JUNIOR CAMPAIGN on the field with 130 tackles on defense and nine receptions for 300 yards on offense. While he drew some recognition from college coaches towards the end of the 2002 season, it was difficult to stand out on the No. 1 team in the nation stacked with Division 1- and NFL-caliber talent.

From the graduating senior class, Maurice Drew was the biggest name and accepted a full-ride scholarship to UCLA. Damon Jenkins went on to Fresno State. Demontae Fitzgerald to Montana State. Erik Sandie to Colorado State. John Chan and Cole Smith to the Naval Academy.

Johnny Dempsey: "A buddy of mine I used to play football with at Skyline High School in Oakland was scouting for Cal-Berkeley. I told him during Terrance's junior year, 'Listen, my cousin go to De La Salle. Next year he gonna be a senior, you better get on 'em now!' He didn't believe me."

TK's junior class was the most talented in De La Salle's history. No one could argue that TK, Jackie Bates, Cameron Colvin and Willie Glasper all had the athletic potential to play on Sundays. Glasper had been named a Students Sports all-American cornerback as a junior.

John Chan: "They were all freaks of athletes. TK was a good linebacker, but he got lost in that defense his junior year."

Beyond the "Big Four" of De La Salle's 2004 class, the rest of the junior roster was also littered with Division 1-caliber athletes such as T.J. Ward, who had finally hit his growth spurt as a junior. Football ran in the family. Terrell Ward Sr. had played safety at San Diego State and was drafted by the Philadelphia Eagles in the seventh round of the 1980 NFL draft. Now, T.J.'s father coached De La Salle's secondary.

Of the Big Four, there was a feeling that TK in particular wasn't maximizing his enormous potential.

Justin Alumbaugh: "TK took some lumps his junior year. I think it was one of the first times that he didn't perform at a level that he wanted. He was certainly good, but he wasn't great. He improved throughout the year but you could tell that he wasn't as committed. It wasn't that he was hugely lazy or anything – but he wasn't really a grinder and he wasn't putting in as much as he could.

"Junior year he wasn't really able to harness his competitive spirit because he hadn't put in enough work. He was more athletic than guys, but he was weaker and slower than some of them. He struggled with the physicality in some matchups. He avoided some contact. He wasn't scared, but he just wasn't strong enough or physical enough to be able to do it. He knew that he wanted to do something different, so he committed himself to it."

"I was going into my junior year, so I was taking cues from the guys who would be seniors and the leaders of our team," explains one former player. "At times, TK held back – whether it was in a drill, in the weight room, gassers or film review. It was frequent at the beginning of that offseason that you'd hear TK get called out in front of everyone for not giving maximum effort.

"The default is when you have a talented player like TK – you let those things slide. One of the things the De La Salle program prides itself on is that the standards apply to everyone. There isn't special treatment. It's expected that everyone does the summer workouts and abides by the team's rules. Especially for a high-profile guy like TK, it's not good for the team. It sets a bad example – the notion that you can get by off of your talent and that you don't have to give everything for the team. At the end of the day, it wasn't enough to have a talented TK, we needed the best TK. We needed him to be a part of the team. That's giving everything you have in the drills and leaving nothing off the table when it comes to the work you put in."

T.J. Ward: "Before our senior year, Coach 'Baugh was hard on TK and really challenged him. He wanted TK to be more a student of the game instead of just using his athleticism to make plays. He knew that if TK became a student of the game and got that intellectual part down, he would dominate."

Jackie Bates: "They were telling Terrance he could be the best player to ever come out of De La Salle. They didn't want him to make a mistake. They had such high expectations because they knew he hadn't even come close to peaking. Junior year, he'd make plays all across the field and Alumbaugh would still be on him. There were some days where he'd be irritated and tell me, 'Oh my God, why they riding me so hard?' But at the end of the day, you see the bigger picture and what Alumbaugh was trying to get across. He was a phenomenal coach. He knew what he was doing, he knew what he saw in Terrance, and it stuck with him. They brought the best out of him."

Steve Fujimoto: "TK had proven he was good junior year, but not great. He was slacking a little on drills or he'd show up a little late. At De La Salle we don't let that slide. Coach 'Baugh was on him because that's what Coach 'Baugh did. You knew he liked you and cared about you if he was riding you, and he rode TK hard. During films, after films, during practice – TK was getting it all the time from Alumbaugh. Then, at the end of the season, the coaches called TK in and had a talk with him. When they pulled someone in, everybody knew about it."

Justin Alumbaugh: "We pulled TK in during the offseason, right before we started offseason workouts. We told him, 'If we're gonna be successful, we gotta have leaders. But leaders first and foremost have to lead by action and lead by effort – and that's something he'd never done before. *Nobody's going to listen to you unless you're puttin' in the work.*

"He says, 'I got' chu coach.' And he put on that big ol' smile and almost a little wink. I'm thinking, 'Alright, he understands what I'm getting at...'"

TK had to cut out all distractions to fulfill the potential the coaching staff saw in him. He had to buy in, which meant focusing exclusively on football even though he continued to draw interest in baseball. One all-star team from Richmond offered to pay his way to play baseball in Australia for two weeks.

Landrin Kelly: "Terrance really turn't the light on that summer after the coaches challenged him. They told him he needed to step up and be a leader and a captain on the team. He told me, 'Dad I'm goin' for it. I ain't playin' baseball this summer. I've got too much to work on. I'm just gonna stay home and work out for football. I want me a scholarship.'"

Lanny Kelly III: "He was so excited for his senior season. He saw it as his time. People in Richmond challenged him. 'Ya'll not gonna be undefeated this season. Who ya'll got now? Who's gonna run the ball? Ya'll don't have no more stars on the team.' They didn't see Terrance as a star. He played his role at tight end and linebacker, but Maurice Drew was the big talk his junior year. He wanted college coaches to know who he was. He took on the leadership role. His mentality was, 'We're not gonna lose this year, not in *my* senior season.'"

Justin Alumbaugh: "He showed up in the weight room after we talked to him and had a completely different attitude. He was working his ass off. He had so much credibility because he was so kind to everybody and so likeable. So with him working hard – that really held a lot of clout. Other guys perked up and started working harder because of that. Everybody jumped on board.

"He was honest with himself. That's not easy for most teenagers to do. Most people in general are not all that honest with themselves. He told me, 'I was lazy, I was weak. I've had it easy. I have so much I wanna do, so much improvement I wanna make.' He was diamonds in the weight room after that. He was running, pushing other guys. It was like he was a completely different athlete as far as dedication."

Terry Eidson: "He came on the second half of his junior year playing tight end and linebacker. We really knew we had something with him. We could see the potential as to how good he was gonna be. Different kids respond in different ways. When we got on him about things after his junior year, he responded. He was very honest about his effort and took it to heart. That's when I knew he could be something special. He had the talent, but you could see he also had that desire to be better and that he was willing to change."

Lanny Kelly III: "Every time I saw Terrance that summer, it was in passing. He'd run in Granny Bev's house, eat, then grab his cleats and drive to Concord to hit the weights, work on footwork or talk with the coaches."

167

Steve Fujimoto: "Whatever the coaches said to him – that really sparked something. He really stepped it up in the weight room after that, right there with Biller and I. He was our best player and we knew that. We needed him to be the best he could be. We told him, 'You're doing everything that we're gonna do, so get ready.' When he got tired, if he had to do another set, we said, 'Nope, you've got another set. Let's go.' He got bigger, stronger and faster every week. Equal or better than me in strength. He wasn't as strong as Biller, but nobody was. TK's skill-level jumped enormously over that summer, more than anyone else on the team."

Jackie Bates: "A De La Salle workout is equivalent to two workouts for someone else. Leg press after squats. We're adding stuff to our workouts where Alumbaugh has to tell us, 'You guys need to take it easy.' We're grinding man. Running extra. Watching extra film. We're in that mode. It's like, 'We gotta uphold this streak and have the best season we can.' I'm thinking 2,000 rushing yards, nothing less.

"TK was so focused that summer. He prepared himself, ate right and worked his tail off. Terrance knew he could play and had been more of a natural before that summer – his game wasn't built around just being a muscle-head. But he really stepped it up as a weightlifter that offseason. Squattin' low, ass to the grass. The strides he made were crazy. His power cleans went up ridiculously – he was cleaning 300 pounds as a senior, pulling that off the ground and catching it in a front squat. You combine that with the talent he had? Man. Keep in mind this guy had the reach of an NBA guard with those long arms."

Bob Ladouceur: "TK was a good leader in the weight room, he worked hard in there. He put on a lot weight between his junior and senior year. And it was good weight, muscle weight."

Back in Richmond, friends and family noticed the difference.

168

Mary Kelly: "Physically, it was like he had transformed overnight. It wasn't like I saw him every day, more like every month. But it was unreal how fast he bulked up."

Louis Montgomery: "You could see the transition. Every time I saw him, I thought, 'Damn he gettin' big.' I asked him, 'Boy what you been eatin'? Damn boy you gettin' taller too? Damn!'"

Jeremy Williams: "He was a kid – then all of a sudden he was grown. It was like Quinton Ganther, who was the stud of every league in Richmond growing up. But Quinton looked grown like that when he was 12. With TK, it was like all of a sudden he got big that summer. We were like, 'Boy what'chu doing? What they got you eatin' up there at that school?'"

Jackie Bates: "By the end of that summer, TK was college-ready. Landrin drove TK and I to Stanford Nike Camp that summer. We both had a good showing in the drills. Terrance squatted close to 500 pounds there."

Kevin Lopina: "TK hated to lose in conditioning. If you beat him, he'd let you know he wasn't losing next time. If you lost, he'd let you know it. He'd challenge you."

Drew Curto: "He put a ton of good weight on that summer, and he started to tear it up in the 7-on-7 summer passing league. We played local teams and TK started to shine – scoring touchdowns left and right. You could see he had made that next step and turned a corner. He came out of that summer our most improved player."

Erik Sandie: "The difference between TK's junior year and senior year was enormous. I remember coming back the next year and watching him play – it was like he was a completely different person. Like he had flipped the switch. I thought to myself, 'That guy got big.'"

Cole Smith: "At that time, Chan, Sandie and I are playing D1 football. TK had always been a lanky, fast, athletic kid. But when we came back to watch the guys below us, it was like, 'Wow he's a beast.' It's a different level. Now, he *looks* like a D1 athlete. It was like he had finally tapped into the potential he had."

Justin Alumbaugh: "TJ and TK were both of a similar mindset – they made a huge transformation between their junior and senior years. They had similar personalities. They were both affable guys, nice, fun to be around. They pushed each other without any animosity."

T.J. Ward: "I had always been undersized so I didn't play much junior year, but going into senior year, I was ready. Of TK, Jackie, Cameron, Willie and myself, I was the only one not on the map. I didn't hit any Nike camps where my name would be out there like those guys. So I knew I needed to come into my senior year and ball. But TK really stepped up that summer. I seen him in there studying and watching film like he was in college. He really knew the playbook."

Justin Alumbaugh: "As a junior, Terrance understood what I was talking about in terms of film review and the mental aspects of the game, but he hadn't fully committed to it. It takes a lot of studying and extra time put in. You have to visualize what will happen on the field – 'If they're going to run this specific play, and we're in this defense – this is exactly where I should be on the field.' Once he understood the importance of it and how integral it was to his success and the team's success, he was quick and *very* intuitive."

Lanny Kelly III: "He always had his playbook. If he was sitting there with his playbook and the TV was on, you could tell his mind wasn't on TV – the TV was watching him. You could see him going over plays in his head, visualizing how the game would play out from the tight end and linebacker positions."

On the field, TK and Parker would again lead De La Salle's defense as one of the top linebacker duos in the country.

Junior lineman Scott Hugo, from Alamo, recalls competing against TK in practice every day.

Scott Hugo: "I was the scout team center as a junior. It was a trial-run game each and every week – I had to block either TK or Parker. Those two set the standard for me when I think of great linebackers. They were the heart of the defense and are inseparable in my mind. When I watch any linebackers today, I look at whether they read an offense like TK and Parker. They were an incredible team and I had to bring everything I had to not to get annihilated by them. It was a really formative experience for me both as an athlete and as a person.

"TK had a kind of fluidity about him at linebacker. When I went out to try and block him, it was really hard to pin him down. Then, when that moment came for the hit, my God, he could deliver. Some of the wallops I took from him, I'm glad I still have my head on straight.

"With Parker, there was a directness to the way he played, a conservation of energy and movement. When he read the play – he was on a straight line. He was strong, well-built, fast. He packed the punch of a bulldozer. They had complementary styles of play.

"Besides having a healthy dose of fear at every practice, what I loved about those two was that that they weren't mean about the competition. TK and Parker never tried to embarrass me. They'd tease me and challenge me, but it was never mean-spirited.

"If I made a block against either of them, the coaches ran the exact same play again. Now Parker and TK were tough enough when they had to read what's going on. But when they know the exact play? They'd both call out to me before the play, 'Hugo....*I know you're coming!*' That healthy fear I had would elevate to a downright panic.

171

"There was one time in particular. We run a play up the middle called '14 Counter Drive,' where I'm the lead blocker going up against the inside linebackers – Parker and TK. He must have been off balance – because I go out and knock Parker down on the play.

"TK and Parker were the best linebackers I would ever face – so to put down a good block on Parker was a huge feat. Parker gets up. His face is red; his eyes tear up with rage. As soon as I did it, I realize I've stirred the hornets' nest.

"Coach 'Baugh calls out from the sideline, 'OH MY GOD. DID YOU JUST SEE HUGO LAY OUT HANKS.' So Coach 'Baugh and Coach Lad smile at one another. They say, 'Run the 14 Counter Drive again' loud enough for everyone on the team to hear it. So now I know I'm a dead man.

"Parker lines up ready to rip my head off. TK lines up next to him staring at me. He has this huge grin on his face, and he says, '*Hugo, you're in trouble…*'

"That's TK's sense of humor. That's the stuff I smile about thinking of the two of them. I've never seen two individuals who read the field faster. They made me a better player, and I learned what it takes to be great from them."

TK had made an impression at the linebacker position, but in Richmond, the family wondered why he wasn't getting a shot at running back given his size and athleticism.

Johnny Dempsey: "We always felt TK should have been playing running back instead of tight end and that he should be getting more of the limelight. So we had to remind everyone to be patient. On an outstanding team like De La Salle, it's hard to be recognized because everybody's great. It's one unit."

Landrin Kelly: "Going into that senior year, it was like he had totally changed. It was like he understood everything I was telling him as a young boy. I asked him, 'Why you ain't in the backfield? It was you, Jackie, Willie and Dominguez – ya'll was the freshman running backs.' 'Dad, I'm just concentrating on defense. I ain't even worried about it. Me and Parker rotating at tight end and I'm playing linebacker. I'm cool.' "

Whether at tight end, running back or linebacker, TK had finally bought into the De La Salle program and its ethic of hard work and selflessness. Challenged by teammates and coaches, he put in the extra effort to get to the next level and now looked like a Division 1 football player. As colleges across the country soon realized, TK was only scratching the surface of his huge athletic potential.

Parker Hanks, TK

CHAPTER 20

Disrespect

TK TRAINED FANATICALLY over the summer and became bigger, faster and stronger every week. Outside of class, he studied De La Salle's playbook or relaxed with his closest friends on the football team. On the 'other side' in Concord, TK let his guard down because there wasn't jealously and hate that permeated certain neighborhoods back in Richmond.

Paul Webster Jr.: "In Richmond, you have to watch your associations. It's something you learn growing up. 'Watch who you be around.' I had to be there to let TK know at all times, even if I was mad at him, 'Yo. *Watch the people around you.*' "

Paul Webster Sr.: "The conversations we had with TK and Lil Paul during that time was, 'Watch who you be around. Watch out for the element.' If you a football player – you need to be around other football players. Look around to see what doesn't fit. If one of those people ain't doing something – you gotta get rid of him. Tell 'em you'll come back to them later."

Paul Webster Jr.: "We had met Larry Pratcher through our friend Markel. They were both from Central Richmond. We were close to Markel because we grew up playing baseball with him – he was on the Bad Boys team we competed against back in Little League. So whoever Markel bring around is good – its 100 percent. Larry Pratcher was a cool dude. Him and Markel was real good street dancers."

Louis Montgomery: "I knew Larry Pratcher from high school. He was more TK's friend than mine. I knew of him before, but TK brought him into the circle. Our group, we got along with everybody because of sports."

Landrin Kelly: "I didn't know Larry Pratcher until they needed another player for the Richmond Police Activities League basketball team TK played on. TK and Markel vouched for Larry and he played on that team with 'em. They won a championship at Cal-Berkeley in a 10-team tournament. I brought the team to my house after they won and cooked 'em steaks, baked potatoes and crab legs."

Paul Webster Jr.: "The only time TK wasn't as humble was when we was in a crowd of athletes. TK, Markel and Larry were all athletes – they all played on the Richmond PAL basketball team together.

"TK ragged on Larry about small stuff, like what he was wearing. But that's how we grew up – it's all about teasing. We talked about each other. What you did wrong. 'You weak.' 'You struck out.' 'I did this and you did that.' TK was a little harsh on Larry in that way – he did to Larry what Terry and everyone else used to do to him when we were young. He talked about him, joked about him."

In the summer of 2003, TK participated in a 3-on-3 basketball tournament at the Nevin Community Center, in the heart of Central Richmond's violent Iron Triangle. The event drew a crowd.

Paul Webster Jr.: "TK, Larry Pratcher and our friend Chuck were on the same team at the tournament. So you got a crowd of people watching."

Anthony "Ace" Brown: "TK ain't weak. Whatever team he on, he gonna be noticeable. He making people 'ooo and aww' out there. He was dunking and there were girls there."

Landrin Kelly: "Terrance was going from the rigid structure of De La Salle to playing ghetto ball. It was two steps and to the hole. That's what got 'em mad."

Paul Webster Jr.: "So TK rags on his teammate Larry, from Central, during the game. Larry's little brother Darren was there."

Darren Pratcher was 14 at the time.

Paul Webster Jr.: "TK ragged on Larry about small stuff, but Larry didn't fight back with TK. It was just like TK didn't fight back with Terry when we were kids. Larry just said, 'Whatever, whatever' to TK. And everybody else laughing.

"Now Larry and them was less fortunate. So you got a little brother that look up to his big brother, and here's this cat TK who think he all that. 'You got everything and we ain't got nothing, and you think it's cool to talk about my brother.' That creates animosity.

"The little brother Darren was feeling he had his big boy pants on. His attitude was, 'If my brother ain't gonna say something, Imma say something. Who do you think you is coming to our hood doing what you wanna do?' So Darren said something to TK. When Darren said something, TK bagged on Darren and Darren didn't like that."

176

Louis Montgomery: "That's how we played. Whether I'm winning or losing, we talking shit. I'm doggin' you. That's just how we grew up."

Lanny Kelly III: "I learned not to talk back to Terrance when he was in any sort of competitive situation because he took it serious. Darren said something to Terrance at the tournament, and Terrance kind of ragged on him in the heat of the game. You got emotions going and you not trying to lose. There were girls around and Darren was embarrassed by it."

Paul Webster Jr.: "At that time, gun violence was real serious. Being from Southside in Central, you don't know who funking with who. Somebody may only know you as being from Southside. That could be a problem."

Landrin Kelly: "On the Southside, people had it a little better. Not much, but the Southside had a little bit better neighborhoods. They called us Southsiders the pretty boys. Terrance had his own car, he had money, he went to private schools and he was a ladies' man. Now he comes to Central and wins this tournament. That's where the problem started."

Darren Pratcher grew up in East Oakland – at one point in an apartment on 79th Avenue and later in an apartment on 90th Avenue. Both were extremely rough, violent neighborhoods. Darren's mother held down two health care jobs as a certified nurse assistant. His father worked nights.

Paul Webster Jr.: "East Oakland – they real big on gunplay – they known for that. The mentality over there is, 'If you disrespect my brother or my set, Imma knock you down, Imma kill you.' That's the way it is over there."

David Brown [former Contra Costa County deputy district attorney]: "Darren Pratcher's parents did the best they could. They were hard-working. They were caring. They knew the dangers of the locations they lived in. They were trying to improve on where they lived and get out of there. They did a remarkable job in attempting to stop Darren from going down a bad path."

In the fifth and sixth grades, school records showed Darren doing well; A's and B's, honor roll. His behavior was good and he received good comments from teachers.

In 2000, the Pratcher family moved from East Oakland to a one-story house in Central Richmond on Pennsylvania Avenue. Darren was 11 years old and in the sixth grade when the family moved.

Anthony "Ace" Brown: "Darren and I were friends growing up. We went to junior high together for two years at Helms Middle School. I used to hang out over at his house in Central. He had a mother, father and older brother in his house. Nine times out of 10, black males born in Richmond is not gonna have that. You usually have your dad in one place and your mom in another. He had both. Where they stayed at in Central might not have been the best place, but when I knew him in junior high, we was trying to play sports and everything."

Darren's grades fell in the seventh grade. In separate incidents in August 2001 and October 2001, he was written up for "defying school authority." He attended eighth grade sporadically, maybe two times a week.

Robert Turner: "The hardest place in Richmond was always North Richmond. But in the 1980's, everybody else in Richmond wanted to show they were as tough as North. Central started getting a reputation for being hard. Southside started getting tough.

"I've been coaching and teaching in Richmond for over 30 years – I've met a lot of Darrens. With Darren, when you're moving from East Oakland, which is real hard, to Central – you gotta find a way to fit in. In Darren's case – I think he wanted to be hard. He wanted to show he was just as tough in this new environment over in Central. So he went to something he knew. For some people, the hard life isn't the easy way out; it's the only way out because it's the only thing they know."

Pastor K.R. Woods: "I personally think the problem today has to do with the culture – the suggestions that are given to young people through the music that they listen to and the videos they watch. Violence and street life is glorified, and that trickles down. When you got people – I'll use Lil Wayne as an example. He's a brilliant musician, but he's glorifying street life, whereas he is far removed from street life. To a young person, it's like, 'Hey I want be hard too. I don't want to be a sucker.' So it's the environment and the influences. It's a culture of showing respect. It's almost a badge of honor for some young people to participate in violence."

Quinton Ganther: "We were all so close-knit when we were young. With the kids today, if you don't catch these kids by 11 or 12 and guide them – they're lost to the streets. Kids don't go to each other's houses and play football or baseball anymore. The video games are a big problem. Nobody's outside playing anymore, and that's probably because of the violence."

Paul Webster Jr.: "If you went out and surveyed people in Richmond, a lot of them could have been something. But a lot of them *chose* that quick money, or to have a name, or be a killer, or a drug dealer or whatever else – because somewhere down the line, it's who they got affiliated with. 'Everybody else is like this, so you know what, Imma be a part of that too.'

"It's not just from our generation. It's from our fathers' generation as well. They could have gone a lot farther in life but they *chose* the streets. It's the environment. It's, 'Forget college or going pro, I need shoes.' It's, 'I see how to get money and I wanna get money right now. I wanna be around money – the videos, the rapping and all that. I don't wanna be that different dude.' "

179

Robert Turner: "I read an article years ago – it was a letter between two of the Grand Wizards of the Ku Klux Klan. The letter said, 'We're gonna go out of business. Blacks are killing each other. This rap music is worth more than anything we can do. Let's just sit back and watch 'em kill each other off.' And it's true. We call each other the N-word, which I cannot stand. We call our women B's. And they're just sittin' back laughin' at us – they love it. A lot of young people think it's fun, but to me it's not. I think it's had a negative effect on a lot of our lives. We need to be more in-tune to our history – then we'll be more inclined to help each other because we've lost a lot of respect for each other and we stereotype each other."

David Brown: "It's a matter of association. If you're 12 or 13 and you associate with older people who have stopped going to school and taken up a violent lifestyle – you start to emulate them and do the exact same thing. If they start to believe that education is not going to improve their lot in life – you do the same. You stop trying to better yourself through the school system and education. When Darren started associating with gangbangers, their mentality started influencing his behavior and conduct."

In middle school or early high school, one of Darren's friends was shot and paralyzed. Others were murdered. His brother Larry was shot in the foot.

Paul Webster Jr.: "We had just met Larry. We were all at a hall party at Lefty Gomez, which was shootout central. There was a big fight. Bullets started flying and Larry got shot in the foot. TK and I followed the ambulance from Rodeo to Brookside Hospital in San Pablo. We stayed and made sure Larry was cool. We saw his family and left later that night. The next day we came to the hospital and checked on him."

In the ninth grade, Darren began avoiding areas outside of Central Richmond such as North Richmond, South Richmond and Hilltop mall out of fear for his safety. School records show further decline. On February 20, 2003, he was written up at school for fighting. On April 16, 2003, a school report documented Darren's involvement in an unprovoked attack on a female student with two other boys.

*　　*　　*

Meanwhile, TK's de facto step-brother Brian James was heading down a similar path.

Landrin Kelly: "I coached Brian since he was 6. He was a good kid. But when he got to about 12, I noticed he started veering off."

Robert Turner: "Brian was my student at Adams Middle School. I had him for sixth, seventh and most of eighth grade before he got kicked out at the end of the year. He was somewhat respectful, but he could also be a little brat and a jerk. He was a really mischievous person. He also didn't know what was going on as far as his father not being around."

Lanny Kelly III: "Brian James and Darren Pratcher hung out in the same circles. They knew the same people. As time went on, it seemed like Brian got more distant from TK and I. You could tell there was a change in him. Him and I stopped hanging out. If I showed up at Landrin's new house, he'd either leave or wouldn't be there at all. As time goes on, people change, things change. You start to separate yourself from certain people.

"The last time Brian and I hung out together, I remember we were around Nichol Park at Landrin's old apartment. It was late night. I was young – definitely too young to be leaving the house at 12 o'clock at night. Brian says, 'You wanna go to this party?' 'What party?' 'It's over in Southside by Kennedy.' Now from Nicholl Park to Kennedy, that's not too long of a walk. But at 12 o'clock at night in Richmond? That's a long walk.

"So we walk to the party. As soon as we get there, first person we see is TK. I tapped him on the shoulder. He turns around, and at first he's excited, 'Heyyy! My lil cousin, what you doing here?' Then he's like, 'Hold on, you supposed to be at my dad's. It's late, how'd you even get here?' I told him we walked. He was upset with Brian for asking me to leave. He let us stay for a little while, but then he gave us a ride back to the house and made sure we got in straight."

Landrin Kelly: "Brian's girlfriend Candy lived in Central at 7th and Nevin Avenue, which is right where Darren hung out on the corner every day. Brian and Darren starting hanging a little tighter after I moved up to Hilltop. Brian spent more time down there in Central, and he started coming home with new clothes and new shoes every few weeks. People were telling me, 'Your stepson just bought an ounce off me!' He was coming in the house late at night, high, eating all our waffles – I recognize the munchie signs. After that, it was rebellion with Brian.

"I could see Brian getting a little jealous of Terrance and how everyone spoiled him. But Terrance had earned that treatment, whereas Brian was more irresponsible. When he got older, Brian felt he should be getting the same treatment as Terrance even though he was cutting class, bringing home D's and F's.

"One time I come home early from work over the summer – Brian and his friend cut class and had some little broads coming through my house. I was like, 'I'll whoop both of ya'll ass!' But I wouldn't discipline Brian – I made his momma do it. So I got on the phone with Terrance, because ya'll about the same age, and he can woop ya ass. So Terrance rushed over to the house looking for Brian and they got into it."

Lanny Kelly III: "TK and Brian's relationship seemed playful. But at times you could tell there was animosity from Brian towards Terrance. When they got into it, he'd say, 'You ain't really from Richmond. You a private school kid. You think you better than me? You ain't better than me. If you wasn't that big, I'd whup you.' He'd say this as if he were playing, but you could tell there was some seriousness behind it.

"Terrance didn't buy into it. He was like, 'My dad with your mom, we're pretty much brothers.' He'd go back-and-forth with him a little bit, but Terrance was playing. Brian may have held a grudge."

CHAPTER 21

Breakout

THE DE LA SALLE SPARTANS were once again ranked No. 1 in the nation heading into the 2003 season. TK's senior class was loaded with Division 1-talent and had significant experience on both sides of the ball. But there were chinks in the armor.

Senior wide receiver and defensive back Cameron Colvin, a five-star prospect ranked by Rivals.com as the No. 2-receiver in the nation, was ineligible for the first six games of the season. Jackie Bates, a four-star recruit expected to be the team's featured-running back with the departure of Maurice Drew, was also banged up with a sprained ankle.

Nevertheless, De La Salle ripped through its first two opponents – Archbishop Mitty of San Jose and a tough Palma-Salinas team, ranked No. 18 in California, by a combined score of 82-0.

TK, Parker and the rest of the defense were a stone wall through the first two games. T.J. Ward already had a pair of interceptions, while

TK had splash plays in both games – a devastating, momentum-changing block in the Mitty game and a fumble recovery against Palma.

Parker Hanks: "In the Palma game, they drove down into our red zone. They were still in the game, down 14-0. They snapped it. TK came in from one side and I came in from another. We knocked this dude and forced the fumble. That was really the back-breaker."

Lanny Kelly III: "That senior season, Terrance was so dialed-in. The day before the games, he was off his phone. He put it aside so he wouldn't be distracted. He'd sit in his room and zone out on the task at hand – the upcoming game on Friday night. Every game was a big game. He didn't want to be on the team where the streak ended. He didn't want that to happen – he felt that would tear the team apart. For him to go undefeated until his senior year and then lose a game – that was unacceptable to him."

Kevin Lopina: "If we weren't playing well, you could see Terrance get in the zone. He'd make a huge hit and spark the whole team. He'd change the momentum of a game in a play."

Justin Alumbaugh: "TK's senior year, he had great ideas when we were prepping for teams. He'd say, 'Coach can I line up over here so I'll have a better angle if they run this play?' He was diamonds."

T.J. Ward: "TK knew the opponents. He was running through holes before the ball was even in the running back's hands because he knew the plays so well."

Parker Hanks: "TK and I had the scouting report down to where we'd call out plays on the field and we were right every time. We were the most vocal guys on the defense and gave tendencies off to other players. As the other team gets set, we'd say, 'It's a sweep left.' 'Counter this way.' 'Power that way.' "

Even with lopsided scores in the first two games, there were question marks on offense given the tough upcoming schedule. The most glaring was at running back. All-American cornerback Willie Glasper had filled in capably out of the backfield for Jackie Bates, possessing speed that also made him an effective receiver and dangerous kick returner.

Chris Biller: "On offense, we had stalled out a bit. We weren't that great against Mitty. Not that explosive against Palma. Willie had some big runs, but he wasn't a natural between-the-tackles runner. Dominguez went down and Jackie got banged up."

Parker Hanks: "TK was in the coaches' ears about moving him from tight end to running back. That was a big thing – TK knew the plays. He kept telling the coaches, 'Just give me a shot.' "

Terry Eidson: "We had running backs down for the week, so we put TK back there in practice as a single back. It was, 'Zone-read and go.' We handed him the football. It wasn't a lot because we still felt OK at the position – just a few plays."

The Spartans now hosted St. Francis, ranked third in the Bay Area. The year before, the Lancers had played De La Salle tough and lost 14-0, De La Salle's lowest offensive output since 1989.

St. Francis' 2003 roster featured three-year lettermen in key positions – quarterback Kyle Spraker, 6-0, 240-pound running back William Taufoou, and receiver Daniel Descalso, with a pair of Division 1-prospects in the trenches.

Parker Hanks: "St. Francis was a big game. I didn't have my best game the year before. They had a couple big players that were talking shit."

T.J. Ward: "It was an eerie fall night. The sky was two-toned. I felt weird. My patella [kneecap] had been sore earlier in practice and it felt funny in warmups."

186

De La Salle's pre-game went as usual. The players rallied into a huge circle on the sideline that turned into a mosh pit.

Lanny Kelly III watched every game next to Bevelyn, Chastity and Johnny Dempsey in the center of De La Salle's home stands.

Lanny Kelly III: "TK was never that hype player. He wasn't the guy getting the team pumped up, jumping around. He was like the calm before the storm. He was one of the last ones out and he had this slow trot about him. It would look like he wasn't totally into it, but that's just how he got into his zone.

"When De La Salle got fired up in their circle jumping up and down – you'd see TK walking around the perimeter of it. It's not that he wasn't into getting hyped with the team. He was saying his prayers for the team while he walked around them. He prayed for the team – that everyone would play their best. He prayed for victory and no injuries.

"Then out of nowhere he ran, jumped and tried to touch the middle person's helmet from the outside – it looked like his whole body was lying on top of the pack. That's when you knew he was game-ready."

The game began with a scoreless first quarter. De La Salle was once again sluggish on offense, but had a seven-point lead after a short touchdown run by Willie Glasper.

T.J. Ward: "It was the second quarter. I was on defense playing my deep half of the field. I'm reading the quarterback. He gets flushed out of the pocket, so I break up the field towards the sideline. If the QB tries to throw across his body – I know I'm going for the pick. As he runs to the sideline, sure enough he throws the ball across his body.

"I see him throw it, so I break up the field for the interception. The receiver doesn't see the quarterback throw it, so he runs up the field. We collide knee-to-knee. I try to get up, but pain shoots up through my whole leg.

"Willie was playing left corner. He runs over and looks at me, then down at my knee. His eyes pop wide open. He looks toward the sideline and starts waving people over like, 'Get somebody out here.' I got carted off the field and they took me to the hospital."

Shortly after T.J.'s injury, Jackie Bates suffered an injury to his foot on a punt return. Though TK hauled in a touchdown reception at tight end before the half, the team's morale was low after losing two future-NFL players to season-ending injuries in a matter of minutes.

The third quarter was another defensive battle, with De La Salle adding a field goal to open the lead to 17-0. Then, senior running back Mike Dominguez was sidelined with an injury.

After a St. Francis touchdown reception on a long bomb, De La Salle suddenly found itself in a dog fight against a tough team.

Terry Eidson: "All of our runners got whacked, one-by-one. We were hurting. So I say, 'Hey, let's give TK the ball and see what happens. At least we know he's one of our better athletes.' "

Bob Ladouceur: "We became depleted of running backs. Terrance remembered the plays. So I stick him back there by himself in a single-back set."

Landrin Kelly: "I was up in the baseball bleachers with my brother, my uncle and my cousins. I saw that they put TK in the backfield. I was shocked – we'd been waiting since his JV year for him to have the chance to run the ball."

Justin Alumbaugh: "When Terrance made the switch to running back, it completely changed the dynamic of our team. The linemen loved him. Terrance was one of those linemen because he had played at tight end. He worked hard at that craft – he didn't take his blocking lightly. Those linemen were tough guys and he had their respect. The entire line lit up like they had just got a Christmas present when he got in the backfield, and they fought their asses off for him. They literally blocked harder with him back there because they knew that he was gonna run hard, and he did – he ran hard and fought through tacklers."

TK ripped a 15-yard run with his first handoff.

Chris Biller: "Terrance was a savvy player. I'm pulling, playing guard. So I run from my side of the line to the opposite side to block out in front for him. He was smart, he'd grab your jersey and kind of lead you – he was right in my ear, whispering, 'Go Bill…go Bill…' Think about a guy whose is calm enough in the middle of a play – especially at running back – to grab to you and guide you as you block in front of him."

Parker Hanks: "The coaches call the next play, '18 Veer.' I was at tight end following behind TK on the play after he broke through the line. TK ran over a safety, just bulled him. He took it 65 yards to the house. We were all so juiced for him."

Landrin Kelly: "He came towards the end zone closest to us. I was like, 'Damnnnnn, there he gooooooo!' He pointed at us as he crossed the line."

Johnny Dempsey: "He had his moment. I sat back with a smile on my face and said to my Aunty Bevelyn, 'I told you! I told you! We just had to be patient. God has a time and place for everybody.' Everything fell into place. We knew that was his last day playing tight end on offense."

Drew Curto: "He blew that game wide-open. He was a beast – physically bigger and stronger than you, but also fast and agile. When he started running downhill, you weren't tackling him. You'd have to take him low because if you tried to tackle him high, he was gonna run you over."

Jackie Bates: "I was out and Terrance stepped up to the plate. These guys on the other team are looking at him like, 'I don't wanna tackle that guy.' Not only was he powerful, he was shifty too. He was a problem.

He hit the line full stride and ran people over. He was like other elite De La Salle running backs, but bigger – D.J. Williams and Kevin Simon are the only ones I can think of that could run like that, but were that big."

Paul Webster Jr.: "To see him change from – us being the little chubby kids – to now he's totin' the rock at halfback – that was something special."

Johnny Dempsey: "Landrin drove straight to my house in Oakland after that game to get the tape. I didn't mind staying up late for Terrance, because he would do the same thing for me or anybody else – that's the type of guy he was."

T.J. Ward: "I was at the hospital in pre-op before surgery after the game. My knee had swollen up so big that they couldn't pull my football pants off, so they had to cut them off. My whole family was in there crying. I'm hurtin'. I'm crying – I didn't know what was going to happen. It was a sad moment.

"TK and Cameron Colvin came to see me that night. When TK walked in, they pulled the sheet back so they could see my knee. He says, 'Daaaaaaaang, boyyyyy!' Everybody cracked up. I was hurtin', but I couldn't help but laugh. That's just TK for you."

Landrin Kelly: "TK didn't get home that night 'till late. I put the tape in and we watched it. He gets the ball on tape and I'm riding him, 'Look at'chu! Look at'chu carryin' the ball loose like a loaf of bread!' 'Dad, I still ran for 150 yards and two touchdowns!' 'Still what?! I want the fundamentals to be down! If I'm lookin' at this, what you think the scouts are looking at?'

"We'd go over it back and forth, play-by-play. It was a battle, a challenge. A competitive thing. We'd be up until two in the morning going over the tape like that."

TK sheds tackles against St. Francis, September 26, 2003

CHAPTER 22

The 5.0

THE **SPARTANS BLASTED** through a highly-ranked Foothill team 48-0 in early October. Next, the team prepared for a flight to Southern California to take on La Costa Canyon of San Diego.

Chris Biller: "We all hop on a school bus at De La Salle to leave for Oakland Airport. TK's car broke down on I-680 in Pleasant Hill, not far from school. Terrance calls, so Drazba and I go get him. We pick him up off the shoulder on the freeway.

"If my car breaks down, I'd say, 'I have to take care of my car, I'll catch you guys later.' But Terrance was just like, 'Nevermind my car, I gotta get on the plane.' I don't know who came and got his car, but it got figured out."

Landrin Kelly: "Terrance drove my momma's Honda out to De La Salle. She called me. 'The car stopped on Terrance.' So my dad drove out to Pleasant Hill to jump it. The alternator had gone out, so he had the car towed back to our house in Richmond.

"I flew down and watched the game with my mom, my sister and Nicole. Terrance ran for four touchdowns and they won 28-7, but the play wasn't up to the standard and expectation held by the coaches. The line play was a little sloppy. The coaches knew that Evangel Christian was coming into town soon all the way from Louisiana. Evangel was ranked second in the nation behind us going into the season, so the guys needed to be sharp.

"When we got back in town I decided to get Terrance a new car. I'd been thinking about it even before my mom's Honda broke down on him. He was doing everything that I wanted him to do and I wanted to surprise him. A friend I worked with offered to sell me a 1981 Mustang 5.0. I had saved for it so I bought the car.

"I walk in the house after the San Diego trip and TK's on the couch. I told him, 'Huh, go test this car out. See how you like it.' I threw him the keys. 'Dad, you bought a new car?' 'Yeah.' He went and drove it down the block. He came back so excited.

"Dad, this is phat! This tight. This nice! Man, dad.'

"OK. That's your car.'

"You lyin! You lyin!'

"Naw man, that's your car. I bought that for you.'

"Dad, but you driving this?' And he looked over at my old 1963 Oldsmobile Cutlass Supreme.

"It ain't about me, it's about how my kid look. Your kid supposed to look better than you.'

"I'll take this Cutlass dad, you take the 5.0.'

193

"Naw, this yours, dude. I want you to shine.' He was so excited. He grabbed me and started kissin' on me and hugging me and kept saying, 'You lyin' dad!'

"You deserve this. You doing everything you supposed to do… so, this is for you, baby.' And he jumped on me, just so happy.

"But there's one thing you gotta do. You gotta follow directions. And that means when I tell you to do something, you do it. Because I'll take it from you. I'll put you on restriction.' "

Johnny Dempsey: "Landrin pulls up at my house the day before and says, 'I just bought this car for my son.' 'What? You bought him a 5.0?' TK came the next day to my house and showed it to me. You could tell he was so happy to have his own car. He took me for a ride. A lot of people get things and they don't want you around. He wanted to show me what his father did for him."

Lanny Kelly III: "That same weekend he got the 5.0, Terrance came to Berkeley to pick me up in it. His horn didn't work, so I just sat by the window and waited to hear his engine. It was so loud you could hear it coming from down the block. When he pulled up, I said, 'Alright dad, TK's here, I'm going.'

"He loved that car. That's where I got my love for muscle cars from. I run outside and hop in the car. He's outside looking at the ceiling of it, the windows and the rims. He says, 'Aww, I know what I'm about to do…I'm about to put these types of tints on it.'

"And the next week, he had matching tints. Then he says, 'Aww, I'm about to put a TV in it.' This was way before people were putting TVs in their cars. Next thing you know, he had a TV coming out the dash with a DVD player. 'Aww, I'm gonna put some speakers in it.' Then he got speakers, two twelves. It was a hatchback, so the box touched his back window.

194

"He wasn't close to being done with it. He talked about remodeling the engine. He wanted a 302. He wanted glass tack mufflers because he loved the loud roar. He loved driving a stick shift and he talked about converting it to a stick.

"After I get in, he puts his hand on the top of my head, rattles my neck around and asks how I'm doing, if I'm ready. He cranks the stereo and the bass rattles my chest. The whole car shakes and I can't hear. I look at him, he's laughing – he's talking to me but I can't hear him because it's so loud.

"Every time, Terrance peeled off. He loved to hear his tires squeak. He liked to accelerate fast just to get it out of his system before he slowed back down and started cruising.

"Riding with him, I felt like I was in a different place, like I didn't have any worries. I knew he'd take care of me. I definitely knew I was gonna eat because he loved to eat. I can't remember riding with him in the 5.0 where it wasn't a nice day. We always had the windows down, the music loud. I didn't notice anything else on the road. It was just me and him."

Tra'Meka Kelly: "Terrance tried to have sex talks with me. I was only 13 or 14. He set it up when we were riding in the 5.0 so I can't get out. It was the most awkward thing ever. Terrance turns down the music and he says, 'So…'

"No, no, no. Are you serious? I'm not having sex, dude.' He looks over at me and says, 'But if you are, you know these boys don't like you. They just want something.' 'Oh my gosh that is so gross you are so nasty you cannot talk to me about sex,' and I turn up the music on him.

"He turns the music back down. 'I'm just tellin' you. They don't like you. They don't think you're pretty. They think you're ugly. They don't want nothing from you. They want one thing, and do you know what that

195

one thing is?' 'Nope. You know what, conversation over. I'm turning up the music.'

"I had to shut him down, it was so awkward. But it's a brother-sister thing, so I understand. If he didn't, who would?"

Mary Kelly: "He'd drive to see me in that thing. He lit up when he talked about it, and he was very proud that his dad got him that car. I told him, 'Mr. T, be careful in that thing, that's a fast car.' 'Alright, Mookie, alright.' He wanted to soup the car up and add components to make it faster. He was naming things I didn't know about. I figured the car was fast enough as it was."

Steve Fujimoto: "We used to race our cars down Treat Boulevard in Concord. He had the 5.0 and I had a Trans-Am. Every day after practice we'd drive side-by-side. He'd look over at me and we'd race. So we speed down the street and I get nervous. I'd think, 'OK I need to slow down, I'm gonna get a ticket.' But TK wouldn't slow down, he just gunned it. We must have done that 20 times down Treat. He'd talk shit that he won. He talked about how much better and faster his 5.0 was than my Trans-Am. We argued a lot about the two cars."

Jeremy Williams: "That was one of the cars back in our time – either a Mustang or a Camaro. We'd hit donuts, fishtail and burn rubber. We were kids with V8's, so we were speeding and racing. He had Flowmasters on there and it had that loud sound. We had some times in there.

"The only time we came into contact with the police was because of tickets. Speeding tickets or mirror tint tickets. TK and I both had our windows tinted so you couldn't see inside the car. Back then in Richmond, it was real bad. A lot of stuff was going on and they pulled people over to see who was who. We were older, so we got pulled over all the time. They'd run our license and ask us, 'What you got – probation? Parole?' We were like, 'Man, we're kids. We never been to Juvenile Hall.' We was always legit besides the speeding."

Jackie Bates: "It was a beautiful car. He got a $200 ticket for that mirror tint. He used to pick me up in that thing. He was already the man, but after he got that 5.0, those girls were really looking at him."

TK's growing circle of admirers went beyond people looking for a ride in the 5.0. His name was in the papers weekly with each De La Salle win. He started at tailback and inside linebacker for the best team in the country and was a good looking, easygoing guy.

Jeremy Williams: "He had these two national championship rings from De La Salle. He'd wear them two at a time. They was hella big. I'd say, 'Let me see those right quick. Let me see if this work. Let's see if they know who you are yet.' If a girl walked by, I'd say, 'Hey, I'm THE TK. Have you read about me? Did you see me in the paper?' He'd laugh and say, 'Boy you stupid.' "

Chastity Harper: "I put up with a lot when it came to other girls. They'd call me and threaten to come to my house and beat me up. Random girls showed up to his games and cheered for him. Our arguments were him trying to convince me that the girls were either just friends or after him.

"He'd stick up for me when girls tried to fight me, or call them on three-way while I listened. He'd tell them to stop calling. We actually broke up over it once. I came home crying and my parents noticed because that's not the type of person I was. My mom called Terrance and told him, 'This is unacceptable. I'm not going to let her talk to you if this continues.' My mom called Bevelyn too and she reassured me, 'No one is ever coming around us or our family except you. No one is calling here.' "

Paul Webster Jr.: "TK and Chas, their relationship had its ups and down. They always seemed to find each other no matter what problems they had. But TK was well-liked amongst the women. He was way off in Concord so these Richmond girls don't know nothing about him except that he go to De La Salle and he a big football player. So you got a popular dude who dresses well and drives, and they know nothing about him…except that he a big football player. Chas did go through a lot with phone calls and rumors. These other girls were just jealous because she was wifey."

Jeremy Williams: "TK calls me and says, 'Ey man come to this prom with me!' 'I don't have nobody to pay for this prom dude. It's not gonna work.' 'C'mon man it's one of Chastity's potnas, she cute!' 'Bro I can't go.'

"We used to play around. I'd tell him, 'I'm booked.' That was the cool thing to do at that time – you go to as many proms as you can. St. Mary's prom, El Cerrito prom, Pinole prom, Fairfield prom. So you got the same guy at all these different proms, all within a week's time, in all the different pictures."

Landrin Kelly: "In his junior and senior years, he went to a ton of proms. He was a hot commodity. I told him, 'Check this out dude, you gon' have to repeat some of them suits. I ain't about to buy you a new suit for every prom!' "

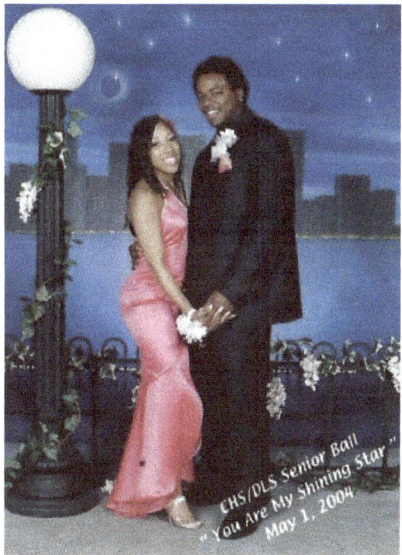

TK and Chastity

CHAPTER 23

Coming Out Party

AFTER A 63-7 DEMOLITION of nearby Freedom, TK and the Spartans prepared for the game of the year. Evangel Christian Academy of Shreveport, Louisiana was rated No. 2 in the country behind De La Salle heading into the season. ECA was a two-time defending 5A state champion with a blue chip roster.

It would be the first high school football game ever broadcast live on national television. Ten months prior, LeBron James starred in the first-ever live national telecast of a high school basketball game.

De La Salle's marquee matchups with the streak on the line the year before were St. Louis of Hawaii and Long Beach-Poly. TK had played well, but the pressure of the spotlight had been on seniors such as Maurice Drew.

Parker Hanks: "Coach 'Baugh brought us in to watch film of Evangel Christian's star running back Jacob Hester. There was some special clip of him. We were all ready for the game, but they were lighting that fuse early in the week. We had articles posted on our lockers with quotes. We also posted pictures of their faces – some of the big lineman, Hester, their quarterback, the receivers."

Hester, known as the "Freight Train," was 6-0, 240 pounds. As a junior, he rushed for 1,600 yards and 24 touchdowns and was named Louisiana's 5A offensive MVP. TK and Parker Hanks had the task of shutting him down.

The game was played on a clear October Saturday at Diablo Valley College in Pleasant Hill. Television news vans cluttered the packed parking lot and ESPN raised two massive portable light towers high above the field for the broadcast in addition to the field's regular lights.

Johnny Dempsey: "We had to hustle some tickets just to get in because the game was sold out and there was nothing at the gate. We found some kid who sold us two tickets. It was a big game, a big stage. We got in there and let Terrance know where we were sitting. There were cameras around so we left him alone after that. I knew he was ready."

Landrin Kelly: "I watched the game from the back of the end zone with Jackie and T.J in my work gear – hard hat and combat boots. T.J. and Jackie were both on crutches. My mom, my nephew, my cousins – my sisters – everybody was there in the stands."

Parker Hanks: "Evangel had a spread offense – shotgun four-wide – which opened up a lot of space on the field. So TK and I had to audible a lot in that game to adjust to the different receivers moving around. We'd come out and change the coverage because we knew what was coming."

Landrin Kelly: "First play of the game, Terrance recognized the play from film. He called an audible, jumped up to the line and hit the dude deep in the backfield for a 10-yard loss."

Kevin Lopina: "A lot of people doubted us going into that game. I was a first-year starter at quarterback. Cameron Colvin hadn't played yet.

My season ended with an injury in that game and that sucked – but Terrance carried us and took over on both sides of the ball. That game was really his coming-out party."

The game was never close. De La Salle dominated in all facets and went on to win, 27-10. TK finished with 106 rushing yards and two touchdowns along with a handful of key tackles on defense.

Terry Eidson: "TK took over the game. He was just awesome. After that, he really became a top recruit."

Louis Montgomery: "I watched that game on ESPN. I told other cats at school, 'Look at him! I know that cat, look at him!' It made me proud."

Johnny Dempsey: "After that game, things were starting to take place as far as scholarship offers. It didn't surprise me at all. I was like, 'I told you so!' I was so thrilled that everybody else knew about my cousin."

Paul Webster Sr.: "All that shit we did when they were little, it paid off now. We groomed the boys for this. We started to pull back and listen to them more. Our kids made us proud in high school. TK did such an excellent job at De La Salle – you wouldn't have thought he was raised in no South Richmond. You raise kids to be champions and they'll be ready when the time comes."

Mary Kelly: "I got phone calls. 'Did you see him on ESPN?' Did you see High School Sports Focus?' 'Oh yeah!' I came to the important events outside of the games – but I also didn't want to cause any problems. My mother-in-law Bevelyn and I talked a lot during that time. She said, 'Mary Lou, you do what you feel is best, you don't want to hurt nobody's feelings.' We had our moments and our times. TK knew I loved him."

Quinton Ganther: "I was at Citrus Junior College playing football at the time. It was great to see somebody from the neighborhood that you grew up with doing it. This little clumsy, chubby kid from the neighborhood had finally grown into himself. He caught up to his body and he was a monster."

Landrin Kelly: "When we went to the barber shop in Richmond everybody talked about him. They had his newspaper articles on the wall. They said, 'I seen you in the newspaper man!' I'd get the newspaper articles every week, blow them up and stick 'em on the wall in his room."

Paul Webster Jr.: "For TK to stay humble around all that, that's something special. From weak TK to raw TK, he never changed."

Jeremy Williams: "He was a real humble person. Even with all the scholarship offers and his name being in the paper, he didn't think he was better. You wouldn't even know about all that. He was just cool. He didn't act funny. He didn't change nothing."

After his performance against Evangel Christian on ESPN, scholarship offers from schools across the country poured in. USC, UCLA, UC Berkeley, Fresno State, Oregon, Oregon State, San Diego State, Utah, UNLV, Washington, Washington State, Colorado, Arizona, Arizona State, Michigan, Nebraska and Wisconsin all offered TK full-rides.

TK diving tackle against Evangel Christian, October 24, 2003

CHAPTER 24

You Gotta Earn It Dude

TK'S DEDICATION AND COMMITMENT had changed between his junior and senior years at De La Salle. He assumed a leadership role on and off the field. Nevertheless, he continued to struggle with the 40-minute one way commute and demanding schedule. After film sessions with Landrin until the early hours of Saturday morning, he had to be out of the house by 7 to make De La Salle's morning practices. Mid-way through his senior season, TK still showed up late to morning classes, practices and team meetings.

Bob Ladouceur: "He was showing up late to practices and to first period at school. It was nothing dramatic. He wasn't being disrespectful to anyone. But for a team leader, you gotta always be out in front and showing by example. He wasn't doing that. He would kind of slide a little bit. The rules are the rules. We warned him about it."

Parker Hanks: "TK showed up to practices as the team is running around the track. We all noticed and we'd give him shit for half-assing it or call him a 'Jaker,' which basically means slacker. The coaches either kept him late or ripped into his ass."

Steve Fujimoto: "We'd point him out in front of the whole team when he came late. But it got to the point where we were like, 'Fuck it. If he's gonna show up late, he's gonna show up late and there's nothing we can do about it.'"

Chris Biller: "We finished Friday night games at 10 p.m. We shower up and leave school at 11. He's gonna grab food on the way home like we all did. Then get up and drive 40 minutes to school and be there at 8:30 a.m. That's tough, but it's a good life lesson about De La Salle – it doesn't matter that you drive in from Richmond and no one else does. The lesson is, 'When you leave here, the world isn't fair – no one else is going to give a shit about you.' That's why De La Salle wins. They don't cut you any slack."

Bob Ladouceur: "He kept coming late, so we brought him in after practice and said he was gonna sit against Pittsburg. He was a tough guy and a quiet leader. He was competitive. He knew he let his teammates down and put us in a difficult position. He had such a huge responsibility to the team at two important positions. It's difficult to find a replacement there to keep the caliber of play up. He felt really bad about that."

Pittsburg is a blue collar town 20 miles north of Concord, and its football team always has talent and speed. The Pirates were the last team to beat De La Salle before the streak began, winning in the North Coast Section 4A championship game in 1991.

Parker Hanks: "It was after a Wednesday practice, the last full-pad practice before the game against Pittsburg on Friday night. I found out TK got benched. I was disappointed in him because he was my wing-man and I told him that. He was always the dude next to me. I didn't feel comfortable playing Mike linebacker without him there. The defense wasn't as sound without him. There's chemistry between those positions that's unique. We'd fill holes in the same progression. TK was irreplaceable."

Landrin Kelly: "I didn't find out Terrance was gonna sit until I went to watch the game. I asked him about it, and he told me he overslept and was late. With my schedule, I was dead tired at that point and slept in on Saturday mornings. I told him, 'This is your fault. If this is your business and this is what you want, you have to do this on your own. You gotta deserve it and you gotta earn it dude.' Terrance could be a lazy-ass kid. It wasn't our job to wake him up at that age. We had to make him responsible for his own actions too."

Despite TK's absence, De La Salle still rolled over Pittsburg, 26-0, showing the depth and talent of the 2003 team. Nevertheless, he did not take the benching lightly.

Justin Alumbaugh: "In the following Thursday night meeting at one of the player's houses, TK broke down in front of the team and the coaching staff. He was upset that he had let everybody down. He was a tough kid. He didn't show his emotions a lot. He was so likeable and he had already earned a lot of respect. When he broke down like that, it added a new dimension to him and it added a new dimension to our team – our team broke down with him. It was a profound moment for our guys."

Parker Hanks: "TK was soft-spoken and quiet. He didn't speak much in front of us at those Thursday night meetings. He held his hooded sweater over his hands and wiped his nose and eyes with it as he talked. When that happened, it was big. We all respected TK already and we respected him even more after that. He used to sit in the back of the room during film review and doze off. After that night, he sat in the front row with all the starting linemen through the rest of the season."

Steve Fujimoto: "TK was No. 1 on the field. He never gave speeches – he was always just the best player. After the coaches sat him against Pittsburg, he stood up in front of us. He was wearing a big hooded sweatshirt – he always wore a big black puffy jacket or a big hooded sweatshirt. It was the first time I'd seen him like that – he got some emotions flowing in him. He apologized to the whole team for showing up late and slacking. He said he wouldn't do it anymore and that he wanted to be the No. 1 guy and a team leader. We all bought it. We took his word for it as to what he was gonna do, and he did it. It was like a switch went off in his head. It looked like he cared more after that. He bought into everything more and he put more effort into the team."

Scott Hugo: "A lot of who we are as individuals is reflected when we make mistakes and when we fail. Rather than being resentful after he got benched, TK stood up and apologized to everyone on the team. It was never an issue again. De La Salle football is about preparing young men for life. For him to own his mistakes and apologize for it, that was him growing as a player and a leader. It set an example for the younger guys on the team. It was a powerful thing."

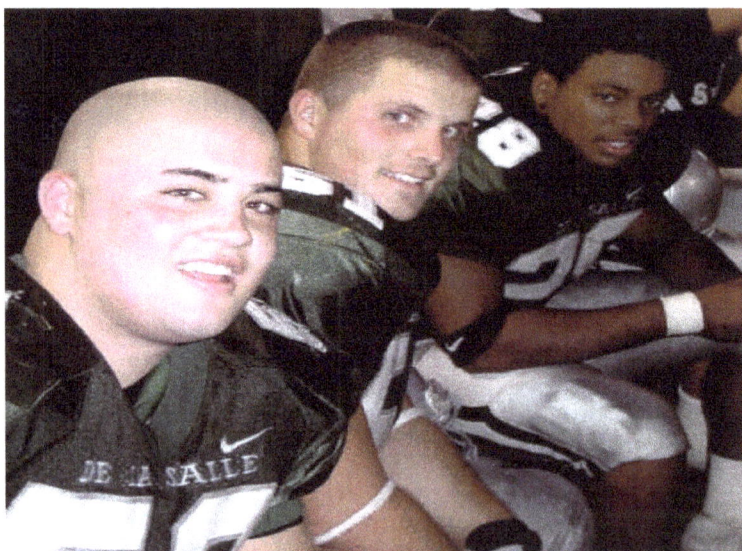

Steve Fujimoto, Chris Biller, TK

CHAPTER 25

Next Level

DE LA SALLE PUMMELED the opposition through the rest of the regular season and playoffs, and then demolished Pittsburg in the North Coast Section 4A final. The win marked the team's 151st consecutive victory and a third-consecutive mythical national championship. The defense allowed only 65 total points all season. The coaching staff called it the best in school history.

TK was named De La Salle's Most Valuable Player, High School Sports Focus Player of the Year and Cal-Hi Sports Bay Area Player of the Year. He was labeled a four-star recruit and collected all-America honors from Superprep Magazine and Prep Magazine. Playing on the best team in the country, he finished the season with 1,023 rushing yards and 20 total touchdowns on offense along with 118 tackles and three interceptions on defense.

Terry Eidson: "TK was going to be a success. Definite pro potential. He was so driven. He was a strong safety-type kid. He had speed and size. Nobody could tell me he didn't have pro potential."

Justin Alumbaugh: "He was getting stronger and that would have continued. His shoulders were big and he had a really lean frame. He became one of the best we've ever had – including as a leader. He had the best unfinished upside I've seen from a player coming out of De La Salle. We've had players leave here more advanced than him, but he had the most unfinished upside. I wouldn't have been surprised to see him in the NFL at all."

Parker Hanks: "TK had as much athleticism as anyone on the team. He wasn't ripped and he didn't have mass like you would expect. He was lanky and looked skinny, but he still weighed 215 pounds. His frame could have put on a lot more weight."

John Chan: "TK was one of those guys that always ended up in the right spot. It comes from playing Pop Warner your whole life but it also comes from somewhere else. If I had a bad week of practice – I wasn't going to play well in the game. TK was one of those kids that had an on and off switch. He could just turn it on. He could just go out and play."

Chris Biller: "I think it's an innate thing. He was just a gamer. A footballer. He hit hard. Super-athletic. He was rangy and could run. He had it. And he hadn't even fully developed. By the end of our senior year, you could see him getting bigger – his neck was gettin' all big. He was just blooming, just scratching the surface. You put him on a college campus – now he lives in the weight room. Control everything he's eating, top-of-the-line food. Tutors. He would have hardened up for sure. He would have been a monster."

TK had advantages over other elite athletes being recruited – he was more than capable in the classroom, maintaining a B-average and scoring over an 1,100 on the SAT. But it was his personality and mental makeup combined with athleticism that made TK a true rarity, that one-in-a-thousand kid. He was popular on campus because of his likeability with faculty and peers. He was one of the biggest, strongest athletes in the school who routinely slept in class by laying his head on classmates — whether they played football or not. He was very much a part of a real sense of brotherhood that forms among seniors at De La Salle coming from different backgrounds.

Steve Fujimoto: "TK was genuinely a nice, chill guy. We all loved TK because he was funny and he got to know everybody. He wasn't a showoff. We were able to become good friends with him because he never cared about anything else — where he came from or anything. We knew where Richmond was and that it was a rough area. None of us had ever been there. But TK never tried to act hard or tough. He got to know you based on who you are."

Parker Hanks: "TK had this loud, high-pitched laugh. He sat with everyone, all different groups at meetings — he didn't just sit with the starters or his boys. He sat with underclassmen too. He was a really caring guy. He came from a different place, but he was the guy laughing and hugging on everyone."

Erik Sandie: "TK was very low-key and didn't like being the center of attention. On the football field — that's when he would shine, but he's not the type of guy who would get a penalty for celebrating either. Off the field, he didn't want the spotlight. He was a Spartan. He was one of the guys. He didn't take himself too seriously."

Chris Biller: "You think of a big, strong, black football player from Richmond. If there was one guy who could have said, 'I'm from the hardest area out of anyone at this school,' it would have been Terrance. Never heard it once. You think about how easily he could have intimidated or been mean to people for whatever reason. Never happened. You'd have these dorky white guys in class joking with Terrance, they called him 'Terry.' "

Justin Alumbaugh: "We had this player, Chris Labee. Labee was a junior when Terrance was a senior. When Labee struggled with gassers,

Terrance tried to encourage him – 'LABOO, YOU CAN DO IT!' There was no real reason for Terrance to be overly nice to Labee. He was a senior and the MVP of the team. But that's just the type of person Terrance was – just a sweetheart of a kid. He was a funny guy, and you could play around with him like that – we'd always razz each other. I remember talking shit to him about how I could kick his ass in basketball. He said, 'Coach, you're pretty good, but you don't got it. You're not like me.' "

Jackie Bates: "TK could fit in everywhere. Just because you're a black guy and a big stud linebacker, that doesn't mean you need to act like you're better than people or walk around with your nose up. No. Terrance possessed a quiet confidence. He'd never try to down you or make you feel beneath him. He knew he was a good player and knew he was gifted, but he got along with everyone. That's a credit to his family, they raised a well-rounded person. Very intelligent, very educated. He read between the lines and had a great sense of humor, which makes it easy to adapt in any setting. He treated everyone the same. Nothing soft about him, but just a good guy. Really down to earth, fair and non-judgmental. Just a hell of a person."

*   *   *

At the end of the 2003 season, TK was the most polished prospect out of De La Salle's 'Big Four' – TK, Jackie Bates, Willie Glasper and Cameron Colvin – the most talented group of seniors in school history. TK had the biggest year on the field but Glasper was a close second and named a *Parade* all-American cornerback. Coaches aggressively tried to land as many of the 'Big Four' as possible.

Johnny Dempsey: "Coaches called me up and tried to get Terrance's phone number. He changed his number because of all the calls. The coach at Cal called me up. He said, 'Which way is your cousin going? Can I get his phone number?' I told him, 'Look man – his junior year, you should have been on him! This isn't my decision to make, this is his.' "

John Chan: "It was an anomaly of a class. Out of all those guys, you were sure TK was gonna make it. You knew Jackie Bates had a chance with his speed."

Chris Biller: "They kept everything in terms of recruiting on the hush at school. There were never any big press conferences or anything. You'd hear about letters and offers, but they kept it pretty mum. Cameron Colvin was the most highly-sought after guy."

Louis Montgomery: "Quinton Ganther and TK were the ones as far as talent and size coming from Richmond. A lot of us from Richmond should have made it. But those two were the ones that you just *knew* were gonna make it."

Jackie Bates: "[USC coach] Pete Carroll came to De La Salle one morning. I was in P.E. class in the locker room near the coach's office. Coach Eidson says, 'Pete's here.' Coach Ladouceur says, 'Oh, he wants to see our guys?' Typically, coaches were coming to see all four of us. Eidson says, 'No. Not all of them. The only one he wants to see is Terrance.' Keep in mind USC was on fire back then. Reggie Bush, Matt Leinart."

Drew Curto: "TK took an official visit to ASU. Terrell Suggs was a senior defensive end at ASU and hosted TK on his recruiting trip. So you had Terrell Suggs, a future top-10 pick and pro Bowl NFL player, taking TK under his wing showing him around Scottsdale. Scottsdale is mini-Vegas – tons of night clubs. It must have been unreal."

Landrin Kelly: "It was too hot down there in Arizona for him. Wisconsin, Colorado, Nebraska and Michigan, they were all too cold. He took a couple trips with Marshawn Lynch to Cal and Oregon. Him and Willie went to USC together. He was so excited. They rolled out the red carpet for him and he loved the celebrity-like treatment."

Jackie Bates: "I committed to Oregon early. I didn't think Terrance was gonna come. But Oregon told him, 'You're gonna start right away. You're the most college-ready of any of the De La Salle players.' "

Jamie Richards Jr. : "I talked to him a couple times before he made his decision to see where his head was at. He was getting recruited at running back and safety. He was like, 'I don't want to get hit. I'd rather deliver the contact.' "

Landrin Kelly: "Cal was recruiting Terrance hard and his trip went well, but he told me, 'I wanna get away, dad.' It was too close. So I told said, 'You make the choice, I can't make the choice for you.' I didn't want to be one to blame if he didn't like it there."

Johnny Dempsey: "Terrance wanted me to be there with him when certain coaches visited. That was so special to me because I played linebacker in high school and I never had the opportunity to get recruited like that. I never could have even fathomed that. He'd call me up, so soft spoken, 'Hey Cousin John, you think you could swing by? UCLA is coming over tonight.' I'd say, 'Sure, I'll come by. I'd love to, thank you.' It was a blessing. The head coaches of these schools were coming over to my Aunty Bev's house in South Richmond with me, Aunty Bev, Landrin and Pops."

Landrin Kelly: "I told Terrance, 'Weigh out your options. Where you at on the depth chart?' He didn't want to redshirt. He wanted to come in and play. He liked the atmosphere at Oregon. It was the right distance – not too close, not too far. They told him he'd be No. 2 on the depth chart at safety and either start or compete for playing time. He liked that Oregon was building around the future. He wasn't going to have to redshirt and fit in somewhere. They were building the team around the incoming class. UCLA was a good option, too, because Drew was there – he hosted Terrance on his recruiting trip – so he could show him the ropes down in L.A. But he was gonna be No. 4 on their depth chart."

TK's decision came down to UCLA and Oregon. Oregon had a leg up because Jackie Bates and Willie Glasper both committed to play for the Ducks. Then Cameron Colvin donned an Oregon Ducks hat live on ESPN's SportsCenter. The group of Bates, Colvin, Glasper, Kelly and Ward had grown extremely close in their four years at De La Salle.

Jackie Bates: "As freshman, we had all talked about our dreams of going to the NFL. As seniors, we're family. We've had four years to grow with each other. Nothing can separate us, we're brothers. We have each other's back 100 percent. We love each other."

Landrin Kelly: "The coaches had already been to Cameron's house in Pittsburg and Jackie's house in Benicia. When they showed up, my mama had a lasagna dinner waiting for them. We ate dinner and they were steady talking to Terrance. Then my mama brought out the peach cobbler with ice cream. They said, 'Aww, when we come here we always get so much!' "

Johnny Dempsey: "It was the last week of the national Letter of Intent signing deadline in January 2004. We sat around the table eating dinner with [Oregon coaches] Mike Bellotti and Nick Alioti [brother of De La Salle assistant coach Joe Alioti]. Terrance had his poker face on the whole time, you couldn't crack him. You could see a little frustration on the coaches' faces. Then Coach Alioti says, 'Terrance, do you even like us? No smile? Nothing?'

"Terrance looks at them and starts to talk. Everybody pauses and looks at him. We couldn't believe he was actually saying something. He says, 'You know, I was thinking...I really like you guys...so Imma roll with you guys.'

"That was his demeanor, he didn't get overly excited. So the coaches look at each other like, 'Did he just say what I think he said?' 'What did he just say?'

"Terrance said, 'Yeah. I'm committing to ya'll.' Then everybody jumped up smiling, hugging and celebrating. It took a while, but everyone was so excited when we figured out he had made his decision."

Willie Glasper, TK, Jackie Bates

TK and Pops, De La Salle graduation, May 2004

eDuck

the Magazine

March 2004 · $4.95
Volume II · Issue Eight

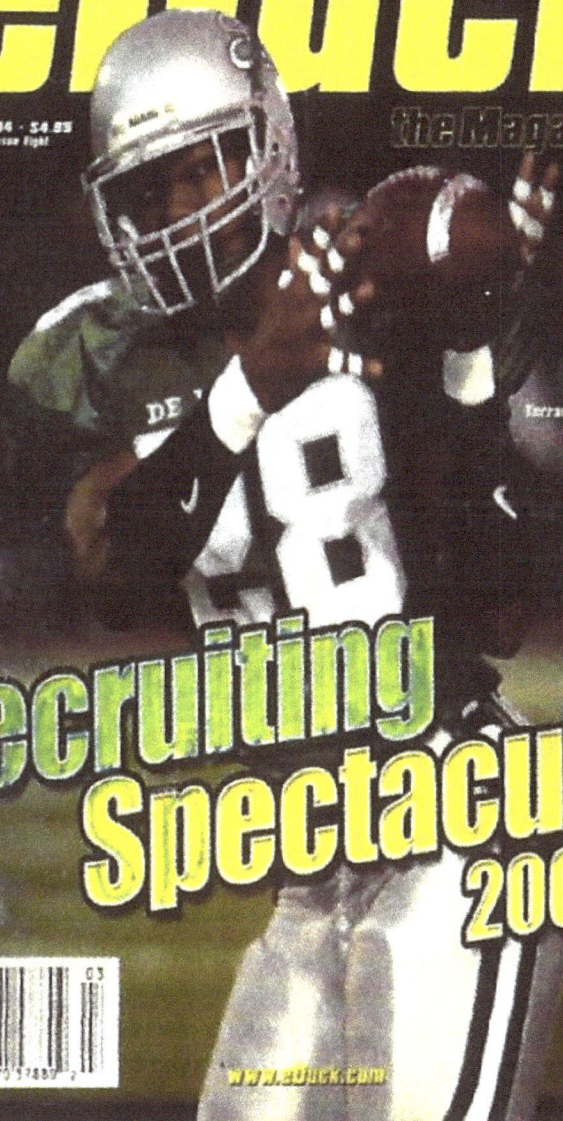

Terrance Kelly

Recruiting Spectacular 2004

www.eDuck.com

TK 2004

CHAPTER 26

Watch The People Around You

PAUL WEBSTER JR.: "TK always talked about how different the people were at De La Salle because there was no jealousy. Everybody love everybody. Kumbaya. World peace. He talked about how parents invited you over to their house or people let you use their stuff.   In Richmond, there's jealousy, hate and other negative influences. The attitude is, 'I never want to see us equal. I'm on top and you underneath me.' "

TK was popular at De La Salle, but he maintained a low profile. In Richmond, he was a hero, and a number of followers from different circles had latched onto him.

Mary Kelly: "Everybody in Richmond rallied behind Terrance. The whole city was like, 'Yes, Mr. T about to do this.' He was going to make it. And he would have hurt himself trying to help so many. That's what I was afraid of – him trying to help too many people, because you can't take everybody with you."

Paul Webster Jr.: "Junior and senior year, you got people from Central coming to see TK's games all of a sudden. I wasn't able to go to his football games because I played, too. So I'd call or send a text message before his games and tell him, 'Bro, ball out. Handle business, I'll talk to you after the game.'

"I'd go over to Granny Bev's and talk with him later on. We'd put on one of his game films in the den, do pushups and lift dumbbells. We'd talk about anything in life, not just sports. With sports, he kept me sharp because he was my competition – I looked up to him as far as what he was doing and that kept me hungry. He made we want to keep playing, keep going.

"People from all over were trying to hang out with him. It's almost like a classic story that you hear when somebody getting a real football deal – people were drawn to the publicity.

"There was a few times where we were gonna to go to a party. He was supposed to come get me. When I call him, he says, 'Oh, my car full. You can't get the car tonight?' 'I don't even wanna go then.' One time that happened and the group he was with, they got into a big fight. I told him, 'Yo, you don't even know them. See what they got you into? And the main person to have your back wasn't there.'

"Every time we were alone chillin', I was on him about it. 'You got male groupies, bro. They your flunkies. I'm not your flunky.'

"Some of these guys didn't have his best interests at heart. I had to tell him, 'Yo, Jordan not the same cat.' He may not have seen how some of these guys were changing as we got older because he was off in Concord every day. They were shying away from what they knew – they used to be athletes like us. Some of them could have gone pro. But they started hanging around the wrong people and stopped playing sports. They started doing stuff they didn't used to do – carrying guns – whatever."

Chastity Harper: "I knew who Terrance's friends were that he grew up with like Paul and his friends from De La Salle like T.J. I always questioned anyone outside of that circle of people I felt comfortable with. I would be nosy and ask him, 'Who are these people? Why are you hanging with them? What are you guys gonna be doing?' I knew the type of family that Terrance came from and what was instilled in him when he grew up. It wasn't always the case with some of the people hanging around him as we got older – they had a different agenda."

Landrin Kelly: "Terrance got a ticket over in Central. They stopped him because he was a youngster and they wanted to know who he was in that nice car. After that, my mom got more worried about him going down there and told me to talk to him. So I sat him down and we had a big argument about it.

"Imma take the car back if you keep going over there.'

"C'mon, dad, I ain't into that stuff.'

"Naw, it ain't that. Niggas jealous of you, they don't like you. They don't wanna see you do better.'

"Aww, dad, they ain't trippin' off me.' I was just keeping it real with him."

Paul Webster Jr.: "Granny Bev called me around that time. 'Hey baby.' 'Hey Grandma.' 'I'm calling to talk to you about your brother.' 'What about him? What's wrong?' 'Nothing wrong. I know you guys grew up with Markel and Jordan and all them, but I don't really like him being from Southside hanging over there in Central. When he come late at night, I be worried about him. Sometime he don't call – when I go to sleep he's not there and when I wake up, I see him asleep on the couch. You know it's getting kind of violent nowadays and I just don't like him being over there. He don't know what he's getting his'self into.' 'Oh he just hanging out with friends – they know TK ain't that type of kid. They

223

know he's not into guns or violence. He's just over there playing basketball and hanging out. Even the guys doing bad know he's not like that. But I'll tell him to calm down and come home at a reasonable hour.'

"Every time after that when I saw her, she said something like that to me. 'Tell him to stay out of Central.' 'He's still stayin' out late.' She figured, with our relationship, he'd listen to me. But after a while, you hear it from so many different people that it gets annoying – and it draws you closer to where people don't want you to be.

"After that, TK and I argued about it a lot. I used to cut hair back in high school to make a few dollars. He needed a line for his graduation pictures. He had a little fro and he wanted to grow dreads so I lined him up. I even cooked for him.

"I tell him, 'Granny Bev don't like you being over there in C-side.' 'Why she worried about it?' 'I know you over there with these guys we grew up with since T-ball. But we in high school and everybody separated, you really don't know what they doing in they side of life. Blood people jealous of you cuz. These are not your friends bruh. They might smile in your face, but they saying the only reason you getting all this publicity is because you went to De La Salle.' 'What do you mean? We grew up with these dudes. Not hanging out with them would be like not hanging out with you!' 'Bro, none of these guys wanted to be around you like I wanted to be around you until your fame and your car came around. They talked about us. We was the fat boys. Now all of the sudden, because you doing your thang, they want to use you for what you got. Why they saying things when you not around to Chas? Why they saying other things when you not around and I get around? Limit yourself around them.'

"I could see how maybe he thought I was jealous. I told him so many times, 'I hope you don't think any of this coming from any sort of jealousy.' We went back and forth like that. He needed to hear it and I was on him tough. I can see how I almost sounded like a nagging parent or a jealous girlfriend. We almost kind of fell out a little bit after that. Either that or he had so many people wanting to be around him, he just forgot about me. For his graduation party, I didn't get a call from him. Everybody knew about it but me."

Landrin Kelly: "For Terrance's graduation, we had a barbecue at my house in Hilltop. He had his boys from De La Salle and his Richmond potnas there. They was intermingling with each other and there was no conflicts, no jealousy, nothing. It was cool. We had about 70 or 80 people there. People came in and out all day. I put 12 slabs of meat on the barbecue and my mama made potato salad."

T.J. Ward: "Cameron Colvin and I went to TK's graduation barbecue at Landrin's house. He had all his guys from the city there that he grew up with and a bunch of our teammates from De La Salle. Just to see how both sides admired him and loved him – it was good."

Tra'Meka Kelly: "It was a big deal for him to graduate. Everybody was excited for his next chapter in life. I was glued to his hip, following him around. Then he tells me, 'So you next.' I'm like, 'OK, time for me to leave. That's my cue – here you go with the lectures.' "

Landrin Kelly: "Brian was there and he was feeling kind of jealous – I could see it on his face, how outgoing we was for Terrance with the new car and the celebrations. He was around it all the time because we all lived together. I'm like, 'This my son, where your daddy at? He should be doing this for you.' Besides, Terrance had risen to the occasion. He had done everything right and he deserved it. If you do right, you get it. I'd give Brian money every now and then – but you gotta deserve it to get it from me. I'm not just giving you money when you cuttin' class and smokin' weed.

"That summer, Brian got a little summer job painting houses for Chevron. So he was having a little money. He took that money and used it to buy weed so he could sell more. Brian and Darren Pratcher bought a little car from a dope fiend for like $300. They were selling weed, got in a high-speed chase with the police and ran into a pole. Both boys jumped out of the car and tried to run. They caught Brian, but Darren got away on foot.

"Brian got charged with evading police in a car and so now they got him down at Juvenile Hall. After they released him with an ankle monitor, he came back to my house on house arrest. I was hella pissed off because now these probation officers can come and check out my house anytime to do random drugs tests or whatever. I wasn't doing anything, but there's strict rules – no firearms, no drugs, no alcohol. Nothing can be in there. It was breaking my relationship with Nicole apart."

*   *   *

Paul Webster Jr.: "TK didn't think I knew, but I saw him watching my baseball games. My dad was at all my games, so of course they talked. He'd say, 'Don't tell Paul I came.' After the games, females told me, 'Your brother TK was here. He just left.' I'd text him after. 'Thanks bro for showing your support.'

"After that happened a couple times, I called him. 'Cuz why you ain't stay after the game? They told me you just left not too long ago?' We went back and forth. He came to my next game at St. Mary's and we talked for a while, hung out and got food.

"I think he seen my letters and what I was doing on the field – so that reassured him I wasn't just jealous. He asked me what I thought about going to Oregon with him. I could walk on to either the football or baseball team. We were gonna get our own apartment and Landrin lined up a job for us moving furniture. I didn't know where I was going as far as college or anything else, but I had confidence in myself to walk on. It sounded like a good thing.

"When TK said that it meant a lot to me. He wanted me up at Oregon with him not just for the ride and fun of college life, but to help him stay on point. He had faith in me to keep us both above water and keep our head on straight. I just needed him to keep his head on straight while he was still in Richmond."

CHAPTER 27

The Vision

TRA'MEKA KELLY: "I told Terrance, 'I'm coming up to Oregon with you.' That was my plan. 'I'm going with my brother.' I told him, 'You gonna have to find some way to make me your assistant or something. I'm gonna date one of your football player friends.' He hated that. 'Just kidding. Just kidding.'"

Landrin Kelly: "Terrance went up to Eugene for a month to learn the system and bulk up. He left for camp a week after graduation. He worked at a moving company up there, and I got him a bike to get around campus. He really wanted his car and hated riding around on the bike, but he had a great camp up there. He stayed in Eugene all the way through the 4th of July."

Quinton Ganther: "I had just transferred from junior college to play running back at Utah, and TK was new at Oregon. We were both going through the transition together and we started talking a lot more. We got close again, like family. We helped each other out through that period. I told him, 'We're blessed. We're making it out. Don't ever lose sight of that – what we've come out of.' Towards the end of his camp in July, I told him, 'Don't go back. Stay out there. Enjoy it. This is college. We worked so hard to get to this point and we're finally here.' I knew what the Bay Area was and how it can get."

Anthony "Ace" Brown: "It was exciting to see him go up to Oregon. We was all happy for him and telling him, 'We don't want you out here in the streets of Richmond, stay up there. Get up out of here. Stay at Oregon.' "

Landrin Kelly: "I didn't want him to come back to Richmond. Niggas was getting killed. Niggas was goin' to jail. He was supposed to stay up at Oregon for the whole summer, and we would just come up there for the first game in September and buy him a car. But my mom wanted him to come back to fix his ticket. She said, 'I don't want my baby on TV. What if he gets a warrant and they come get him?' You know how grandparents think.

"So he drove back to the Bay Area with Dennis Dixon, who lived in San Leandro. I drove over to San Leandro and picked him up from Dixon's house. When I got him, he was really feeling himself. I asked him about Eugene and he was like, 'This is where I want to be, they're gonna take care of me. I'm alright dad, I just need a car.' He wanted to drive his Mustang back up to Eugene. I told him, 'No, just wait 'till September when I get up there for your first game and I'll buy you a car. You can fly back and forth and you'll have a car in both places.' I didn't want him to take no risks. So we bickered back and forth about that like father and son do."

Louis Montgomery: "When he came back from Eugene, I went over to his house. He showed me his Oregon cleats and all that Oregon stuff that he had. I'm like, 'Man, you got the O's on! You about to do this!' He was doing what we had all dreamed of – going to the next level."

Josh Dozier: "I hadn't seen TK for about a year. We had that kind of relationship where we didn't have to see each other all the time, but as soon as we did, it was like we'd been hanging out every day. He called me on the phone when I was driving and says, 'Hey man what are you doing?' I'm at the light waiting for it to turn green. He says, 'Look behind you.' I look behind me and there he is. He says, 'We're gonna get together and do one last sleepover thang – play a bunch of video games, get a bunch of pizzas and just kick it.' I was excited to hang with him again because TK, Jamie and I hadn't seen each other as much after he went to De La Salle. We were gonna do one last little hangout right before everyone went to college."

Tra'Meka Kelly: "When Terrance came back from Oregon, we were together every weekend. When you get into high school, you still close to your family, but you want to go off with your friends. But every Friday, I'd get out of school and say, 'Terrance you coming to pick me up?' Then he'd come get me in Vallejo. We'd hang out all weekend and then he'd drop me off on Sunday. We'd go out to eat or just hang out at my dad's house in his room, watch movies and eat junk food. We loved the Mexican Pizza from Taco Bell."

Kevin Lopina: "When other graduating seniors got their scholarship offers, they were done with De La Salle, ready to go off to college. But Terrance did summer conditioning and weights with us in Concord after he graduated. It was almost like he was still a part of the team. He worked out with us, pushed us and coached us. The coaches knew they could trust Terrance to say and do the right things, and they gave him free reins to do that."

Lanny Kelly III: "After TK came back from Oregon, I got to go with him to work out. It was a Saturday morning. He woke me up. 'C'mon, you about to go work out with me.' I'm looking at him, and keep in mind I'm a little small guy at that time compared to him. I'm thinking, 'What?! Work out with you?'

230

"So we ride to the gym in his 5.0. It was a very nice day in Richmond; a life-changing day for me. It kind of came out of nowhere because we had never talked this deep and he had never gone into this much detail about the plans he had for his life. He talked about his dreams. They were bigger than his family and bigger than the Southside of Richmond. He wanted to represent the city of Richmond and the Bay Area as a whole, not just the Southside. Not just the Kelly family. He talked to me about how he planned on doing positive things in Richmond. That when he left, he would never turn his back on his city. That he would be back.

"He told me, 'We gonna get Granny Bev a big building so she can do her day care thing, and maybe start a school.' He had this vision of being the change in Richmond.

"We get to the gym and I just sit back and watch because the weights they used were heavy. He really showed me work ethic at that time. I had seen him in social settings with friends or family, but to see him in business mode – it was like he was a whole different person. It wasn't all that laughing, messing around unless they were in between sets. It gave me a better understanding of why he was so good on the football field.

"Even though the person he was working out with was older, it seemed like Terrance was in charge. He was very motivational and determined. He pushed his workout partner, 'C'mon, one more set. We can do it. One more set. Don't stop. Don't stop.' "

Paul Webster Jr.: "Everybody knew that TK was going to the League, man. And everybody knew he'd try and put Richmond on his back."

Sondra Dempsey: "Terrance was genuine. He wasn't boasty. He wasn't arrogant. He wasn't haughty. You never heard him boast about football or anything. The success didn't change him. He was just Terrance all the time.

"Our main focus with Terrance was not him being a football star. Our main focus for Terrance was that he would overcome what was going on in the immediate area where he was raised, and that his mind would be renewed. That he would get a good foundation by way of college. My sister Bevelyn wanted him to be restored from what he had seen, from what was in the atmosphere all around us. She wanted him to go to college and come back with a different mindset."

Paul Webster Sr.: "We had a sense of accomplishment as parents. It gives me the chills thinking about it now. Those were some of the best days, right after our boys graduated. You feel real good about yourself as a parent. We didn't hold nothing back as far as celebrating accomplishments.

"I don't wear pro players' jerseys because I'm not in awe of nobody – but I wear TK's jersey because I'm in awe of TK. It was like a three-month high where you just get up in the morning and you happy about everything. It's that sense of accomplishment because it's something you done that turned out right.

"It was just good to take a deep breath, because we had it hard. Raising those boys wasn't easy, and our moms was proud of us too. It was euphoria going around, like it was almost too good to be true.

"TK would have got his degree, gone pro and run for mayor. He would have fixed a lot of things in Richmond. He would have given back. He seen and appreciated the work that the Grannies was doing. He knew why he was making it. He knew that if more people got the kind of attention he did – we'd have more TK's. He knew he had the help of a support system. You give a kid the right support system, you won't get all of them, but you'll get the majority of them, and he knew that. He had a purpose."

Landrin Kelly: "I came back from coaching baseball one day and sat next to Terrance. He was watching a game on the couch. I wanted to quit. I was like, 'Man, I'm tired of coaching these bad kids, I ain't coaching this year. I'm just gonna travel and watch you play.' 'Naw dad, who gon' save these kids like you saved me and my friends?' "

Father-son, 2004

CHAPTER 28

Crabs In A Bucket

LANDRIN KELLY: "That summer after he came back, TK didn't spend much time down in Central. He'd drive through there and say, 'What's up,' to a few people, but he wasn't stupid. He'd heard enough warnings from everyone around him. He was just in and out of there."

But in the summer of 2004, merely driving in and out of Central Richmond carried heightened risks. In April, a high profile 'Shot Caller' was gunned down in Central Richmond near Nevin Park after surviving three other shootings in 2003. The victim's name was Rommel.

Landrin Kelly: "Rommel played football with Terrance when they were 10. I coached him. He wasn't as big as TK, but he was a pretty good player. Rommel was a laid-back, cool dude. He was suave, a ladies' man, and got along with everybody. But he got caught up. He quit playing football in Midgets and started in the streets. When Rommel was in the eighth grade, he drove up next to me in a brand new BMW. He says,

'W'sup Coach? How TK doing?' I say, 'Aw, you know, working hard.' I drove a little Toyota Bucket at the time.

"Rommel got killed because of jealousy. He was a young go-getter and he was getting money. He was a year older than TK. He was one of the stars down there in Central. It wasn't a big shock when he got killed because he was a part of the streets."

After Rommel's death, Central Richmond and in particular the area around the Nevin Center was on edge.

One witness testified that he didn't want to hang out in that area because, "Somebody got killed down there. People was coming through there shooting. And I'm not from down there and I'm not fixing to be in no crossfire. At the time, there was a problem if you're down there and not from Central Richmond. I didn't want to stand outside because there was something going on between North Richmond and Central Richmond. They funking. People get killed down there. I could be outside, and they happen to ride past and think I'm somebody."

Another witness lived in the Barretts, a massive cluster of three-story apartment complexes wedged between Barrett Avenue and Nevin Avenue and surrounded by seven-foot high spiked fences. The Barretts apartments were known as a "rowdy" hotbed of criminal activity, with fences chained 24 hours a day.

As the Barretts witness testified: "Someone got shot or killed down there bi-weekly, monthly. Someone gets shot, you hear the gunshots, you come outside, see who is on the ground, see if you know them, and if you don't, you just go back on about your normal life. And if they still alive, you see the helicopter come down right outside my patio window. It's Kaiser Hospital, you see the helicopter come airlift them. And if they are dead, you will see them pass – you see them laying there for about eight hours, nine hours something. I've seen that numerous times."

Paul Webster Jr.: "Rommel was a go-getter. He was smart. He was savvy. He started out at 12 getting money. Rommel's demise was about haters. They were hating on him because he was a young stud and he was making all the old cats look stupid. He was like the Nino Brown of Central – he was giving little kids money, buying 'em ice cream. He influenced a lot of people."

One of those people was 15-year-old Darren Pratcher, who now went by the street nickname 'Money D.' Darren spent ninth grade at Richmond High School attending classes sporadically. He received D's and F's in many cases.

A Central Richmond witness described Darren Pratcher as, "Medium-build. You wouldn't think that he was 14 or 15. His appearance, he doesn't look that age. I think he was about 5-9, I'm not sure. He is kind of thin, but he wears a lot of heavy clothes so he looks much older. Shootings that occur around our neighborhood is not based upon age, really, because everyone grows up so fast and they have their own minds and they do what they want to do, because they think they are grown. So someone that is the shooter at 14, 15 is no big surprise."

Another witness from Central Richmond: "As far as ages, don't nobody in the hood where I come from look at how old you is. You can't just look as far as age, you can't look at somebody depending on the age. *Age ain't nothing but a number.*"

David Brown [Former Contra Costa County Deputy District Attorney]: "Darren was relatively immature. There's two types of maturity. There's regular maturity that we all have growing up, then there's street maturity. I think street maturity – he was average or above that. As far as social maturity, he was behind on that. Darren idolized gangbangers. If you want to be like them and you feel disenfranchised from the community in general, the gang acts as sort of a surrogate family. You adopt their thoughts, their processes, their behavior and their conduct. You adopt the attitude of, 'You can't let somebody punk you. You can't let

236

somebody disrespect you. You gotta stand up.' It's about retribution and retaliation. If you don't like somebody, you use physical force against them."

Anthony "Ace" Brown: "It's easy to fall into that type of stuff when you see it around you every day. When you see people having guns. When you see people shooting just because they from a different area. It's easy to fall into that."

Another witness testified: "Darren acted like he was hard. I'm pretty sure people saw him as a tough guy because he knocked my little cousin's teeth out. He let somebody ride a bike, and then whoever he let ride the bike the first time, they let my cousin ride. After my cousin got on the bike and brung it back, Darren said it was gone too long and knocked his teeth out."

On June 12, 2004, Darren Pratcher was apprehended by officers during a routine traffic stop with a loaded handgun in his front pocket. Darren argued that he had found the gun in the bushes and was going to use it for protection. He was booked and sent to Juvenile Hall.

The next day, a Contra Costa County mental health staff member administered a yes-or-no questionnaire to Darren. The document is standard intake procedure typically administered within the first 48 hours of a first-timer's admission to Juvenile Hall. If the subject's answers raise flags, additional questions are asked or a recommendation is made that the juvenile get mental health support while incarcerated.

Darren Pratcher answered, 'No' to a number of questions indicating that he might be suffering from post-traumatic stress disorder such as: whether he had been jumpy or hyper; whether he had ever wished he was dead; whether he had nightmares bad enough to make him afraid to go to sleep; whether he ever felt like hurting or killing himself; whether he ever had a bad feeling that things don't seem real, like he was in a dream; whether he had given up hope for life; whether he had ever had something very bad or terrifying happen to him; whether he had ever been badly hurt or in danger of getting badly hurt or killed; whether he had a lot bad thoughts or dreams about a bad or scary event that happened to him.

Darren answered 'Yes' to: whether he had been drunk or high at school; whether he had used marijuana; whether he had seen someone severely injured or killed in person, not in movies or on T.V.

The mental health specialist marked down that his results were, "Generally unremarkable. Patient is stable, calm and cooperative."

After his release from juvenile hall, Darren Pratcher and TK once again crossed paths at the annual 3-on-3 basketball tournament at the Nevin Center in Central Richmond.

Landrin Kelly: "Terrance and his team didn't get in the tournament in 2004 because they had won it the year before. So TK went to the tournament and accepted last year's trophy with his team. Everybody coming up to him saying, 'W'sup man, I see you gettin' off!'"

One witness recalled: "We was at the tournament, off to the side of the court in a big crowd of people, while other people playing basketball. People saying, 'What's up' to me. I'm saying, 'What's up' to people. TK saying, 'What's up' to people. Darren standing there. TK say, 'What's up' to Darren. And Darren just looked at him like he ain't never said nothing."

Darren Pratcher egged TK's 5.0 as he left the Nevin Center after the tournament.

Chastity Harper: "I saw the egg on his car later that day. I asked him what happened. He said, 'Some guy egged my car.' 'Who was it? Why?' He didn't make a big deal out of it. I thought it was a prank or something, because to him, it was nothing."

Louis Montgomery: "I asked TK what happened at the tournament. Whatever the situation was, he wasn't concerned about it. He said, 'I'm not paying attention to that. I don't have a problem with him. I don't know what his problem is.' He wasn't too concerned about Darren because he knew where he was going. TK was like, 'I'm leaving. I'm going to school; I don't have a problem with nobody.' "

After the tournament, another incident took place between TK and Darren at a house party.

David Brown: "There was some animosity at the party for whatever reason, but it was never fully brought out in our investigation. Somebody had told us that it was over a girl. Terrance and Darren had some words and Darren felt disrespected."

Anthony "Ace" Brown: "Darren was part of a group from Central that didn't want outsiders coming in. Their mentality was, 'We're tripping with you because you not from Central. If you not from Central, you from the outside and you a sucka. Can't no Southsiders come in here.' Darren was probably just trying to feel cool. Trying to make a name for himself by doing something."

Jeremy Williams: "I heard about the basketball thing, but I think the problem between them was really about girls. People in Richmond be embarrassed to say, 'I don't like you because the girls all want you.' They not gonna tell you that. They too prideful. They not gonna admit that. They gonna say it's about something else – so that it looks like it has nothing to do with a girl. There's no way to know the real reason for the problem. But I can tell you my opinion is that it was pure jealousy. Whether it was about TK being athletic or about girls – it was pure jealousy."

Robert Turner: "It's like crabs in a bucket. Everybody trying to get out of that bucket, and as soon as you get to the top they'll pull you back down. That's the mentality of some of these kids – they don't want to see you succeed."

Paul Webster Jr.: "If you talk to most of the hood dudes around Central that we used to play basketball with, they had nothing against TK. What happened at the party was about Darren's brother Larry. TK used to rag on Larry. Not in a serious way, but he was hard on Larry. That was nothing new – we all hung out.

"Darren basically gave TK a warning that night. 'You need to watch who you're talking to. You ain't no hood nigga. You can't go around talking to people like you're Mr. Untouchable.' His mentality was, 'You talking down to my brother? You're not the king of nobody. You're not exempt from being hurt.'

"At the same time, TK was probably like, 'Who is you? You're a little kid. Who are you talking to?' But Darren was starting to get, 'With the Shit,' as we would say – being down, being a hood person – playing with drugs, guns and all that bad stuff. Trying to make a name for himself."

Tra'Meka Kelly: "You from Richmond and you go to De La Salle High school and you have a full-ride to Oregon? My brother had nothing but the best – a nice car and every pair of Jordans you can think of. People are going to be jealous of that where we come from."

On August 9, TK drove Brian James to his girlfriend Candy's house in Central Richmond off the corner of 7th Street and Nevin Avenue to pick something up.

"We got there and I said, 'Be right back out,' " Brian James testified. "TK stayed out front and sat in the car while I ran in and out. As I'm leaving Candy's house, Darren and some people were on the corner in front of the house. I say, 'What's up' to them as I walk toward TK's car. Darren says, 'Boy, it ain't cool to be bringing people over here.' TK ain't

240

hear it. Darren didn't say it directly to me. I heard him say it as I'm walking past.

"I knew they had something going on, but I didn't think it was that serious. I didn't tell TK what Darren said because TK already knew. TK didn't even look at how much Darren didn't like him. He took the boy as a joke. He didn't really care or trip off of having problems with him. He looked past him, because he just knew he better than him. He just knew he had something going for himself. If TK was around him, he'd be like, 'Man, what is up,' and he'd just keep going."

CHAPTER 29

The Day You Went Away

LANDRIN KELLY: "I woke up at 4 a.m. for work at 5. TK only had two days left in town. I had two plane tickets on my dresser – one for him to get up to Eugene, and one to come home on break. I had $1,000 for him to take up there and live on. That morning, I went into his room before I left. Terrance was sitting in there lifting 50-pound dumbbells while Chastity twisted his dreadlocks. Turns out she had to be at the airport at 6 a.m. because she was heading off to Spelman in Atlanta for college. 'Aw dad, what'chu leaving for? I thought you were just gonna stay home for Thursday and Friday?' 'Naw, I gotta get to work and make sure you be alright and make sure everything right around the house.' 'Aw man, I'm gonna take care of you dad.' 'Well until you start taking care of me, Imma keep gettin' up and going to work.' "

Chastity Harper: "We walked down the street together later that morning to my house and he basically saw me off. We talked about whether we would stay together and have a long-distance relationship. We agreed to do it. It was that young love. 'We're gonna get married. We're gonna have kids.' My mom ended up taking me to the airport."

242

TK then drove to the courthouse to take care of his ticket while Landrin went to work.

Jackie Bates: "I talked to TK about his ticket that day – it was about the window tint on his 5.0. He told me, 'Yeah, I gotta pay the fine and take the tint off my car.' 'What are you doing tonight?' 'Man, I'm going to play basketball tonight. You coming?' 'No I can't make it.' "

"I got off work around noon," Brian James testified. "I got a ride home from my brother – TK. We hung out for like – not that long, because he had to go somewhere. So like TK picked me up and we went home to Hilltop. Then we came back out to Richmond and he dropped me off at Nichol Park. I played basketball. Then I walked to my girl's house in Central."

Paul Webster Jr.: "TK came by my house and wanted to hang out. He said, 'Bro, you coming with me?' I had to do something for my little nephew birthday party. I said, 'No. Go ahead. Ya'll have fun.' "

Tra'Meka Kelly: "I was riding with my friend near the YMCA in Richmond and I saw Terrance standing on the corner in some basketball shorts. Terrance never wanted me to be in Richmond, so when I saw him I was like, 'Oh my God that's my brother,' and I tried to sink down into my seat. But then my friend stopped the car in front of him.

"I said, 'Hi Terrance.' 'What are you doing over here?' 'Oh I just came from the hair shop.' We talked for a while and then he left. I called him later, 'Terrance can I use your car real quick to run to the mall?' 'I don't know, I'll see, because I'm about to go play basketball.' "

Later in the afternoon, Larry Pratcher, Darren Pratcher, Markel and Ram, 18, – all from Central Richmond – were hanging out around the basketball courts in the center of the Barretts apartments complex.

Ram testified: "Darren and other people around the neighborhood were shooting a pellet gun at targets and at people. So

243

Darren shot my ex-girlfriend Kelly with the pellet gun. She says, 'Don't shoot me again, that is disrespectful.' And Darren says, 'I will shoot you again.' And he was getting ready to shoot her, so she threw off her backpack and was ready to fight him.

"I broke it up. 'Come on man, it ain't cool like that, you going to go to jail for hitting a girl, and you already been to jail. Watch out, watch out, watch out.' So she like, 'All right, all right.' As she's leaving the Barretts, she says, 'I'm going to call my daddy,' and I heard her on the phone with her daddy naming off people who was there that had something to do with it.' I went to my girlfriend Camila's apartment in the Barretts, I was laughing like, 'You should have seen what happened.' "

Landrin Kelly: "I came back from work around 1 p.m. and fell asleep on the futon watching a baseball game. Terrance came in the house in the late afternoon, jumped on me and started kissing me on my face and tickling me. 'Dad, dad, lemme use your car!' 'Man, get your big ass off me!' 'Let me use your car!' 'Why?' 'I wanna go play basketball with Ace and Chuck.' 'What's wrong with your car?' 'I only got one headlight lit.' 'Man I gave you money to fix your light the other day all you had to do was go to the store and get a bulb!' 'I know I didn't do it, I been at court fixing my ticket and seeing everybody.'

"He was going up to Hercules to play basketball with his friends. Now, they really strict up there in Hercules and they'll profile you – they would have pulled him over for sure with a headlight out. Plus, he had just cleared up a ticket.

"I didn't have to work Friday, so I was gonna cook and have him a little sleep over with his friends the next night because he leaving. I tell him, 'I got a full tank of gas. There's $15 on my dresser. Get'chu something to eat because I ain't cookin' tonight.' So after that, he drives my Oldsmobile out to Hercules with Ace and Chuck."

Anthony "Ace" Brown: "TK was kind of like my big brother, he treated me like a little brother. He always came down in his 5.0 and kicked it with me and Chuck. We'd play video games, workout, or talk mess to each other. On Thursdays, we liked to go up and play basketball at the rec center in Hercules because they had courts.

"So we drive up there in Landrin's car. It didn't have a radio in it at the time – so we talked the whole way there, laughed and cracked jokes. We talked about how TK going to the NFL and what position he gonna play. He wanted to play running back, but they were gonna put him at linebacker or safety."

"It was dark out," Darren Pratcher's mother, Muriel Pratcher, testified. "This person came to the door. He was banging, roughly banging. We didn't open the door. My husband Larry Sr. asked who it was. The person banging didn't say who it was at first. He said, 'I'm looking for Darren,' in a rough voice. Then he said that Darren shot his daughter with a BB gun. His daughter was also with him, and she was explaining the same thing – that Darren had shot her with the BB gun.

"We opened the door for them. The man looked like he was under the influence, that he was intoxicated. After five minutes, they left.

"Later, both of my sons came home. I told Darren that a girl and her father had come looking for him. He looked shocked. Darren and Larry Jr. left the house at some point after that."

Michael "MG", 18, lived in the Barretts and had known Darren Pratcher for "roughly a year or two" at that time. He described the Barretts apartment complex as "just a kicking spot, a fake bar where everybody just hanging." He was storing a .22 bolt-action rifle in his room for a guy who went by the name of Cool Aid.

MG testified: "Darren came to my patio window. He asked me to hold his pellet gun. He said, 'Let me get Cool Aid gun.' I said, 'Cool Aid going to come but... all right. I mean, hey, it's – it's your cousin, your brother, whatever you want to call him, it's his gun.'

"So why wouldn't I give him the gun? I let him in and I went upstairs. I got the rifle out of my closet. I wiped the whole rifle down with a sock, because if you use a towel, you don't get all the fingerprints off. I wiped my fingerprints off it because if you take it out and go kill a person, my fingerprints aren't on it. I ain't got nothing to do with it. That is just how I was raised. I put it in a black nylon fishing bag, pinned it back and gave it to him. He went out the front door."

Ram: "I walk back to where we were all hanging out before. Larry, Markel, Darren – they all like for real serious. They tell me Kelly's daddy had come back with her. He was threatening that he was going to kill everybody, like making death threats. I seen they had a long thing wrapped, I guess it was a gun, wrapped in cover. So I call up my girl to give us a ride to 6th Street to get another gun because Darren is my friend, and I wasn't going to let him get beat up by an older man. We needed a gun just in case he come back, we going to fight him. We wanted a better defense. If anything was going to occur, we were ready."

Camila, the girlfriend, subsequently drove Darren, Larry, Markel and Ram to 6th Street, where they were unsuccessful in obtaining another weapon. Camila dropped the group off at Candy's house on the corner of 7th Street and Nevin Avenue because, "that's where they used to hang out."

Taylor Davis, Candy's mother, lived directly across from the Barretts at the corner of 7th and Nevin. She later testified: "I had a lot of issues with kids hanging out in front of my house. The Barrett security guards would run them away from there, and then my house is directly across so they'll run over to my side of the street. Sometimes it be like 15 boys out there shooting dice, gambling on the sidewalk. I tried to call the police one time and they told my kids, 'Your mama can't tell us to get off the sidewalk, we not in her yard.'

"That's why I'm barring up my yard, fencing it around. As long as I don't bother them and stay to myself, they don't bother me. I wouldn't try to handle things myself because they have sent threats to me.

"That night, it was very calm. And usually it's not like that. Usually the boys be standing out on the Barrett fence. But that night it was calm. Nobody. Nothing. It was a very strange night."

Upstairs in Taylor's house, Brian James was hanging out with his girlfriend, Candy. He testified: "TK already knew he was going to come get me later on that night wherever I was at because we lived together. I left him a message on his friend's phone."

Jeremy Williams: "I was at a friend's house off 30th Street in Richmond. When I talked to TK, he had just finished playing basketball. He was dropping off Ace and Chuck. I told him to come over. He said, 'I'm fittina pick up lil bro, then I'm gonna meet you.' "

Landrin Kelly: "My mama called me. 'Landrin, where your baby at?' 'Aww, he went to play basketball.' 'Tell him to get home. He got to finish packing his bags. Call your baby.' "

Anthony "Ace" Brown: "TK gave us a ride home to Richmond from Hercules. Landrin called TK a bunch of times while we were in the car. It was getting late. So TK called him back. TK and Landrin were going back and forth. It was kind of hostile. TK was like, 'Man, I'm gonna bring your car back!' "

Josh Harvey: "I used to pick up Brian at my little cousin Candy's house sometimes. When I couldn't pick him up, somebody else like TK would. TK called me that night. He's like, 'Man, can you pick up lil Brian?' 'Naw, I can't do it right now. My car's down, you know how my Oldsmobile be.' I was stuck in Emeryville. My radiator was down – it had a hole in it. I had to put some water on it to cool it and start my car back up."

"TK got my message, and he called me back," Brian James testified. "He said he was going to come get me. He was like, 'Just be outside.' I told him, 'Naw, I don't want to just stand outside, because it's dangerous over there in that neighborhood. Just call me as soon as you get outside and I am coming down.' 'Alright.'

"It happened quick. I say – like no more than four minutes, I can't say how many minutes, but he was there quick. He called me and told me he was outside. I said, 'Alright. I got my stuff ready and ran downstairs. Then I remember. I forgot my phone, my charger and my jacket upstairs.'"

Ram: "Me, Markel, Larry and Darren were sitting around in front of Aunt Tay's house. I was telling Markel, 'Let's go home.' I had known Markel since I was like 5 years old. I had just met Darren and Larry two years ago. In them two years, we had grown close together, so I was praying for all of our lives. I was going to grab it – the gun – and we was leaving.

"Then a car pulled up. We was all scared, nervous and like seeing who it was. Then a voice yells out, 'Larry, check it out.' Larry went to the car and talked with his forearms and elbows resting on the passenger door. When Larry went like that, I turned my head because I knew it was all right, it was somebody that he knew. Darren was still there at that point, but he all of a sudden just disappeared.

"Larry and the person talked for a minute, then Larry walked back. I asked, 'Who was that?' He said, 'TK.' He said they were talking about a basketball thing today. The next thing you know, I heard a pop."

*　　　*　　　*

Two years later, Contra Costa County Deputy District Attorney David Brown stands in front of a jury in the midst of closing arguments:

"We're here because of this lying murderous thief. He doesn't steal tangible items. He doesn't steal things you can hold. He stole the most

248

important things a man can possibly have. He stole potential, he stole hopes and he stole aspirations.

"He didn't steal it in a brief manner. He did it in a deliberate, vicious, horrific manner. A cold-blooded ambush of a guy that he didn't like and he didn't think should be in that neighborhood. A person that he had problems with."

Brown shapes his hands as if holding an imaginary rifle, sights and aims at defendant Darren Pratcher.

Brown: "On August 12, 2004, just two days before Terrance Kelly began his education at the University of Oregon on a football scholarship and gone on to perhaps an NFL career, this man stole a life."

Brown pulls the trigger of the imaginary .22 rifle, then imitates racking another bullet into the chamber.

TK grimaces from the impact of the first shot to the top of the head. The Oldsmobile rolls forward. Darren Pratcher moves with the car as it rolls, pulls the bolt backwards to re-cock the spring, then forward to lock it. He aims through the open passenger-side window, fires the rifle again and hits TK in the cheek.

Mr. Brown: "Stole a man's dreams." Brown racks the imaginary rifle for the second time.

The Oldsmobile bumps the car ahead and stops. TK opens the driver's side door as Darren cocks the rifle and fires a third shot into his back.

Mr. Brown: "Stole a son." Brown racks the imaginary rifle a third time.

TK lays face down on the street with one leg trapped in the car. Darren walks around the car until he's directly above TK. He cocks and reloads the rifle for a third time. Aims and fires a fourth shot into the back of TK's head.

Mr. Brown: "Stole a citizen of the world."

CHAPTER 30

Vengeance Is Not Ours

RAM: "I heard a pop. I looked back and I seen Darren with the rifle and popping. Pop. About five seconds and another pop. Then I ran."

After the shooting, Darren hid the bolt-action rifle in Taylor Davis' side yard and fled the scene.

Paul Webster Jr.: "Years later, I finally got a version of the story from people who were there. Markel and Larry were near the window talking to TK. Darren came up behind them and said, 'Watch out.' By the time they looked back, he started firing and they ran away.

"If somebody say, 'Watch out' and you see gun flashes – you gonna run. I've been in that predicament before. You don't run to the bullets. You run away from them."

Patrick Smith worked as a field operations supervisor for a security company inside the Barretts that night. Sometime around 10:40, he heard what sounded like three muffled shots: "They were not rapid – there were a good two to three seconds in between. I saw three black male juveniles running. I observed another black male juvenile follow the same path they did about three seconds later. The fourth juvenile was running a lot faster than the first three.

"I also heard a juvenile run into the house at 7th and Nevin, yelling that somebody was bleeding and to call 911. The juvenile was upset, screaming. The juvenile got the head of household from the Nevin residence, and she went out there and started screaming the same thing. So I immediately called 911 and I called Richmond Police and attempted to get emergency services on the way."

Ram: "We all running. Then, all of sudden, me and Markel went one way towards Markel's house and Larry and Darren went another way toward their house."

"I get downstairs, I open the door," Brian James testified. "He usually right in front of the house. He wasn't outside. I mean, he wasn't right there. I didn't see anybody outside. I am just thinking like, 'Where he at?' I walk out.

"I turn to the right and see the white Oldsmobile. I'm like, that's the car. But usually you could see somebody head and stuff all in the car when you walking up, you know what I'm saying? I didn't see him, but the door was open, so I am thinking like he kneeled down.

"I just walked in the middle of the street, and I seen him on the ground. And I just take off to him. I run over there. And then, I just seen him on the ground. I seen him bleeding and stuff. And then I go straight back to the house. I'm yelling in the house – like call the ambulance – man – my brother outside – he on the ground. I don't know what is wrong, he is on the ground. I just seen a little blood, but then when I came back, it was a lot of blood."

"I was in my bedroom that evening," Taylor Davis testified. "I didn't hear any gunshots. We had TV's on and music on. Then I heard

Brian knocking at the door real frantic. My daughter opened the door and Brian said, 'Call my mother, something is wrong with TK.' So I went downstairs and went out the door. And TK was lying on the ground face down with one foot still in the car.

"I am a nurse by profession. I went over and felt for a pulse. He had a slight one, but he was bleeding very heavily. The car was still running. I directed my daughter Deena to go around and cut the engine off.

"All the kids crying. I'm crying. Brian was sort of hysterical. Kaiser is about a block away. I told him to run to Kaiser to see if they could bring an ambulance down here or somebody could come and help us out. And he went down there and he came running back and no one came. So maybe a few minutes later the police and stuff came."

"I was panicking," Brian James testified. "I ran to Kaiser Hospital across the street from the house. I was telling them like, 'Man, my brother, something happen on 7th and Nevin, my brother on the ground – like I need help.' They was just like, 'What is your name?' They wanted me to do paperwork. So I left. I call my mom, I told them to call an ambulance. I'm like, 'Mom, TK on the ground right now.' 'What, he on the ground?' 'He on the ground.' "

Landrin Kelly: "I'm asleep on the couch, Nicole's next to me. Brian calls Nicole and he screams, 'Terrance on the ground.' I'm thinking he collapsed from basketball or something. I jump up in a t-shirt and sweats – no shoes, no socks, nothing.

"So we shoot down the freeway doing 100. I hear the police sirens and the ambulance. I jump out the car, run across the street to where the body was and went under the tape – there's only two cops on the scene. Terrance laying out in the street. The police tackled me and handcuffed me. I'm like, 'That's my baby on the ground, what's happening man, did you check and see if he alive? Tell me.'

252

"They released me. Next five minutes I hear my mama coming across the parking lot, screaming, '*LANDRIN???!! LANDRIN???!!!* Is that our baby? Is that our baby?' 'Yeah mama, that's our baby, mama, they killed our baby, mama.' And she collapsed right there from a heart attack."

Tra'Meka Kelly: "I had just left Richmond. I was in Vallejo and got off the exit. I got a phone call that my brother was laid out there. I have no words for that moment. I have no words to describe that feeling."

Mary Kelly: "Tra'Meka comes home from Richmond and we get a call. They told us, 'Something happened to TK.' We drive 90 miles an hour from Vallejo to Richmond. I call Landrin's phone, he's not answering. Then I got a hold of Lajada and she told me. I scream. We pull up out there in Richmond. I see a whole lot of commotion. I see his car. I see him laying there."

Johnny Dempsey: "My sister called me up. I couldn't believe what I was hearing. It was like the world stopped. When we get out there, it doesn't dawn on me in my head that Terrance is still laying on the ground. When I got out of that car, the first person I thought of is Landrin. He was standing there with no shoes on. He held me. He was crying and screaming, '*WHAT AM I GON' DO NOW MAN???? WHAT AM I GON' DO NOW??????*' He just kept screaming that."

Louis Montgomery: "I'm in West Oakland. My mom calls me and tells me what happened. You can hear it, but you don't want to hear it. I say, 'Naw, you playing with me. Don't play with me like that.' I shot to Richmond.

"I parked my car and left it running. I saw his car. I saw him on the ground. I started crying. I saw Landrin. He gave me a big hug, he was crying. He was like, '*Do you see this?*' For somebody you were so close to – I had just seen him two days before in all his Oregon stuff – that just kept flashing in my head."

Josh Harvey: "I got my car started up in Emeryville. As soon as I got to my house in Richmond, I get a call from our close friend. He told me, 'TK was down.' 'What do you mean he's down?' 'Man, he's dead.' 'What?' I hung up the phone and went straight there. I see yellow tape and a crowd of people outside. He was laid out in front of his car on the ground. It was a cold scene man."

Jeremy Williams: "I'm sitting outside my friend's house waiting for TK, and he just never came. Somebody calls me and says, 'You hear what happened to TK?' I'm like, 'No. I'm waitin' on him now. He supposed to be around here.' All these calls flooding in. People asking, 'Is it real?' I'm like, 'I don't know.' That was one of the worst nights of my life."

Anthony "Ace" Brown: "After TK dropped us off, we went in the house and took our basketball stuff off. I got a call 10 minutes later. 'TK got shot. He laying over there by the Nevin Center.' So we go over there. Sure enough, we see all the police and everybody outside. We see Landrin and he went berserk. TK and Landrin, their relationship was one of a kind. Growing up in Richmond, everybody don't have their dad. It was a blessing to have his son and for TK to have his dad around his whole life. For him to see his son who he worked so hard for laying dead in the street? That'll make any man go crazy."

Jackie Bates: "I was in Benicia, Maurice Drew called me from UCLA. He said, 'Youngy. Are you alright right now?' 'Yeah, w'sup man?' 'Someone just told me Terrance just got shot and he's dead.' 'Yeah right. What?' 'Yes. He said Terrance Kelly got shot.' 'Maurice I'm gonna call you right back.'

"First thing I do – I'm calling Terrance's phone – over and over and over. Sometimes I call him, he might not answer – he could be busy. By the fifth or sixth time, I started thinking this shit was true. I started trippin'. I tell my mom, 'I'm going out there. I'm going to Richmond. I'm driving to his house right now.' I'm crying. My mom panicked. 'I'm coming with you, I'm coming with you, Oh my God.'

254

"I call Terrance's house. A woman answered, I don't know who it was to this day. She was so sad. I could just hear it in her voice that it was true. She told me Terrance had been shot, and where he was at.

"I hopped in my car and did 100 there. I got out there, man. Seen everything. Seen Landrin. I hugged him. Landrin was trippin'. I was trippin'. Landrin kept telling me, '*Jackie, ya'll supposed to be going to school. Ya'll supposed to be going to school.*' I threatened people. 'One of you know who did this shit to my brother.' Everyone was quiet. No one had nothing to say. That moment changed my life.

"If I could do it all again, I'd go out there, but I probably shouldn't have been out there seeing that, because that shit really scarred me. It was the worst phone call I ever received. It really changed my life. It was like a bad dream."

T.J. Ward: "I was at home. We had just come back from playing basketball. We were getting ready to play PlayStation. My mom came in the room crying. I said, 'What's wrong?' She said, 'TK got in a car accident.' That's what she heard at first. I call people. My mom wouldn't let me go out there. I call Jackie, he drove out there. He told me, 'TK got shot.' It was devastating. I froze."

Pastor K.R. Woods: "I remember the night of the tragedy when I got called out there. I'll never forget that night. Landrin just hung on me saying, '*Pastor, why? Why?*' And I did not have an answer for him.

"I couldn't even fathom the depth of his pain. I spent the whole night at the Kaiser Hospital emergency room because Mother Bevelyn went into cardiac arrest. She was beside herself with grief."

Chastity Harper: "When I got to Georgia, I was so tired from the red-eye flight and running around that I didn't talk to Terrance that day. I was so exhausted that I turned my phone off before I went to sleep – I never do that, but I didn't want to be bothered. But I randomly woke up in the middle of the night. Something told me to turn my phone on. That's when I got the news."

Landrin Kelly: "All I wanted to do was crawl up into bed with my mama and hold her. They wouldn't let me go see her. My sister Lona and my brother told me, 'No. Mama sick. Don't go there. She can't handle it right now Landrin. If she see you like this, she might stress out. She might not pull through.'

"I'm screaming, fucked up in the mind. Walking around on broken glass with bloody fleet. They had about 10 investigative cops out there. It was the most I'd ever seen at a Richmond crime scene. The coroner couldn't pick him up until they collected all the shells. My baby laid there on the ground for six hours. I didn't leave until he got picked up.

"My baby didn't deserve that."

*　　*　　*

Muriel Pratcher had a brief conversation with her sons when they came home later that evening. Before she fell asleep, she described "hearing that PlayStation game going on in Darren's room."

Muriel Pratcher testified: "Our plan was to go and get Darren's clothes off layaway for school the next morning. And from there, go up to Pinole because we had put a transfer for him to go to Pinole [Valley] High School. Before we did that, I was gonna go to the bank and then go school shopping. So that morning, I called him and said, 'Darren, let's go. We're ready. Let's go do what we have to do.'

"I was stacking dishes. He came in and broke down and started really, really crying – crying and saying that he had to go. He came up to me, fell down on his knees and grabbed me, put his arms around my waist, and told me how much he loved me. I asked him, 'What is wrong? You're really, really scaring me. I can't go through this, I've got high blood pressure. What's wrong?' And he just kept crying. This went on for about

20 minutes. I kept asking him why he was crying, what was wrong. He finally said, 'I did something bad, something horrible.'

"I had seen news reports that morning about the shooting. I asked Darren whether it had anything to do with that. He didn't say anything. He did a nod, and you know, dropped his head. Then he said, 'I have to go.' I tried to get him to stay, but by then, I was upset, too. The next thing I know, he had left.

"After Darren left, I broke down. I cried and Larry Jr. tried to comfort me, you know, telling me, you know, it will be OK. That's when I called my husband. I told him that he needed to come home. When he got home, I told him that Darren did it."

*   *   *

Mary Kelly: "I was in a dark place first. While Landrin and I were separated, I had a child. He passed five months before Terrance did. I was broke down to the point where I couldn't even bathe myself. I had given up.

"Landrin was there for me. He came and he helped. It wasn't no physical thing. It was, 'You have always been my friend, and I'm going to help you.' He helped me get myself back together.

"Five months later and this happens to Terrance. We got back because we needed to help each other get through what we was going through. God put us back together – through loss, through hurt – He put us back together. After that night, I was with Landrin at his house. We were trying to figure things out. 'What are we going to do? How are we going to live now?' And there was a time where we didn't want to go on. One thing that kept us going was that Tra'Meka was still there and we had to take care of her. So we had to figure this thing out."

Landrin Kelly: "I was numb. I couldn't do nothing. I was totally out of it. That's my baby, my world revolved around him. It totally

257

destroyed me. I didn't know where to turn. I didn't trust nobody. I'm drinking, smoking, every day, all day. I'm hearing him call me, *'Daddy! Daddy!'* I'm jumping up. My brother, my Uncle Billy and my wife – they in the room with me, I wouldn't let anybody else around me. They stayed with me in the room for two weeks straight.

"I grabbed my little sister Latonya – she turned her life over to Christ before I did. I asked her, 'Did you see this coming? Why did God do this to my baby? You a spiritually-filled woman, you gotta tell me something!' 'No Landrin, God don't take life, He give life.' 'Well if he was doing everything right, why did He allow this to happen? He could of did something!'

"And I found my answer – in a bottle, and in a joint – until I was passed the fuck out. The reporters come into my house – they didn't know who I was until after the first week. I had my cousin Johnny speak to the reporters."

Johnny Dempsey: "There was so much company coming in and out of there. So much traffic in Landrin's face. They didn't give him time to rest. I don't think he slept for three days. No shower. Same clothes. He was stuck. In a trance. Reporters ran up to the house – it was chaotic – they fought hard to get a story. Before, out of respect, they'd call and say, 'Hey, can we talk.' Then they just started knocking on the door, opening windows. They didn't understand his pain."

Landrin Kelly: "I'm scared, I don't know who some of these people is. I'm really paranoid. Everybody comes over because there's food and people drinking. I say, **'ALL YOU MOTHERFUCKERS GET THE FUCK OUT. CLEAN THE WHOLE HOUSE OUT. I DON'T WANT NOBODY IN MY HOUSE.'** "

*   *   *

Detective Mitchell Peixoto was assigned to the Richmond robbery-homicide unit in August 2004. He testified: "At the scene of the crime, I went with the K-9 to the side yard behind the gate. I located a rifle, a white t-shirt and a black nylon bag. After talking with multiple witnesses, we obtained a search warrant for a residence on Pennsylvania Avenue in Richmond that we identified as Darren Pratcher's home. On August 14, 2004, we conducted a search pursuant to the warrant signed by the judge.

"SWAT hit the house about 2:15 a.m. Larry Sr. and Larry Jr. were taken for questioning. In the master bedroom, we found an Intratech assault type of machine pistol. In Darren Pratcher's bedroom, a .22 Remington bullet was found in a dresser. In the same dresser, we found an item that had the heading, 'Money D' on it."

The document contained rap lyrics written by Darren Pratcher:

> "Us Youngstas heartless,
> now if you ain't from our
> part of town you're a
> fuckin' target, so you better
> smarten up cop't some gats
> and grow some nuts, cause
> some niggas 'bout to die
> and it's not go' be us. All
> you nigga go die, ya'll don't
> want beef with a Central
> nigga get turned into a stick
> figa."

After the search of the Pratcher residence, a manhunt ensued. Darren's picture ran in the paper. The Richmond Police Department sent bulletins out to its seven patrol teams and to its detectives in the robbery-homicide unit.

The manhunt was unsuccessful. Darren was driving around and sleeping in a van.

LR, a 16-year-old resident of Central Richmond, had a short interaction with Darren Pratcher within 48 hours of the shooting: "We had found out it was a killing. I went to the scene. A couple of days later, I was leaving my house and going to watch a girl fight at the park. I had seen this boy name Bear. I got a ride with them in a big passenger van.

"Darren was in the back row of the van. We were going up the street to watch the fight. I heard Darren was involved in the shooting of TK, but I did not too much believe it because I don't believe that he would do something like that.

"When I saw Darren, I was like, 'What's up.' I asked him what happened. He said, 'I had to do what I had to do.' It looked like he was going to cry, but that's just how Darren looks. He looks nervous. He looked me in the eye but he kept on putting his head down. We rode up the street, then I got out to go see the fight. I say, 'Bye.' He said, 'Don't tell nobody you seen me.' "

*   *   *

Pastor K.R. Woods: "Landrin was very broken, and he had his internal struggles. There was a lot of hurt leading up to the funeral services. In the church, we tried to make it a place of solitude, peace and healing for the family. There was a lot of reconciliation of relationships. Landrin contemplated retaliation. Some people encouraged retaliation, and he very well could have had retaliation."

Paul Webster Jr.: "TK had a lot of love from a lot of people, even a lot of bad people. Even I thought about turning bad at the time. I had a lot of hate."

Landrin Kelly: "People coming up talking about, 'Man, what you want me to do, we know who did it.' People ready to do 'em. But my mama said, 'No. *Vengeance is not ours.*' And I had to live by what she said."

*   *   *

On the evening of August 17, Darren Pratcher met with his father and the family's pastor in Central Richmond. Together, they walked into the Richmond Police Department.

David Brown [Former Contra Costa County deputy District Attorney]: "He came in with his father. My speculation is that word on the street got out that Darren had done it. And the word got out that something could happen to him. I think his family figured he had a better chance of survival in custody rather than on the streets. TK was very well-respected in the community. I never got the feeling that all the neighborhood guys in Central disliked TK or that any group of people disliked him."

Detective Mitchell Peixoto testified: "I got a call from my sergeant at the time, approximately 6:30 p.m. I was told Darren Pratcher was in custody. My sergeant asked me to respond to assist in Pratcher's interview at the Hall of Justice.

"Myself and Detective Jose Villalobos advised the defendant of his *Miranda* rights before the interview. He told us he wasn't at the scene of the crime. We spoke for probably a little over an hour. He was sitting down, talking to us in a pretty normal conversation. When we asked him where he was on the night of the shooting, he said that he was, 'Chilling with Big L.'

"Then, I asked him if he watched the show CSI and got to asking him about a gray beanie he had left at the crime scene. And it seemed the whole interview changed gears there. His demeanor changed, he became very apprehensive, sat back a little bit, started talking a bit faster. Seemed to me he was worried.

"He said, 'I had lost a beanie.' He kept asking me what color beanie was found. We did not tell him. At some point after this, the defendant terminated the conversation.

"Later, we were transporting Mr. Pratcher to Juvenile Hall in Martinez, California. He asked to talk to us further about his knowledge of the case. I refused to talk to him until we got to Juvenile Hall and parked. Once we parked, I audiotaped the conversation. He changed his story that he was, in fact, at the scene when the murder occurred. He said that he saw it. He was there, heard the shots. He was probably the last one to run away from the scene and that's why everybody thought he did it. And most likely he left the beanie at the scene."

During the course of the two interviews, Darren Pratcher lied 35 times.

*   *   *

The news stunned residents across the Bay Area and devastated the De La Salle community. Three weeks after Terrance's death, the football team lost its first game in 12 years, ending its record 151-game win streak.

But this paled in comparison to the effects of the tragedy in Richmond, Berkeley and Oakland.

By the mid-2000's, violence had already spiraled out of control in Richmond. TK's death led to a crisis. In June 2005, Richmond's city council requested a declaration of a state of emergency because of the dramatic rise in the city's homicide rate.

Paul Webster Jr.: "There was a lot of anger in Richmond. Everybody had love for TK. From Pony baseball to Steeler football. He was a good kid. He was a nice dude. Everybody was rooting for him. Everybody wanted to brag about him.

"Then here come this kid who, for a dumb, petty reason, take what everybody was gonna experience. At that point, it did have a big impact. For about two months, it was like, 'What is Richmond coming to?' Then after those two months, they went right back to killing.

"What Darren did set a whole new mark for why people kill in Richmond. For us, you didn't have too many vendettas as far somebody wanting to kill somebody through high school. There was shootings happening, but it was older people. Terry was an accident. They thought he was somebody else. But from the 20-28 age range, those killings is different. There is animosity or a vendetta for killing somebody."

Quinton Ganther: "It hurt me so bad. [Head coach] Urban Meyer was very supportive at Utah. We were in the middle of training camp and he got me a flight to go to the funeral. There were so many people there. That was a tough time for the whole Bay Area, not just Richmond, because everyone was touched by this. It's different when you got kids in the streets – so when something like that happens – you can accept it and deal with it. Here you had the guy that was doing all the right things. Landrin did everything he could to keep him out of that life. He was going to make it out. He would have been in the NFL *for sure*. And his life was cut short due to stupidity.

"Those are the ones you can't accept. It's a tough pill to swallow. After TK, no one was safe. There was no longer any of the free passes for kids that we had when we were young. There's no more unwritten rules. Everybody's a target. There's no more, 'Off limits.' "

Landrin Kelly: "A lot of these kids around Terrance lost hope after he passed. They went to the streets. Selling dope. Killing people. A handful of 'em are in jail. Another couple got killed. You got people where – they used to play on the same teams. They used to spend the night at each other's houses. Their daddies were best friends. Now they out there shooting each other and robbing each other."

Anthony "Ace" Brown: "You didn't want to be in Richmond after that. You seen how careless people be. You love the city but you can't stand to be in it because of all the tragedies that go on. There was nobody else doing what TK was doing except Quinton Ganther, and Quinton was older. TK was going to be the only one that made it out after Quinton."

Jeremy Williams: "If TK was still alive, he would have been for Richmond what [Seattle Seahawks running back] Marshawn Lynch is for Oakland. He would have put Richmond on the map. Darren ruined everything. He changed everybody's life. TK was a positive thing for the whole city of Richmond. Finally, you had a success story coming out of our city. He came from a nice family that did the best they could. He ain't been in no trouble. Everybody supported him. And then this happens. It's just inexcusable.

"When things happen and someone dies, people always say, 'Oh he was a great guy.' No. Here you actually had a really great person. He was a good role model for people coming up under him. That's somebody you could model your life after."

Tra'Meka Kelly: "Once my brother died, Richmond went downhill – there were murders left and right. After this happened, I couldn't go back to Richmond. Everything there was a reminder. I didn't want to go to my Grandma house. I didn't want to do anything. I had lost my baby brother prior to this and Terrance helped me get over that. So I had no one to lean on or talk to. I just closed down."

Lanny Kelly III: "After Terrance passed, the division in Richmond got worse. Southside versus Central versus North. Terrance had friends in all the different sections of Richmond. He represented Richmond as a whole. He didn't want any of the division in Richmond. He never got a chance to tell people that. Of course, he couldn't say to that to his

264

Richmond friends. They'd say, 'Aww, you a sucka, trying to be a peacekeeper,' or whatever. This is the normal trash talk that they would do for anything positive."

Johnny Dempsey: "When I was growing up, they didn't tell me how many people was gonna die on me, or how many people I was gonna lose to gun violence. It's hard to adjust. I have these conversations with people all the time. I come from Oakland. Oakland and Richmond are real similar. People from the outside will ask me, 'What can we as society do to make things better as far as the violence?' I tell them, 'Nothing.' Because it all starts with parenting. It all starts at home. You have babies having babies – there's no guidance. There's nobody to teach them.

"Terrance grew up in Richmond, California, but he knew right from wrong. He knew that hurting somebody was wrong. Certain things were instilled in Terrance that weren't instilled in Darren Pratcher. It's sad. I feel bad for Darren Pratcher. My heart goes out to him because he's sitting in jail right now for the rest of his life."

At trial, Darren Pratcher's defense counsel argued that Darren suffered from post-traumatic stress disorder (PTSD) as a result of growing up in violent neighborhoods. Dr. Howard Friedman, a clinical neuropsychologist, met with Darren three times in 2006 in order to evaluate whether certain emotional difficulties might have been present and affected his behavior during the shooting.

According to Dr. Friedman, the information provided by Darren Pratcher in the clinical interviews was consistent with his suffering from chronic PTSD. Darren also told Dr. Friedman that he had taken one tablet of ecstasy within an hour of the shooting and had also used marijuana.

Darren's counsel argued at trial that on the night of August 12, 2004, Darren was jumpy, agitated and scared due to credible threats that Andre Jones, a man with a reputation for violence, was looking for him because he shot Andre's daughter with a pellet gun. Darren obtained the rifle for protection against Andre Jones and hid the weapon in Taylor Davis' side yard. When Terrance Kelly pulled up at the corner of 7th Street and Nevin Avenue that night, he was driving a 1963 white Oldsmobile Cutlass Supreme rather than the Mustang 5.0 that he normally used to pick up Brian James. Darren did not recognize the white Oldsmobile and thought it was Andre Jones. He grabbed the rifle out of fear for his life and shot Terrance Kelly in a case of mistaken identity.

The narrative above conflicts with several facts: Multiple witnesses testified that Darren Pratcher had a motive to kill because he had problem with Terrance Kelly. When TK pulled up to the corner of 7th Street and Nevin Avenue, he called out to his former teammates and friends Larry Pratcher Jr. and Markel Robinson. TK had dreadlocks at the time, while Andre Jones was bald. Larry Jr. and Markel approached TK in the vehicle and talked with him about basketball through the passenger side window. After Larry Jr. acknowledged TK, Darren went to the side yard and grabbed the rifle. Before he started firing, Darren called out to Larry and Markel, "Watch out."

After deliberating for five days, the jury reached the verdict of first-degree murder for Darren Pratcher. Judge Laurel Brady focused on the firing of four bullets from a bolt-action rifle:

"The fact that Mr. Pratcher was 15 at the time is truly a tragedy for society, but it doesn't change the outcome and it doesn't change the fact that Mr. Kelly is dead. Whether it was a 40-year-old, a 30-year-old or the 15-year-old, the end result is the same...I think that there was a lot of thought, whether misguided or not, is separate. But an awful lot of thought went into this act and a great deal of coldness to allow someone to shoot into an occupied car at someone who's clearly not a threat; and not just once, but four times. I think you could even explain the first one in some fashion, but two, three and four, I don't know how you explain them."

Darren Pratcher was sentenced to 50-years-to-life in prison for the murder of Terrance Kelly.

*   *   *

After the trial, rumors swirled around the possible involvement of Brian James in the shooting. Did he set TK up? Was he complicit in the killing? These questions remain unanswered. Many have an opinion.

Anthony "Ace" Brown: "Brian, Lanny III and I grew up playing on Landrin's teams. I knew Brian personally since we were young. He was a cool dude. He just hung out with the wrong people who made some decisions that wasn't in his best interests. He didn't have no bad intentions whatsoever. Some people have Brian confused as always being in the streets or a being bad guy. But if you really knew him, that wasn't really him. He was a good dude."

Lanny Kelly III: "With how everything happened, I feel it could have been prevented. If Darren is telling Brian, 'Don't bring TK around here,' Brian could have related that to Terrance – 'Hey, this guy feeling some type of way about you, watch your back.' More than one person knew about Darren's hostility toward Terrance and everyone had Terrance's number. It could have been squashed. Someone could have said, 'You two need to talk before this get out of hand.'

"There was different things that could have happened to prevent it from going down. Brian was at the house where it happened. This is just my personal opinion, but I'm sure he knew what was about to go down or what could have possibly gone down – to the point where he could have told Terrance, 'Don't come.' Someone could have said something to prevent it."

Landrin Kelly: "When it happened, everybody was out at the scene crying. Brian's mom took him in the car because he was in shock. I don't think Brian understood what was about to happen, and I don't think

267

he took Darren seriously when he said, 'Don't bring TK down here.' Brian was probably like, 'Why you trippin'?' "

David Brown: "At trial, I had questions about Brian James that were never answered. There were some disconcerting inconsistencies in his testimony. Some people had the impression that he might have been complicit in the killing."

Paul Webster Jr.: "TK took Brian under his wing. He didn't treat him like no red-headed stepchild at all. When we went to parties, TK would take Brian along or drop him off where he wanted to go. He taught him how to drive a stick shift and let him drive his car. I remember a few arguments, but it was petty stuff.

"Everybody bragged about how great TK was doing, and Brian outcast himself because he wasn't doing nothing with his life but gettin' in trouble. With the way Brian's life went after TK passed, I don't know if it was eatin' at him or what, but it went downhill, and maybe guilt about TK led to his demise.

"Everyone asks the question, 'Was Brian in on it?' Unless Brian knew Darren was going to do it or saw him with a gun, there was no reason to warn TK. He knew that TK and Darren had an argument, but how was he supposed to know that Darren would shoot?"

Grand jury and trial testimony reveals that Brian may have smoked marijuana prior to the incident. Brian James and Darren Pratcher later fought while both were in Juvenile Hall.

Brian James' involvement in the killing of Terrance Kelly will never be known. In 2006, he was shot and killed at a public venue in view of roughly 100 witnesses. His murder remains unsolved.

Robert Turner: "I coached Brian for three years and in my heart I don't think that Brian actually set TK up. He may have thought that they could run into each other, and that TK may end up kicking Darren's ass. I don't see it as a setup. Unfortunately, I think it was fate. God had something to do with putting them all together that night."

CHAPTER 31

Redemption

JOHNNY DEMPSEY: "Landrin and Bevelyn hadn't even seen each other since it happened. Imagine what the emotions were like when she got out of the hospital. That was their baby. They both broke down. It was the day before Terrance's funeral."

Terrance Kelly's funeral was held on August 19 at Hilltop Community Church in Richmond. Over 3,500 mourners packed the large interior chamber and overflowed into a second. Attendees came from everywhere, from Richmond and Oakland's poorest neighborhoods to the wealthy suburbs of the East Bay. Younger friends and family from the neighborhood wore airbrushed white t-shirts adorned with TK's picture and various slogans. The church lobby reeked of marijuana. Former teammates, opponents, classmates, teachers and coaches funneled in to pay their respects.

Josh Dozier: "Hilltop Community is my regular church, and that church is not little. There were so many people there that it got to the point where it was standing room only. As close as Jamie and I were to Terrance, we were sitting up at the top. It was surreal to see that many people devastated by the same event, to see how many people TK touched and how many people cared about him."

Scott Hugo: "I'll never forget watching Landrin walk in to the funeral. He was a man broken under Heaven. I've never seen an individual so completely crushed."

Landrin and the immediate family wore all white tuxedos and dresses and sat at the front of the church. Pastor Woods sang *The Presence of the Lord Is Here* accompanied by a choir as the auditorium filled.

Scott Hugo: "One of the first things they said was that this was a celebration of TK's life. It was something special. It's a very unique way of dealing with tragedy. It's a way of acknowledging that everyone that there had stake in TK."

Before De La Salle coach Bob Ladouceur took the podium, the mood inside the church was almost like a party – jubilant and uplifting – a true celebration of TK's life. Pastor Woods, the choir and the band clapped, sang and played their instruments while the audience cheered. The horrific act that had brought thousands of strangers from every demographic together had to that point not been mentioned.

What came next sucked the air out of the room and silenced the crowd. It was the embodiment of the man behind the speech – *intense*. More than any particular game in Ladouceur's mind-boggling win streak, this speech was the pinnacle of his career.

A round of applause and shouts of encouragement rang out as he prepared himself:

Bob Ladouceur: "All right, I'm feeling a little bit better."

More applause, encouragement, instruments and chords followed before he spoke again.

Bob Ladouceur: "When it's all said and done though, I just can't see how any of us can feel good about why we're gathered here today – When Terrance, who's so well-loved and well-respected, is taken from us in the prime of his youth, by an act so despicable and senseless that it defies all wisdom and comprehension. It's just hard to feel good about anything.

"In fact, now, we are all engaged in a battle, and that battle is difficult and fierce. The enemy – despair. The battle is against anger, hate and vengeance. The enemy is our broken spirit and our hopelessness.

"But it's a battle we all must fight. Why? Because Terrance would want us to. And that's what he would do. That much I do know about Terrance. So even though we don't feel good. We must seek and find good.

"Even so, we can't help but ask, 'Where is the good in this situation?' Well, the good is right here, and it's in front of us [Ladouceur points to Terrance in his casket].

"…The perfect way to carry this forward is to remember Terrance. What do I remember about Terrance? I remember the first day I saw him. He was that awkward freshman that was all arms and legs with an infectious smile. A coach couldn't help but notice the grace of his athletic ability. That, coupled with his strong academic performance, and we knew – Terrance was on his way to greatness.

"I remember when we pulled him up for the playoffs his sophomore year. He was still that skinny kid that was taking taunts from our seniors about how they were gonna, 'Bust him up.'

"It was kind of a rite of passage for our sophomores that were good enough to come up to the varsity. He quickly earned their respect as a football player. There was one sophomore kid that nobody was gonna bust up.

"It was from there I learned the toughness and grittiness of Terrance Kelly. He wasn't going to back down to anybody on the field of play. He combined that competitive attitude and his athletic ability into a winning combination, and had Division 1 schools fighting for his services. It was his athletic ability they were after. Little did they know that they were going to get the complete package along with it.

"The University of Oregon knew this. With Terrance, they were going to get much more than just a good athlete. Terrance was a good player, but more important, he was a great person. I have heard Terrance described as a gentle giant, and that he was. He wasn't particularly big, especially for a Division 1-football player, but he always looked physically big in my eyes. I am convinced that it was his stature of character that gave him an extra two inches in height, and 20 pounds in weight.

"Quiet and introspective, Terrance was a listener that learned quickly. He was not just a student of the game, he was also a student of life. He spent his four years deciding what kind of person he wanted to be, and what he wanted to become. And he was making all the right decisions.

"The one characteristic of Terrance that I admired most was his gentle nature. I had a strong feeling about this, and last Friday his teammates gave witness and testimony to that truth. Terrance wouldn't and couldn't harm anyone.

"I never saw him angry or confrontational. I never saw him cruel, disrespectful or mean-spirited. I know words hurt him. And when I felt he wasn't maximizing his potential, he got sad. I know he didn't want to disappoint others, and he didn't want to disappoint me. He cried when he felt he let his teammates down, and he would have done anything, or played any position, if he knew it would have helped his team.

"All this spoke volumes about Terrance's capacity for love. He cared about others. He loved people, and we loved him right back.

"My lasting memory of Terrance will be his beautiful smile and infectious laugh. The smile and laugh always said to me – this world is a good place. He made me feel good in his presence.

"I truly believe with all my heart that Terrance is alive and with us here right now. He is alive because he is a part of me. If you loved him, he is a part of you also. I will honor him and keep him alive everyday by remembering him and living the lessons he taught me.

"To the Kelly family – Landrin and Bevelyn – my heart breaks for your loss, and I pray for your recovery. God bless you both. And please, take some solace in the fact that you did a fantastic job.

"You raised a beautiful child. You did it right. You're a shining example for all of us.

"To Justin Alumbaugh, our one Lasallian educator who spent the most time with Terrance and had the most influence on him, I want to thank you. I know Terrance loved you very much. You, Terrance and Parker made an awesome team, and I'm sorry for your loss.

"To the Amigos, I know you guys loved each other dearly and were the closest of brothers. You guys are gonna have to carry Terrance with you every day. Share your triumphs with him, and pray for his help in your time of despair – he'll be there.

"Today is the day we let go of Terrance and turn him back to the Father, so He can love him more than we ever could. So Lord, bring peace to our gathering, and all the love that's in this room.

"Bring peace to Richmond."

*   *   *

Landrin Kelly: "I'd look at my mama after the funeral and we'd both just break down and cry. Every time she'd see me it was, 'Baby is you all right?' 'I'm all right mama, I'm tryin' mama. I'm all right mama.'

"I started going to church every Sunday with her. Some of the things the Pastor said were related, some of the words were sinking in. My Pastor kept me reading, kept me in the Book. He gave me a book, *Purpose of a Driven Life*. He told me, 'Each day, read one chapter. Then live your life by that chapter. God only breaks you down to the bottom so he can build you up. It ain't you doing the work, its God doing the work through you.'

"I needed something to lean on and that really got me through. He was speaking to the congregation, but I listened and applied it to my life. I really got into it. That got me through September."

Pastor K.R. Woods: "In our individual time, Landrin and I talked about the life of Job. How God allowed him to go through suffering, but brought him to a place of peace. We talked about him finding that new normal in his life. How it will never be the same, but how he could channel that energy in the right direction – to use the strength of his wife and his family.

"One of the big things for Landrin during that time was, 'TK was my only son. My only son.' I encouraged him to put that energy into his grandchildren and his other children. It was a tough time – a lot of tears at the altar. Every week for months and months I'd sit with the family – Landrin, Lanny Sr., and help as much as I could to mend them back to health."

Landrin Kelly: "I leaned on my brother, my wife and my Uncle Billy a lot during that time. I was just walking around the house crying all day. They took me wherever I needed to go and stayed with me all day and all night.

"My brother told me, 'Man, when you were young and on drugs, we couldn't stop you from robbing people and doing wrong. Terrance was your angel. He was sent to change you. And when He felt you was established and well off, God called him home.'

Landrin Kelly: "My mama used to tell me, 'My baby up there by his'self.' 'Naw, mama, Grandma up there. Cousin Tony, Grandpa up there.' 'Naw my baby ain't never been nowhere by his'self before.' She was like, 'I got to go.' I talked to her at 11 p.m. on October 6. She asked me, 'Baby, is you gonna be all right?' I guess God seen her heart because the doctor say she had lost 10 pounds in September, and that all her vital signs were good and she was gaining strength. On October 7, 2004, my mama died of a broken heart. They couldn't find nothing wrong with her."

Pastor K.R. Woods: "Mother Bevelyn's health was never the same after the tragedy. She literally died of a broken heart. For Landrin to be able to deal with all of that back-to-back, it says how incredible of a man he is. Because that kind of thing will make you lose your mind."

*   *   *

Landrin Kelly: "He say He won't give me no more than I can handle. I say shit, I couldn't bear my son leaving, now you gonna take my mama too? It had me lost for a minute. It had me confused. What should I be believing in? What should I have faith in? That'll make you lose your faith."

Mary Kelly: "God sent people our way. People started coming aboard. People that loved Terrance and what he stood for rallied behind us. People that didn't even know Terrance, but heard about the story came aboard. It grew from there."

Landrin Kelly: "My good friend Jarvis Brown, he ran the baseball league that Terrance played in and I coached for. Jarvis said, 'Man, you need to do something. This is the right time. You've got so many supporters behind you. You've been coaching and working with kids all your life.' He came by and picked me up every day to get me out of the house. Jarvis was best friends with Willie McGee. Those two really pushed me out there. Willie McGee provided my initial funding to cover the startup costs for a nonprofit corporation – the 501(c)(3) filing fee, insurance, stuff like that. That money got me started.

"Next, we demanded that the city open the community centers in Richmond that had closed. These kids had nowhere to go and no place to be educated. When you have no money and nowhere to go – you're going to sell drugs, steal, rob – whatever you have to do to make it happen."

Donna Kelly: "It's important to our family that TK's death not go in vain. Children should not be segregated for economic reasons. All children should be given the same chance. The elimination of programs for children brings about jealousy. When my grandkids came along, the amount of money we had to pay for them to participate in organized sports and activities was excessive. We came from a strong family, so we would get together to raise money so our grandkids could participate in these programs.

"When I was growing up and when my children came along, the recreation centers, little league sports and things like that were at a very minimal cost, if a cost at all. With TK and my grandson's generation, the amount of money that it took for those children to participate meant that the less fortunate kids could not participate, and that breeds jealousy.

"I've seen little kids look through the fence at kids whose parents could afford to pay. They knew they played just as well, but their parents didn't have the financial support to allow them to play. I've seen that in the last 20 years, and it's getting worse and worse."

Landrin Kelly: "The initial idea was to create an after-school program for these kids who had nowhere to go. I started putting in work late October, early November 2004. Jarvis and his friend Janett helped me set up my bylaws, email accounts and wrote everything out for me. We got supplies – computers, brochure materials and stuff like that for the kids. I took seminars in downtown Oakland where they trained us how to run a nonprofit organization and how to run a board meeting.

"We knew we needed big names to support us. We got Dr. John Wilhelmy – the team doctor for De La Salle whose sons Sean and Chris played with Terrance. Coach Lad and Coach Eidson both came aboard right away as well. It just grew from there."

Billy Dempsey Sr.: "Landrin was out of it for a while. He didn't think he could do it. I was right there with him every day pushing it – going to Richmond City Council meetings. Through encouragement, with his family, he did what he thought he couldn't do – work with other kids."

Scott Hugo: "Landrin could have self-destructed. I don't think anybody would have blamed him – it was the likely outcome with the pain and suffering he had to deal with. He's one of my heroes. To take that kind of pain and suffering and make something constructive and beautiful out of it is such a special thing. It's a testament to human resilience. It's a testament to our ability to find elements of redemption in even the most tragic of circumstances, and even the greatest of adversity."

Pastor K.R. Woods: "Landrin was a broken man. But amazingly enough, he was able to turn that pain into power *quickly*, and channel that power by establishing the T.K. Youth Foundation. He did that within months of his son being slain. It was incredible.

"It would be easy to be bitter with people and bitter with God. That he was able to handle his grief – and then have the mentality of, 'I'm gonna help these kids, instead of retaliate against them' – it's special. It's a story of tenacity, faithfulness, and trust in your faith, trust in knowing that a brighter day's coming.

"With Landrin and his family, they have been a light amidst the darkness. They didn't just forsake the city that took their loved ones. They said, 'I'm gonna do something about my city. I have love for my city.' "

In early 2005, the Terrance T.K. Kelly Youth Foundation held its opening ceremony at the Martin Luther King Jr. Center in Richmond, where Landrin and Mary held their wedding reception back in 1996.

CHAPTER 32

TK Lives

OVER A DECADE after the tragedy, the village that raised TK and gave him an avenue to succeed now does the same for at-risk inner city kids across the San Francisco Bay Area.

Landrin Kelly: "My sister Lona always took care of Terrance's paperwork and helped him with school work. She was the second mama, and she's my mama today. Once she saw that I was serious about doing the foundation, she really got behind me. She handles the TKYF's paperwork and works as an educator with the kids. Her best friend Dr. Lilia Chavez works on my board. She has a Masters and a Ph.D. in psychology. She writes the violence prevention programs for us.

"When I was doing something wrong or Terrance couldn't talk to me about something, he'd confide in my older brother. He was there for Terrance whenever he had a problem. Today, my brother works as a counselor for the kids in our program and mentors them."

Kamron Akukuro, from Antioch, recalls his participation in TKYF programs.

Kamron Akukuro: "What Landrin and Mary are doing, it changes a lot of people's lives. Some kids might not get the message and go back to what they were doing, but other kids get it. Adarius Pickett was a guy that came through the foundation and now he's playing football at UCLA on a full-ride scholarship.

"Landrin basically adopted us into his family. He treated us like one of his kids. He was like that uncle that I never had. If I ever had a problem or needed advice – he was there to mentor me. The foundation helped me understand that when stuff gets hard, you can ask for help.

"Landrin always told us stories of TK – that what made him stand out was his heart. When the playoffs came along at De La Salle, the coaches brought all of us running backs in to watch film of former De La Salle greats run the ball. D.J. Williams, Maurice Jones-Drew, Terrance Kelly, Terron Ward. You could see that TK ran with a lot of heart. He was just unwilling to go down."

Lamar Harris: "I was born and raised in Richmond and I'm currently a senior at the University of Oregon majoring in business with a minor in communications. I first heard about the TKYF when Landrin gave a presentation at my middle school on what the foundation does. I was 12 when I started in the program and I'm still working with the TKYF as a volunteer today. With Terrance, I wanted to be like him – how he carried himself, the student that he was, the athlete he was, the son that he was. That's why I chose Oregon, I followed him up there. With Landrin's programs, you learn about the good, the bad and the ugly of life. You learn about life choices – whether they will lead to opportunities or consequences. You learn that life is much bigger than you are. The foundation opens up a whole new world for young people beyond a street corner or area of the city they live. It allows them to grow, to expand their thinking and change their perspectives in life."

Mary Kelly: "The foundation has grown from an after-school program, to a tutorial program – to now we've tapped into things that are far beyond what I ever could have imagined. We've met over a thousand kids and we've made a difference. Not all of them… I've lost some kids to prison or violence. But we've improved kids' grades, granted money for school and got these kids jobs.

"I run the girls program now. Some of these girls are as hard as the boys – already in gangs, already heavily involved in drugs. Some of these issues are beyond my skill. We have to bring in drug counselors, people that specialize in gangs and violence prevention. We never knew in starting the foundation where it was going to take us. But God continues to send the right people our way.

"It wasn't mandatory in the past, but it is mandatory now that we have family involvement with the program. After we got the parents involved – we had mothers and fathers in tears at our meetings. The kids give us anonymous messages for their parents and we meet with the parents. Then we have the kids go down to the center and make lunch for the parents. We read messages to these parents from their kids like, 'I wish my mother paid more attention to me.' 'I wish my mother know I try my very best.' I have parents coming back saying, 'Thank you. Thank you. You don't know what you're doing for my family.'

"I work 40 hours a week and then I do this with the rest of my time. When I'm doing this, I'm dog-tired, but it's a great feeling. The foundation has grown much bigger than I ever could have imagined, and it is helping us cope with everything we've been through. And I know that it's making my mother-in-law proud, because that's what she was all about – helping people in any way she could."

TK's teammates have also carried on his legacy.

Quinton Ganther: "Every college game I played, I dedicated it to TK. TK was on my wrists my whole college career. I couldn't do that in

NFL because they'll fine you. But he was close to my heart, always, through my career on the field.

"Today, I'm a college football coach. I recruit the Bay Area, and my goal is to sign one or two players out of Richmond every year. Every year I wanna come back and give a scholarship and an opportunity to get out of that situation. My goal is to give these kids a shot like TK had and to teach them. It's a way for me to give back. I signed two kids out of El Cerrito this year. The tragedy still impacts me and affects me, and now I want to touch someone else's life in memory of him. His memory still lives on."

At Terrance's funeral, no one looked more shaken than his friend and teammate from De La Salle, T.J. Ward. After the funeral, no one was more determined. Ward walked on to Oregon's football team in 2005 and earned a scholarship. Over the next four years playing defense back while battling injuries, Ward developed a reputation as one of the hardest-hitting safeties in the country. In 2010, he was drafted at the top of the second round of the NFL draft, 38th overall, by the Cleveland Browns. Ward was named to the Professional Football Writers Association NFL all-Rookie team after an impressive debut season playing safety and earned Pro Bowl recognition in 2013. After signing with the Denver Broncos in 2014, Ward was again selected to the Pro Bowl and named a 2nd Team all-Pro by the Associated Press.

T.J. Ward: "My path to the NFL was not easy. I walked on at Oregon. I had more injuries in college. I've tried to progress the way TK would have wanted me to, the way I know he would have. I have a tattoo of on my shoulder to honor his memory and remember him every day. I hope this sheds light on what Landrin is doing with the Foundation."

Jackie Bates: "The day after Terrance passed, I went and got a tattoo and had shirts made. My whole career, from college to the Kansas City Chiefs, I wore a back plate with his picture on it. No matter where I played, I had my back plate out. People always said, 'I heard about your friend. God had a plan.'

"TK was an old soul. To be honest, a lot of times he kept me in line and I missed that after I left for college. He'd tell me, 'Hey man, chill out, it's not that serious,' or he'd say something funny to make me think about a dumb decision before I did it. That's the type of wisdom he had.

"After he passed, I got into alcohol and went into a really bad depression. I was fighting everywhere I went. I was mad and I didn't know why. It really fucked me up. But time heals things. It's still a beautiful thing to know someone like that."

Paul Webster Jr.: "You wanna talk about a good dude – that was most definitely a good dude. When you lose someone like that, who has such an effect on people's lives – I went into a depression for about a year. But with all things, you come out of it. Having him in my life and going through everything with him – it was a joy. Every day when I pass where his last breath was taken, or look at our baseball pictures growing up – or just me talking to my grandma everyday – he still live on."

Erik Sandie: "Every year, there's a banquet for TK at De La Salle put on by the TKYF. Every year, on the day of the event – myself, Wilhelmy, Fuji, Biller and a bunch of the guys – we'd go golfing that day and have a beer for him. About four years ago, we were at the banquet and Coach Lad challenged us to do more for the foundation. He said, 'You know this thing might not last forever, it's on you guys to keep his legacy alive as well.'

"Biller calls me the next day and says, 'We already golf every year. It makes sense to put on a golf tournament to raise money for the foundation.' Biller was playing professional rugby at the time – so he couldn't do as much in terms of the logistics of making it happen. So Sean Wilhelmy and I took the reins in putting together the TKYF Annual

Golf Tournament. We've raised a good amount of money each year doing that.

"Landrin has lived a harder life than most people. You can see the pain in his eyes that he has to live with. He really lives for the foundation and the benefit of those kids. He works so hard and gets hardly any credit for it.

"There's not a two-, three-day span that goes by that I don't get a phone call from him. Landrin lost his son. When you lose your son, you lose not only your pride and joy, but also the support system around you – because your family is supposed to always be there for you. We hope to be seen as part of Landrin's family."

*   *   *

Despite the efforts of family and friends to carry on his legacy, there remains a sense that TK could have accomplished more. The question is often asked, 'What if he was here today?'

Landrin Kelly: "If Terrance was here, he'd probably have the resources and the funding to do more. All I know is that I work harder today than I did when he was alive."

Josh Dozier: "To this day, you still see so many posts on Facebook or Instagram and all that when it's his anniversary or his birthday. When someone dies – they'll post about stuff like that for a year or two, but not over a decade later. So many people are still posting about it – how hurt they are that he's not here."

Chris Biller: "He did everything right. He accomplished everything. Ready to go. Two days before leaving. He was the sweetest kid. Quiet. Mellow. Never mean to anyone. Never bullied anyone. He was 10-out-of-10. When you think about how flat-out tragic the whole thing is, it still hurts. I've had a couple really odd dreams involving Terrance – where it's so real that you can hug him. I'm thinking, 'He's alive! He's alive!' Then

285

you wake up and think, 'That's odd.' But you still appreciate it. It's kind of a hope thing."

Mary Kelly: "He had us working for him when he was here. And now you just can't help but laugh, because he's got us working harder for him even when he's not here. He's probably up there laughing, saying, 'Mama, I got 'em working,' because we're always working. But the reward is there – we're doing the work for him to help these kids. All that we ask of these kids is that they do not misrepresent that name – that t-shirt they're wearing, that wristband – we ask that they do not misrepresent our son and what he stood for."

Billy Dempsey Sr.: "To this day, he's never left my mind. I'll never forget that smile – that smile used to just melt me. For a good kid to turn one corner and die – it's always stuck with me. I can't forget. It's just a hell of a loss. Because we miss out on what he could have been. His influence on other children – it was unlimited. He could have done anything man."

Paul Webster Sr.: "We put every barrier in place for something like that not to happen. Life is the never the same after that. Not to say life is all bad now – there's still good times – but it will never be the same. You just pray and hold on.

"There's no doubt TK would have come back and made a difference. That's why this hurt so many people. This may sound selfish – but it's not about what TK would have become as a person, it's what he would have given back. We lost that. The essence of TK? It's golden. Of course we miss TK – that's my boy. But what he would have gave back? We still waiting."

Tra'Meka Kelly: "Terrance would have made sure everybody had some kind of outlet to become better. That's just the type of person he was. What my dad's doing – I'm sure my brother would be doing the same thing – if not better. Richmond would have been OK, because he would not have turned his back. He would have made sure there was after-school programs, community centers. He was proud of where he came from."

John Chan: "The potential was there. He had the personality and the ability to go a long way and do good things in his life. He probably would have had a positive influence in a rough neighborhood for a long time. He would have given kids a lot of hope – you could see that in the aftermath with what happened to some of his friends – 'This is the kid that did everything right. I'm not even close to that, why should I even try?'

"The foundation has had a really good impact on a lot of lives, but who's to say the things Terrance could have done and brought back to Richmond wouldn't have been tenfold what the foundation has done? There's a lot of good that's come out as far as what the foundation has done. It's just hard to say that it couldn't have been better if he was still here in terms of just giving kids hope. The influence he could have had, it could have been greater. That's where the tragedy still lies."

Scott Hugo: "I've always had a picture of TK everywhere I've gone. It's there as a reminder – that I have the opportunity to continue my education and put my skills somewhere. I always remind myself that I have a duty and responsibility to use them in a way that honors TK's life.

"With the work that Landrin does – if other kids can have opportunities that they wouldn't otherwise have – or a sense of love and support that they wouldn't otherwise have – that's how we can build something positive and beautiful out of TK's life.

"TK's death was a moment where I realized that, with everything going on, I have a responsibility to do whatever I can to try and help be a part of the solution. For me, that's the challenge that is laid before me by TK's death. It's something that stays with me each and every day. And I think it's a challenge to everyone who knew TK. If the people who knew him and loved him don't make an effort to keep him alive, his death loses meaning and we lose a bit of TK in the process.

"So, the challenge was laid before Landrin, but it was also laid before all of us. At the end of the day, what was TK's loss going mean to us? How are we going to honor his life every day? Anger at Darren Pratcher is not the answer. Keeping TK's story alive and using that to positively impact the lives of others – that's how TKYF honors him each and every day."

*　　　*　　　*

Johnny Dempsey: "A lot of times I wonder what he'd be doing right now. What would he be doing in life? And how different things would be as far as our family. When Darren did what he did, it hurt the whole family. There's no more Thanksgiving dinner, we don't do that anymore. From the time I was 3 years old until I was 30, we did that dinner at my Aunty Bevelyn's house every year. When that's gone, there's something out of place. Everybody's breaking off doing their own things, and that's what she didn't want. After Terrance died, they tried to do Thanksgiving dinner. She told me, 'John, I'm gonna need you to bring this, I'm gonna need you to bring that.' But she died a few days later preparing for that meal. When the family tried to do it that year, it didn't feel the same. Everything was quiet. There was a silence. It was hard for her children.

"That's really what Darren destroyed – our sense of family. Our sense of worth. It's different today because my Aunty was the foundation. When you get the family together, it's sad and bittersweet."

Chastity Harper: "Terrance's relationship with his family was very special. They were so close. It's not something you see all the time. When I go to Landrin's now, it's just so different without Terrance there. I miss his presence and the friendship we had. Even if we weren't together, I feel like we would still be friends. Sometimes I wonder how things would be now. What would he be doing? What would he think about me now? How would we connect?"

Sondra Dempsey: "Today, I be wanting to gossip with my sister and tell her something really good and juicy, but then I realize she's not there. I can't call her. There's some things you can only tell a sister. We never judged each other. We could tell each other anything. It was a tragic loss – not only did I lose my nephew, but I lost my sister and my best friend. Ten years later, it's still devastating. We lost a family. We've tried to move forward, but there's still a lot of pain."

Tra'Meka Kelly: "We are a tight-knit family. Once my grandma passed, it did kind of separate things. The holidays aren't the same because my grandma's was the home and the home is broken now. Everybody tried to start their own tradition. I stopped coming around holidays because it didn't feel the same – it was always me and my brother during the holidays."

*   *   *

Landrin today is torn by constant conflict. The tears flow freely when he talks about his son. He is quick to let loose a hearty laugh that masks painful memories. He has hope for the future, but difficulty recalling the past. Every season presents new challenges – TK's birthday in the spring, the anniversary of tragedy in the summer and fall, the holidays in the winter.

"Every day I think about him," he says. "It's rough every day."

But with Landrin and Mary building the TKYF to greater heights, Landrin's life is now defined by the kids in his programs and his grandchildren. The same booming, raspy voice that once molded championship Little League and Pop Warner teams at Nicholl Park now commands respect in an after-school program at the YMCA in South Richmond.

The TKYF's after-school program has been held at the YMCA for the last five years for children aged 6-12. When Landrin speaks, the kids listen. When he individually scolds some for being disrespectful to Shahad Wright, the YMCA program director, many are quickly reduced to tears.

Robert Turner, Landrin's old defensive coordinator at Kennedy High School, now volunteers for the TKYF's E.A.G.L.E.S. and A.N.G.E.L.S. programs, which work with boys and girls, aged 12-17. Turner was one of the few who could feel the depths of Landrin's pain after the tragedy – he has also lost a son and a granddaughter to gun violence in Richmond.

Robert Turner: "I grew up next door to Mary in North Richmond, and I bonded with Landrin because I had already gone through what he was going through, and I still feel a lot of that hurt today. It was fate that brought us together. I've been teaching a long time and I can see where kids are going [Turner currently teaches at Helms Middle School]. Landrin and I try to get the kids where it looks like they won't make it, but we also get some of the good kids. That way the bad kids can interact and learn from the good ones. We take kids from all three communities in Richmond – North, Central and South. What happens is the kids can't stand each other outside of the program, but inside the program they're fine.

"You hear a lot of the horror stories coming out of Richmond, but you never hear the success stories. We've had kids come through our program and graduate from UC Davis, UCLA, Oregon and Stanford. We've got a young man in the program now, Ralphie, who raised his GPA from a 0.1 to a 3.6. A lot of our other kids, they may not have gone to college, but they're working and they're good citizens."

*　　　*　　　*

Deputy Guy Worth of the Contra Costa County Coroner's Division has over 40 years experience in law enforcement and has worked with the TKYF for the past eight. He leads a tour of a group of roughly 30 adolescent boys in Landrin's E.A.G.L.E.S. program through the coroner's building in Martinez.

Deputy Worth addresses the boys matter-of-factly before the session begins, his gaze locked in the distance, drifting to some potentially unpleasant memory. He could pass as your good-natured uncle or grandfather… until he starts speaking:

"I've seen a lot of death and destruction. Everyone here is going to die, and it can happen at any moment. Car accident, shooting – you just never know. Stay in school, stay on track – and you stay out of here."

There isn't much talking as the boys shuffle through the entrance. Inside, they walk past a sheet-covered body with pale feet sticking out and inhale the stench of death. Another deputy, Tim Biggs, takes them step-by-step through the autopsy process in grisly detail.

The Coroner's office is just one stop on the E.A.G.L.E.S. journey that day. After Biggs' autopsy presentation, Landrin, Lona, Mary, Robert Turner and Lanny III, driving in TK's Mustang 5.0, shuttle the group to a funeral home and later to Rolling Hills Memorial Park in Richmond, where TK's memorial and Turner's grandaughter's memorial are viewed inside a mausoleum. On other days, the group will go rock climbing, tackle a ropes course, volunteer at a food bank serving meals to the poor or spend a day at San Quentin Prison. As the teenagers file out of the mausoleum late in the afternoon, one boy remains alone, staring up at one of the tombs with tears in his eyes. His brother is up there.

*   *   *

Tra'Meka Kelly: "I have my own child now, and he feels like he knows Terrance because I don't let him forget. 'This is your uncle. He was a man of God. He was humble. He was a man of his word.' I show my son tapes of our childhood. My son feels like he knows Terrance, and that's how I want people to feel. I want you to feel like you know him – feel connected to him – not just, 'Oh, that's so sad that he died.' He had a great childhood. And while he was here, he didn't want for nothing. He didn't let where he come from determine where he was going.

"My brother was everything to me. I love my brother, but I'm not gonna question God's word. If it took Terrance's passing for my dad to save some other people, then I'm comfortable with that too. These kids my parents help come from all over, not just Richmond. The foundation is only getting better. A building is sure to come, and once my dad gets a building, there's really no stopping him. And when my parents don't feel they can keep going, I'll be here to step up. And when I get old and gray, my son Emaure will be there. The foundation will keep going."

Lanny Kelly III: "Terrance and I were the last two Kelly men in the family. I got to hang out with him in a different light. I know this because he used to tell me – he would never have forgotten where he came from. He had plans to do positive things in Richmond, and I want to have a big impact with the TKYF for him."

Landrin Kelly: "The devil killed Job's family and took his money, but he stayed faithful. Because he stayed faithful and believed in God, God gave him double for his trouble. My story really reminds me of Job. I lost my son, but I got three grandsons to raise now. I had one house, He gave me two houses. I had one car, I got five cars now with vans we use for the TKYF. I just had to believe that He had my back. I'm thankful for what I have today. I appreciate what God has given me. It's by the grace of God, I am able to stand."

Pastor K.R. Woods: "With Landrin, I see a man that has come full circle. He's a leader. He has transformed from a menace in the community to a pillar in the community. It's amazing the amount of people he's been able to connect with in all the different circles, and that's evident in the banquet he has every year at De La Salle, the celebrity golf tournament, the after-school program at the YMCA, the E.A.G.L.E.S. and

A.N.G.E.L.S. camps and groups – all of the things he's accomplished. Yet, he remains himself. He remains Landrin from Richmond.

"As I talked to him the other day, I heard a peace in his voice. He would gladly trade all this in to have his son here. But it sounded like he's come to a place of acceptance. For him to have the courage to wake up every day and have a purpose and a goal in mind, that says something as to the kind of man he is. And the wonderful thing about Landrin is – the best is yet to come."

"Out of every group that comes through our program, if I save one life, I did my job." –
Landrin Kelly

About the Terrance Kelly Youth Foundation

Created in 2004, the T.K.Y.F. provides community outreach for youth ages 5-17 through a variety of cultural, educational and community outreach programs. You can learn more about the T.K.Y.F. at tkyf28.com.

About the Author

Sam Herting is an attorney and author. Sam graduated from De La Salle High School with Terrance Kelly in 2004. You can find more of Sam's work at samherting.com.

Show Your Support

If you liked this book, please help spread the word by leaving us a positive review on amazon.com.

Author's Note

I graduated with TK from De La Salle High School in May, 2004. TK and I were very different. He was black and I was white. He was from a crime ridden, low income community and I was from the suburbs. We weren't friends. I attended classes with him and occasionally ran into him outside of school. From that limited interaction, I knew TK to be laid back, sleepy and funny. He possessed a quiet confidence.

After the tragedy, I attended TK's funeral in his hometown of Richmond, California at Hilltop Community Church with other classmates from De La Salle. It was a surreal experience. We were in a different world and wondered the same thing – why would someone do this to TK? I wanted to find out more.

For years, I thought about TK and the story. But it didn't mean anything because I didn't know anything. To answer my questions, I needed to interview those closest to the story, starting with his father, Landrin Kelly.

I first met Landrin on the night of July 25, 2011, roughly seven years after the tragedy. I didn't know much about him or his family beyond what I had read in the newspapers. But I remembered TK from high school and the sight of his family at the funeral in their white tuxedoes and dresses.

I showed up to Landrin's house with a tape recorder and some prepared questions – very naïve as to what I was about to hear.

In life there are times when you meet someone and everything clicks. This is how it was when I met Landrin. I felt comfortable because of some unexpected similarities. We both laughed in awkward moments. We both had allergies and stomach issues. We both loved sports, especially football. We both had three siblings – a brother and two sisters.

Then our interview began, and the similarities ended.

On the long drive home that night, I realized my life had changed irrevocably. I told Landrin I could deliver his story to the world, and now I had to deliver.

Landrin and I subsequently agreed to move forward as partners. I would research and write the story, while the foundation set up in TK's name would maintain creative control over the project and receive a majority of the proceeds from future sales. My interview process began with Landrin and expanded over the next three and a half years to include, amongst others, members of TK's large extended family, girlfriend, friends, pastor, coaches and teammates. I ended up conducting over 100 recorded interviews, many of which lasted several hours each.

Where collective memories were enough to push the story forward, I let them speak unobstructed in block quotes. Where the people talking were no longer alive today, I filled in the gaps using other interviews, especially my lengthy interviews with Landrin, or with legal records. Some names and identifying characteristics were changed.

None of this would have been possible without my parents, who have supported my efforts on this project for over ten years. I'd like to thank Ann Wyatt and Scott Hugo for providing detailed, time consuming edits to the manuscript when it was needed most. I want to acknowledge the great work done by Damin Esper after Landrin and I decided to hire a professional editor. I owe another thank you to Neil Hayes for helping us on the project and leading us to Damin. Finally, I'd like to thank Landrin Kelly, Mary Kelly and the rest of Terrance's family, friends, teammates and coaches for trusting me to tell this story.

Landrin talks with E.A.G.L.E.S. participants at TK's mausoleum

Landrin, Bob Ladouceur and an E.A.G.L.E.S. group at De La Salle

Mary and Landrin on an E.A.G.L.E.S. rafting trip

A day at the Contra Costa Coroner's central morgue facility, a funeral home and Rolling Hills Memorial Park. T.K.Y.F. programs show teenagers the good, the bad and the ugly.

Landrin and Mary with an E.A.G.L.E.S. group

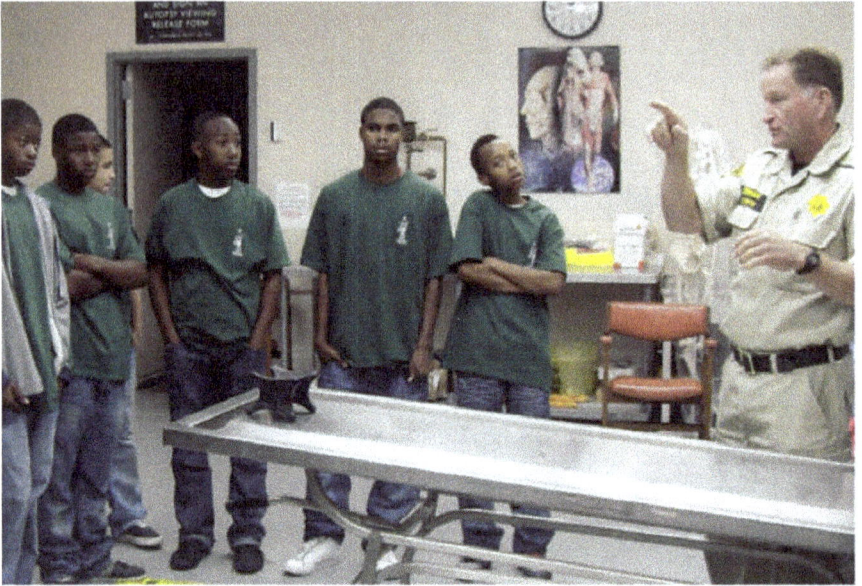

Deputy Guy Worth explains the autopsy process in detail to an E.A.G.L.E.S. group

Landrin and Mary with their YMCA after-school group, December 2014